Person-Centred Practices

Person-Centred Practices

A Therapeutic Perspective

Edited by

Mark Jukes

and

John Aldridge

QUAY
BOOKS

A division of MA Healthcare Ltd

Quay Books Division, MA Healthcare Ltd, St Jude's Church, Dulwich Road, London SE24 0PB

British Library Cataloguing-in-Publication Data
A catalogue record is available for this book

© MA Healthcare Limited 2006

ISBN 1 85642 299 2

Printed by Bath Press Ltd, Lower Bristol Road, Bath BA2 3BL

Contents

Contents

Chapter 14
Working with and supporting men with a learning disability who are gay, bisexual or attracted to the same sex
Neville Parkes and Nigel Hodges

Chapter 15
The person in a relationship: a systemic approach
Sandra Baum and Henrik Lynggaard

Chapter 16
Clinical supervision: the need for an integrative approach in supervising the experienced practitioner
Tony Viney

Contributors

John Aldridge is Senior Lecturer in Nursing (Learning Disabilities), University of Northampton, Park Campus, Boughton Green Road, Northampton NN2 7AZ.

Mark Alison, at the time of writing, was Psychotherapist, West Wales General Hospital, Carmarthen, Wales. He is now Child Psychotherapist, CAMHS, Whakatane, New Zealand.

John Anstey is Professional Practice Lead, Birmingham and Solihull Mental Health NHS Trust, Professional Executive Committee Member, South Birmingham Primary Care Trust, and Specialist Lecturer.

Sandra Baum is Consultant Clinical Psychologist, Newham Primary Care NHS Trust, Newham Community Team for People with Learning Disabilities, Units 7 and 8, Stratford Office Village, 4 Romford Road, Stratford, London E15 4EA.

Jane Bullock is Community Nurse (Learning Disabilities) – Specialist Practitioner, Droitwich Health Centre, Droitwich, Worcestershire Mental Health Partnership NHS Trust.

Cheryl Chessum is Lecturer/Practitioner in Community Mental Health at the University of Central England, Birmingham, and Solihull Mental Health NHS Trust.

David Elliott is Community Nurse (Learning Disabilities), New Burton House Community Unit, Stafford, South Staffordshire Health Care Trust.

Dr Eve Gale is Lecturer, Department of Nursing and Midwifery, Keele University, Keele, Staffordshire ST5 5BG.

Mark Gray is Head of Services, Deafblind UK (Midlands Region), 5 Kirkland Drive, Chilwell, Nottingham NG9 6LX.

Dr Helen Hewitt, at the time of writing, was an Associate Lecturer in the School of Nursing, University of Nottingham. She is now Freelance Consultant and Trainer for the British Institute of Learning Disabilities.

Nigel Hodges is Community Nurse (Learning Disabilities), Oliver House, No. 4 Ivylodge Close, Coleshill Road, Marston Green, Solihull B37 7HJ.

Mark Jukes is Reader in Learning Disabilities, Department of Community Health and Social Work, University of Central England, Birmingham.

Henrik Lynggaard is Chartered Clinical Psychologist and Systemic Practitioner, Camden and Islington Mental Health NHS Trust, Islington Learning Disabilities Partnership, 1 Lowther Road, London N7 8US.

Pam Morley is Senior Lecturer in Mental Health, University of Central England, Birmingham, and Honorary Family Therapist, North Solihull Child and Adolescent Family Therapy Team.

Sarah Newman is Staff Nurse (Learning Disabilities) at 37 Camelot Way, Northampton, which offers short-term care to children with multiple disabilities.

Neville Parkes is Senior Lecturer (Learning Disabilities), University of Worcester, Henwick Grove, Worcester, WR2 6AJ.

Pat Roberts lives in Droitwich and is an active volunteer contributing and committing a large proportion of her time to her local community.

Isabel Robinson is Adult Psychotherapist (UKCP Registered) at Bridge House, Walley Banks, Blackburn, Lancashire, BB2 1NT, Hyndburn and Ribble Valley NHS Primary Care Trust.

Tony Viney is Senior Lecturer in Mental Health at the University of Central England, Birmingham, and Honorary Cognitive Behaviour Therapist, Birmingham and Solihull Mental Health Trust.

Introduction

Mark Jukes and John Aldridge

This book has come about out of our commitment towards person-centred practices, acknowledging how as professionals, and in a post-*Valuing People* era, we need to get closer in knowing the person with a learning disability – their needs, perceptions and their motivations in life, as well as some of the traumas, and distress they experience in everyday living.

This book is not about person-centred planning, but about person-centred approaches in getting to know the person in terms of their individual life-stage development and adjustments.

It is about developing relationships, assisting people to tell their story as it is experienced by them personally.

Once practitioners establish the essence and core of a relationship, the process of person-centred planning can commence.

Summary

This book consists of 16 chapters, divided into three parts. **Part 1** contains three chapters representing the foundations for therapeutic relationships.

Chapter 1: Mark Jukes embraces the broad meaning of person-centredness from a psychological, mainstream healthcare, nursing and person-centred planning perspective. The premise is that the person is of centrality in any of these professional relationships, and that effective person-centred practices are based around skilled interactional and interpersonal processes.

Chapter 2: This chapter pursues facets of the therapeutic relationship as they resonate within the field of learning disability. John Aldridge clearly asserts that the majority of literature in this area has previously been located within mental health and medical–surgical nursing. This chapter comprehensively reviews this stance and places learning disability, the therapeutic relationship into a contemporary focus.

Chapter 3: The final chapter in this section deals with the focus on the human service worker's interpersonal style within relationships. It is here that Cheryl Chessum eloquently explores concepts and frameworks that are essential to examine from a personal and professional domain if we are to develop a sound 'therapeutic' practitioner.

Part 2 deals with the challenging area of understanding and applying strategies in how we can get in touch with people who have profound and multiple disabilities.

Chapter 4: Mark Gray provides an engaging account of zoning theory and how we need to consider the practicalities involved if we are able to identify and teach communication methods, so that people can have a real say in their lives.

Chapter 5: Eve Gale clearly identifies and differentiates between the 'functional' or 'therapeutic' role that touch has in providing and fulfilling a psychological need and therefore quality of life for people with severe, profound disability.

Chapter 6: Multi-sensory environments have been around since the 1970s (some readers may know these environments as 'Snoezelen'), and are a 'collection' of devices that offer sensory stimulation. Sarah Newman gives not only a historical overview of its aims, but also a practical illustration of how MSE can be applied in developing a therapeutic relationship that enables individuals to fulfil their identified needs.

Part 3 is where we take an eclectic journey, examining and applying a variety of psychological therapies in an attempt to discover the person through talking.

Chapter 7: takes us on a largely reflective process between Jane Bullock, a person-centred facilitator, and Pat Roberts, whose personal Making an Action Plan (MAP) is developed.

This process of reflection through adoption of a reflective model identifies quite clearly the essential interpersonal skills that a facilitator requires, and where a model of helping is adopted so as to successfully implement a person-centred plan.

Chapter 8: Helen Hewitt reaffirms that we need to understand as much as possible about who the person is – their identity. The development of life-story books through different formats are explored. Life-story books, as well as being unique to the person, can also act as an important tool for breaking down barriers between service provider and user by creating a better understanding of who the person is – the foundation to good person-centred planning.

Chapter 9: Pam Morley explores the therapeutic approach of solution-focused practice as a means for people with learning disabilities to discover solutions to problems. Principles of solution-focused practice assist a person to decide on their hopes and aspirations for their future and how these can be achieved. Solution-focused practice as a model for achieving personal change is a driver to provide choice for the person, and can assist in empowering them to make choices.

Chapter 10: Mark Alison pursues the more popularly known cognitive-behavioural therapy. As identified, CBT has an excellent record in treating common mental health problems, and applying it to people who have mild learning disabilities and mental health needs.

In this chapter, Mark illustrates this form of therapy with reference to adaptations, attitudinal factors and service issues so as to increase the use of CBT within this field of practice.

Chapter 11 explores transactional analysis as another therapeutic model designed to promote personal growth and change. Isabel Robinson provides us with an integrated approach of this theory through examples within her own practice. Once again, evidence of such a therapeutic approach is noticeable by its absence from the literature on its application or consideration of being beneficial for people with a learning disability.

Chapter 12: Bereavement is an area that has attracted a lot of attention, both in terms of impact and ways in which practitioners can assist people with a learning disability who are experiencing such symptoms of loss.

David Elliott is a well-known practitioner in this area, and in this chapter, he illustrates and discusses a model in helping people where the helper is required to assimilate and demonstrate complex skills in aiding the person come to terms with their loss.

Chapter 13: For some readers within learning disability the very title of this chapter will raise eyebrows. What is neuro-linguistic programming? This form of human interaction has attracted a variety of responses in terms of its utility and application in areas such as nursing, sports, business, sales and education. John Anstey provides an in-depth and practical application of how we need to tune in to people's representational systems, both verbal and non-verbal, so as to work with them in a truly empathic and person-centred way.

Chapter 14: People with a learning disability are already marginalised, and when they have individual traits that can further exclude them from mainstream society, such as being gay, this has a cumulative affect on their exclusion and discrimination. Neville Parkes and Nigel Hodges confront this challenge, presenting a detailed analysis of how as practitioners we need to be constantly vigilant about our personal values and attitudes when relating with people who have an alternative view on sexuality.

Chapter 15: Individuals are part of a system. We all interact with others, within or outside of a family relationship. Systemic and family therapy explores the network of significant relationships. Sandra Baum and Henryk Lynggaard explore how its application can assist people with a learning disability and contribute towards person-centred approaches.

Chapter 16: In this final chapter, Tony Viney, an experienced supervisor of experienced practitioners, deals with the process of supervision for practitioners who are engaged in serious therapeutic work with clients. Engaging with people is an exhaustive process and must not be treated lightly. A collaborative dialogue between supervisor and supervisee that promotes a more creative narrative and visual approach is pursued.

One of the main themes that run through all of the chapters relates to the therapeutic role of the learning disability practitioner. Acknowledgement of this therapeutic role is absolutely vital to the development of a practitioner who is relevant to the needs of people with learning disabilities in the 21st century. In the light of *Valuing People* and other philosophies and policies, all learning disability practitioners, and nurses in particular, have had to re-examine their roles and indeed their very ethos.

In the days of the long-stay institutions, the role of staff was primarily custodial, with a developmental or teaching role added as a poor second. The movement toward a social model of care, the closure of the long-stay hospitals and the development of community living has challenged the very need for learning disability nurses. To an extent, we could argue that learning disability nursing as a profession has itself a relatively poorly developed vision of its future role.

Valuing People, through its largely absent acknowledgement of the learning disability nurse, hints at a lifeline for learning disability nursing in the shape of health facilitation. However, even a cursory examination of this role and its implementation across the country will clearly show that health facilitation is not the exclusive remit of nurses. Health facilitation is not about the delivery of healthcare, but about helping to make healthcare happen. Any reasonably skilled person might do this, and indeed many professionals working in social care have done so very successfully. There is an additional problem that, in focusing purely on a health facilitation role, the learning disability nurse may find themselves becoming no more than a 'middle-person' between the client and the services that really deliver the healthcare. As the strategic level of health facilitation takes effect and generic services improve their ability to deliver high-quality care to people with learning disabilities, we may find that the need for client-level health facilitation diminishes. This is far from saying that the health facilitation role of learning disability nursing is unnecessary. There is clearly a pressing need to help people with learning disabilities to identify and address their health needs, but this is only part of the wider range of roles that learning disability nurses might fulfil.

What seems to have been consistently undervalued and ignored over the years is the potential that learning disability nurses and other practitioners have for therapeutic person-centred work. A broader definition of therapy would seem to include not only the conventional sense of physical and mental healing, but also personal development, positive self-esteem, self-determination and more satisfying lifestyles.

All of the chapters in this book address this broad definition because, in one way or another, they help the individual to 'get better' and to feel better. They all demonstrate that learning disability practitioners have a powerful capability to help individuals to transform their lives in a person-centred way. Although it is essential that clients have access to a wide range of multidisciplinary and multi-agency resources, it is also important to realise our own potential to work therapeutically with individuals and families. We hope that this book will go some way towards offering a vision for at least one of the future roles of learning disability practitioners that will inspire them to explore ways in which they can extend the therapeutic facet of their work and to help to bring about real improvement in peoples' lives.

Mark Jukes
University of Central England, Birmingham

John Aldridge
University of Northampton

May, 2006

PART I

The foundations for therapeutic relationships

CHAPTER I

Person-centredness

Mark Jukes

This chapter identifies the origins of person-centredness and through its definition initially explores the psychological interpretation. Patient-centredness and person-centred care, as these concepts relate within mainstream healthcare settings, are defined and placed alongside a contemporary learning disability context. Finally, person-centredness in learning disability will then be pursued in terms of its recency, interpretation and application through person-centred planning.

Themes of commonality will be extracted, culminating in recommendations for both services and professionals who are aspiring to deliver a person-centred approach within a variety of settings with people who have a learning disability.

Origins of person-centredness

Eastern culture and its institutions are traditionally Humanistic, in the sense that they are centred around the human potential for transcendence or in becoming (Graham, 1986, p. 11). Eastern culture, religion and psychology are synonymous with each other, and hence Buddhism, Zen Taoism and Sufism represent the traditional esoteric psychologies or spiritual psychologies.

From a Western psychological perspective, person-centredness has a more recent history and its roots are in Humanistic Psychology, which essentially represents an emphasis on an individual's own personal 'here and now' experiential processes.

This means that from an individual perspective, practitioner/therapists avoid directing and focusing upon the client's problems, which are perceived to stem from childhood events. This is where a psychodynamic therapist would locate the problems of origin, or, from a practitioner/therapist's assessment and subsequent development of new patterns of behaviour for the future, from which a behavioural therapist would determine and set goals for individuals to make progress on within their personal and social world.

In person-centred therapy control and personal empowerment are transferred to the client and not located within the therapist's locus of control.

Carl Rogers is firmly regarded as the founder, in the 1940s of the person-centred approach, and developed his non-directive counselling as a reaction against the behaviourally directive and psychoanalytic approaches to individual therapy. The person-centred approach was originally called Client-Centred Therapy, as opposed to Patient-Centred, as it reflects Rogers' belief that people, not therapists, know what is best for themselves, and should therefore direct the course of therapy. Cramer (1992) acknowledged that the term 'client' is nevertheless adopted by a number of other therapists outside client-centred therapy to refer to people who seek or receive psychotherapy.

Rogers (1959, 1961) believed that the client-centred approach applies not only to counselling or psychotherapy, but to other spheres of human activity such as education and social relationships.

This extension of client-centred ideas to encompass groups, organisations and society brought about the term 'person-centred' as a way of describing an approach to working with larger groups as well as with individual clients (Mearns and Thorne, 1988).

In terms of the therapeutic relationship itself, Rogers (1957) has emphasised that for therapists to be effective they must internalise and apply six necessary conditions that could release a growth-promoting climate in which individual clients could progress forward and become what they were capable of becoming:

1. Two persons are in psychological contact.
2. The first, whom we shall term the client, is in a state of incongruence, being vulnerable or anxious.
3. The second person, whom we shall term the therapist, is congruent or integrated in the relationship.
4. The therapist experiences unconditional positive regard for the client.
5. The therapist experiences an empathic understanding of the client's internal frame of reference and endeavours to communicate this experience to the client.
6. The communication to the client of the therapist's empathic understanding and unconditional positive regard is to a minimal degree achieved.

These six conditions emphasise the critical importance of the relationship between therapist and client for personality change to occur.

Carl Rogers believed that people were resourceful, capable of self-direction, and have an ability to live effective and productive lives (Cain, 1987). Over the period of development of person-centred theory, Rogers has held a deep faith in the tendency of humans to develop in a positive and constructive manner *if a climate of respect and trust is to be established*. From the outset, Rogers emphasised the *attitudes and personal qualities* of the therapist, and the *quality of the client–therapist relationship* as the prime determinants of the therapeutic process (Corey, 1991 p. 205).

Patient-centred care in mainstream healthcare

Person-centred theory as developed by Carl Rogers became prominent in North America in the 1960s and 1970s, which was also a significant period in both the UK and Europe. The development of new concepts within sociology and psychology was providing people with a new-found liberation in individual thinking and in the experiencing of life.

Table 1.1 The seven Pendleton 'tasks' (Pendleton *et al.*, 1984).

1. Define the reason for the patient's attendance (ideas, concerns and expectations).

2. Consider other problems (continuing and 'at risk' areas).

3. Work with the patient to choose an appropriate action for each problem.

4. Achieve a shared understanding of the problems.

5. Involve the patient in the management and encourage the acceptance of responsibility.

6. Use time and resources appropriately.

7. Establish a relationship which helps to achieve the other tasks.

In terms of medical practice, the doctor–patient consultation at this time was also being put under the microscope, in terms of being part of professional practice where a strong paternalism was traditionally exercised through power exerted by medical practitioners within a consultation.

According to Elwyn (2005), the arrival of audio and visual recording techniques in the 1970s provided an opportunity for the medical consultation to be assessed, and for interactions to be increasingly studied and analysed. This analysis has focused upon the shift from overt paternalism towards individual patient autonomy with more emphasis on the process of the doctor–patient relationship. This can be seen as the beginning of the concept of patient-centredness. It emerged visibly in the early 1980s, when Pendleton *et al.* (1984) suggested that good practice should be based upon what is now known as the Pendleton 'Tasks' (Table 1.1).

Whilst acknowledging that developments in the consultation process have occurred, as in nursing practice, there appears to be also a medical consultation theory–practice gap. As identified by Barry *et al.* (2000) and Campion *et al.* (2002), there appears to be little evidence that doctors employ interaction and engagement strategies such as Pendleton describes within the consultation.

From a personal perspective, I experienced patient-centred care recently when I was diagnosed with osteonecrosis of the left-medial femoral condyle of my left femur. What was meant to be an innocent cycle ride resulted in a swollen left knee experiencing pain, with noticeable debris present around the knee. I self-referred to a specialist knee clinic because existing NHS and Primary Care services were unable to diagnose or refer in a satisfactory time frame (12 months wait for an MRI scan and three months for an appointment with an orthopaedic surgeon).

From the initial download from the knee clinic's Internet site of a comprehensive self-report assessment, to an MRI scan and personal consultation, I felt involved, informed and able to contribute to a consideration of the proposed treatment options in line with my lifestyle and with an assessment of my levels of desired future activity. The relationship with the consultant was engaging and valuing, and certainly demonstrated not only clinical expertise, but warmth and mutual respect through dialogue, which led to consideration of what I felt about the treatment options.

From a self-reflective and critical facility, I was fully aware of the context associated with my situation, in that within a mixed market economy readers might well retort 'You are paying for this treatment, so you would secure such a service!'. Certainly, I was a paying consumer, but my experiences with the NHS, although free at the point of access and treatment, should not (although as demonstrated, they did) have presented an absence in value of me as a patient with an inappropriate attitude, or a lack of skilled communication relative to my temporary disability at that point. I remember quite clearly the GP sitting authoritatively behind his desk, with limited communication, only willing to refer me on my request, with no further attempt at a Pendleton-style of consultation to assess or explore my continuing current situation, or to carry out a further physical examination.

'Patient-centred' means taking into account a patient's desire for information, sharing decision making and responding appropriately, by including the patient's thoughts and wishes in planning treatment management. From a medical and primary healthcare perspective, what patient-centred-ness is *not* is technology-centred, doctor-centred, hospital-centred or disease-centred.

What patients want is care which:

1. Explores the patient's main reason for the visit, concerns, and need for information
2. Seeks an integrated understanding of the patient's world – that is, their whole person, emotional needs, and life issues
3. Finds common ground on what the problem is and mutually agrees on management
4. Enhances prevention and health promotion
5. Enhances the continuing relationship between the patient and the doctor (Stewart, 2001)

During the 1990s the concept of patient involvement in decision-making has moved to a point of centrality within NHS reforms.

The NHS Plan (Department of Health, 2000) provided the impetus for improving patients' experiences, and announced incentive systems to be put into place so as to encourage not only improvements in clinical performance, but also to include patient feedback in a star rating system for performance indicators.

The Bristol Royal Infirmary Inquiry (2001) laid bare recommendations on how to prevent failures from surgeons involved in heart surgery on children, and urged doctors to ensure that patients must be at the centre of the NHS and be treated as partners by way of:

- Involving patients (or their parents) in decisions
- Keeping patients (or parents) informed
- Improving communication with patients (or parents)
- Providing patients (or parents) with counselling and support
- Gaining informed consent for all procedures and processes
- Eliciting feedback from patients (or parents) and listening to their views
- Being open and candid when adverse events occur.

For some medical practitioners this may be difficult to achieve or identify with, due to their value system associated with 'expertness' and being in 'control'. However, in an age of consumerism and individual choice within a mixed market economy, such control will be increasingly less tolerated.

The current scenario is such that patients have access to a variety of sources which extend beyond the doctor. Elwyn (2005) asserts that for doctors, medical paternalism has gone and instead doctors have to play multiple roles of problem solver, guide to the interpretation of symptoms, information navigator, and (where relevant) facilitator of decision preferences within a postmodern consultation.

What does this mean for people with a learning disability?

Communication with the health provision and actually getting to the service remain significant problems (National Health Service Executive, 1999). Most people with learning disabilities do not receive good quality health services. Evidence from research in primary and secondary health provision often finds people and their carers dissatisfied with the care provided (Hart, 1998; Kerr *et al.*, 1996; Mencap, 1997, 2004).

Few studies have been conducted on the experiences of children with disabilities with general NHS services.

Wharton *et al.* (2005) identified concerns relating to health professionals' lack of understanding and knowledge of disabilities, and in particular regarding communication on wards and in overseeing care.

In primary care there are commonly occurring concerns about the lack of time for consultations, which often leads to poor outcomes for the service user along with heavy reliance by professionals on the expertise and communication skills of the carer (Law *et al.*, 2005).

An evolving evidence base on the experiences of people with learning disabilities of healthcare is acknowledging that difficulties do exist in attempting to use and receive treatment within NHS services. These difficulties often commence with poor attitudes and negative views from many healthcare professionals. A study by Slevin and Sines (1996) found negative attitudes from general nurses and attributed such attitudes to a lack of knowledge and having negative and misleading views about people with a learning disability.

Hart (1998) conducted interviews with a small group of people with a learning disability who had received treatment as in-patients, out-patients or day patients in general hospitals. Five themes were identified: fear; general nursing care; communication about treatment; consent to treatment; and communication from doctors.

Findings from this study indicated that people with a learning disability had a fear of hospitals and medical and nursing procedures, combined with a lack of understanding about what was happening to them. From a communication perspective, people with a learning disability, through their accounts, also found minimal evidence of nurses spontaneously interacting, talking and having skills in observation. Doctors' use of jargon added to this detachment in communication.

Barr (1997) suggested that the quality and effectiveness of general healthcare services could be more improved by putting into place strategies such as arranging pre-admission visits, an assessment of individual needs, improved communication, recognition of equal rights and coordinated teamwork so as to improve communication and challenge stereotypes about people with a learning disability.

A major difference which requires emphasis at this point is that medical and nursing professionals within acute and primary care predominantly offer short-time based interventions and tasks. For patient-centred care, as Dunn (2002) observes, being truly patient-centred within, for example, a maximum ten minute consultation, is a real test of resources and traditional working practices

This is juxtaposed by secondary care medical and nursing professionals who can potentially offer more time and therapeutic-based interventions. Therefore, within primary and acute services, professional staff need to examine and focus upon the attitudes and communication strategies open to them within time-limited consultation or interaction phases between patients and clients. This demands additional training and education areas for the present and future workforce and curriculum.

In today's contemporary services acute liaison is being developed by secondary specialist learning disability nurses so as to improve the awareness, education and quality in service provision within general healthcare services. A critique of the literature in acute liaison has revealed that specialist nurses in this area are involved in clinical care, coaching, communication, coordination and championing to ensure that professional staff are working towards patient-centred care (Foster, 2005).

Patient-centred care for people with a learning disability therefore makes similar demands on healthcare and professional services to those of the general population, and thus there is a significant need to pursue a patient-centred focus further.

Scotland, through its review of services for people with learning disabilities (Scottish Executive, 2000), identified a need to undertake a Health Needs Assessment (NHS Health Scotland, 2004) which focuses on the health of children, adults and older adults with learning disabilities. Its aims have been to promote inclusion and to provide a framework for the strategic development and planning of services. It is recognised in this report that many professionals providing generic services have received little or no training in working with people with a learning disability. It is therefore an imperative that if health improvement of people with a learning disability is to take place in Scotland and other areas within the UK, it is important to tackle the unmet training needs of professionals providing services.

Person-centred care and nursing

Since 2001, person-centred care has been embodied within Standard 2 of the National Service Framework for Older People (Department of Health, 2001a), in recognition that excellence in care for the older person within services is an essential target for both professionals and services.

The origins of the person-centred movement are commonly attributed to the care of people with dementia in the UK and appear to have grabbed the attention of nurses in a way that humanistic nursing theory and nursing models seem to have missed (Dewing, 2004).

Tom Kitwood first referred to person-centred approaches in 1988, and distinguished them from approaches which emphasised the medical and behavioural management of Dementia.

Person-centredness in this context is the loss of personhood for people. The aim therefore is for practitioners to work towards the reestablishment of the individual through valuing the person. According to Kitwood the term was intended to bring ideas and ways of working that *emphasised communication and relationships*. This of course was through the influence of Rogerian psychotherapy and its emphasis on *authentic contact and communication*. Person-centredness therefore implies that a relationship coexists between a nurse and a patient/person where a partnership is at the heart of nursing practice.

Kitwood and Bredin (1992) suggest that person-centred practice can be achieved if practitioners:

- Understand user needs
- Engage in positive work with the user
- Place central in all decisions/actions the desire to maintain/improve well-being

In adult nursing this 'working alliance' or partnership between professionals and clients is further amplified by Jonsdottir *et al.* (2004) in pursuance of what constitutes the relational core of nursing practice. This core of nursing practice is seen as an antidote to the existing tensions and challenges from an increasingly technologically driven nurse practitioner (Dewing, 2004). The core of practice is where the processes of unconditional warmth and meaningful dialogue are explored so as to focus on what constitutes the patient's health concerns.

The nurse, through encouragement of conversation, is told about the health issues by the patient in the form of stories or narratives, and the nurse adopts questions for clarification, elaboration and summarising. The approach allows nurses to meet patients where they are in terms of understanding their health concerns, engaging in dialogue with them until a new meaning has unfolded and patients have found a more useful way of living life.

In mental health nursing the Tidal Model (Barker, 2001) was developed, which sought to clarify the discrete roles and functions of nursing within a multidisciplinary care and treatment process. The Tidal Model embraces the importance of interpersonal relationships along with a model of empowerment.

As with Jonsdottir *et al.* (2004), the emphasis is the nurse exploring the person's construction of experience through narrative which employs the concept of the therapeutic alliance. In each phase of assessment and intervention, emphasis is given to engaging the person fully in the process of determining and, where possible, contributing to, the interventions that might meet the person's needs (Barker, 2001).

Nursing practice appears generally to be entering into a phase of practice dissonance, whereby nursing practice is increasingly dominated by a technologically driven, computer systems, prescriptive and outcomes-orientated approach, and as Parse (2004) observes:

> The Person-Centredness called for in Nursing literature where Nurses listen to persons' stories, engage with them in meaningful dialogue, recognize them as human beings with dignity, and respect their unique beliefs and values as a basis for care is conspicuous by its absence in the computerized classification systems.

Brewster and Ramcharan (2005) claim that because person-centred care has been categorised and defined in a number of ways, it leads to the concept being dismembered and constitutes little agreement across care sectors.

Person-centredness does offer different definitions and applications within different care arenas. They do, however, have a common thread which represents a cohesive approach. The person/patient is at the heart of practice and communication along with an attitude of value, equality, respect and partnership in care between the professional and patient/client. The ability to listen, engage and form an alliance is its central tenet.

In care of the older person Davies *et al.* (1999) and Nolan *et al.* (2001, 2002) capture the subjective and perceptual dimensions of caring relationships in the development of a senses framework, where those parties involved in a caring relationship should experience relationships that promote a sense of:

- Security – to feel safe within relationships
- Belonging – to feel 'part' of things
- Continuity – to experience links and consistency

- Purpose – to have a personally valuable goal or goals
- Achievement – to make progress towards a desired goal or goals
- Significance – to feel that 'you' matter

The senses framework in essence is that all participants need to experience these senses if good care is to result. From empirical testing of the senses (Davies *et al.*, 1999), staff have reported that a sense of direction assists in defining best care and highlights what gets lost in evidence-based care.

Nolan *et al.* (2004) believe that therapeutic care requires a shared understanding, and although developed in elderly care the senses framework is a relationship- centred approach that has application across various sectors, including person-centredness in learning disability. The senses need to be experienced by all those in the relationship and nurses should see themselves as one part of a larger social network. As Dewing (2004) suggests, the framework offers a list of indicators that can be used in the context of emancipatory practice development work.

Person-centredness and learning disability

Within learning disabilities over the last 60 years, since the inception of the NHS in the UK, services have largely been driven by approaches emanating from medical, psychological, educational and social dimensions. The movement of advocacy and civil and human rights has put people with a learning disability at the centre of philosophical and policy reforms, with the aim of inclusion within mainstream society and having a voice to be heard.

The past 20 years have seen incremental developments towards individualising approaches from civil rights legislation and professionals in an attempt to value and respect individual rights and needs through shared assessment and care planning.

In terms of person-centred theory, Carl Rogers in 1957 stated that people with learning disabilities would not be able to make use of client-centred therapy, and to date few mental health professionals have been interested in testing this hypothesis (Sinason, 2002).

Through psychotherapy and counselling David Brandon paved the way in 1989 in the UK in publishing *Mutual Respect*, and in his introduction stated: 'Ten years ago (1979) the overall question was, is counselling with people who have learning difficulties possible? Now the question has changed to, how can we do it?' (Brandon, 1989).

Waitman and Conboy-Hill (1992) published further attempts and approaches in psychotherapy towards people with a learning disability in their text *Psychotherapy and Mental Handicap*. In the foreword to this text, Professor Chris Cullen states 'Not only are we forced to consider the intellectually disabled person as a person, but as someone on the same level and with the same needs and demands, as the friend, the family member and the therapist. For many this is not a comfortable message, but it is an urgent one'. Here we are, just over a decade later, still attempting to find ways of becoming person-centred.

According to the Royal College of Psychiatrists (2004, p. 8), people with learning disabilities are still being excluded from therapy and there is no specific training or regulation of this specialist application.

In contemporary services, the climate is changing to one in which an overall willingness from professionals is being pursued in order to explore person-centred theory, not only through dialogue, but also via expression in other media such as art (Rees, 1998), play therapy (Brodin, 1999), drama therapy (Bayliss and Dodwell, 2002), life-story work, as explored by Helen Hewitt in Chapter 8, and Isabel Robinson's work in adapting transactional analysis in Chapter 11.

Within learning disability practice, nurses not only demonstrate a close working alliance with people with a learning disability and their families, but are also in a unique position to promote narratives and to support life-story work, through their access to documentary and family sources, and good practice in fieldwork emulates good practice in research (Atkinson, 2005). This wide acceptance that there are a variety of therapeutic approaches, through adaption or modification of approaches to individual need, is again recognised within the Royal College of Psychiatrists report (2004, p. 32).

It has been found through numerous studies that women and men with a learning disability are at risk from and suffer from abuse (Heibert *et al.*, 1982; Brown *et al.*, 1995). Studies which focus on the effects on emotion, such as that by Barber *et al.* (2000), have demonstrated in particular the processes of person-centred group work when working with a survivor's group for women who have a learning disability who have experienced abuse.

Markwick and Sage (1997) place importance on the attitudes of those in a caring role and who play a crucial role in helping to build positive self-image and self-esteem, where Rogers' (1961) concept of unconditional positive regard can be adopted by healthcare professionals who:

> Prize the client in a total rather than a conditional way... not simply accept the client when he is behaving in certain ways and disapprove of him when he behaves in other ways. It means an outgoing positive feeling without reservations, without evaluations.

Brechin and Swain (1988) have discussed and identified six principles of practice (Table 1.2) for professionals to be mindful of when creating a 'working alliance' with people with learning difficulties. These principles were generated at a time when the authors were developing shared action planning, and the ethos behind this approach was to leave behind the skill development focus of goal planning and individual programme planning. Williams and Robinson (2000) have found that people with learning disabilities are not in control when individual programme plans (IPPs) have been developed, and that IPP was often used as a means of professionals monitoring their behaviour.

Table 1.2 Six principles of practice (Brechin and Swain, 1988).

1. To be an entitlement rather than an imposition
2. To promote self-realisation rather than compliance
3. To open up choices rather than replace one option with another
4. To develop opportunities, relationships and patterns of living in line with their individual wishes rather than rule-of-thumb normality
5. To enhance their decision-making control of their own lives
6. To allow them to move at their own pace.

This approach to assessment is clearly at odds with an approach that emphasises individuals' rights to be valued for what they are and for opportunities for an ordinary life to be made *unconditionally* (my emphasis) (Brechin and Swain, 1988).

What was fundamentally important at this time was that normalisation (Wolfensberger, 1972) and social role valorisation (Wolfensberger, 1983) were being challenged in terms of their imposition on people with a learning disability, and that what normalisation does not do is to prescribe an appropriate style of professional practice.

The principles of normalisation tended to polarise on a style of living, and for workers that emphasis becomes focused upon the aesthetics of living environments which people with a learning disability and their supporters can move towards. Professional workers do not have guidance under normalisation in how their relationships with people will need to change as part of an evolving process.

Brechin and Swain (1988) look towards Carl Rogers as an influence, emphasising the centrality of the relationship between professional and client and the concept of personal growth. They also identify Gerard Egan's work as an extension of such ideas, with the added dimension of generating helping and problem-solving skills, which Jane Bullock adopts in her work as a person-centred facilitator with Pat Roberts in Chapter 7.

In her further work on relationships, Brechin (1998) identifies that good care is best understood in terms of the interrelationships between those giving and receiving care, and that there is a need to identify the 'fundamental similarities' that characterise such relationships.

Person-centred planning in learning disability

There are a plethora of materials, resources, texts, workbooks and articles about what person-centred planning (PCP) is, and how to go about achieving it with people with a learning disability. The purpose of this chapter, however, is not to add to this list but to focus on the issues and skills necessary for the process of person-centredness between the facilitator and the individual so that person-centred planning can be a success.

With regard to the current policy in the UK, two current documents – *Valuing People* (Department of Health, 2001b) and *The Same as You?* (Scottish Executive, 2000) emphasise our responsibility to ensure that people with a learning disability are in control of their own lives. Carers are equal partners in the planning process and person-centred planning is the most effective way of helping us to do this (Bradley, 2004).

As defined by O'Brien and Lovett (1992), person-centred planning:

Refers to a family of approaches to organizing and guiding community change in alliance with people with disabilities and their families and friends. Person-Centred Planning approaches include: Individual Service Design, Essential Lifestyle Planning, Personal Futures Planning, MAPS (Making Action Plans) and PATH (Planning Alternative Tomorrows with Hope).

If one were to map out a time line for person-centred planning, early approaches were developed between 1973 and 1986 in North America through the influence of normalisation. This work spread to the UK in 1979 and Sanderson *et al.* (1997) provide a useful account of how this process has further developed.

To define the difference between PCP and previous attempts at planning with a person with a learning disability, we can compare the locus of control in such approaches.

Approaches such as individual programme planning are often controlled by the multidisciplinary or interdisciplinary team, who determine what is best, often with little consultation with the person's family or significant carers or friends. An assessment is usually conducted which is professionally focused (e.g. nursing, psychology, teachers or occupational therapists), where the planning process commences in areas such as skills to be acquired. Labelling of the individual will ensue in the form of level of IQ, or 'has a challenging behaviour, mental health problem or syndrome'.

In today's mixed market economy an opening in a particular care home at the right packaged costing may need to be filled. The result of these types of meeting may mean that the person with a learning disability has to 'fit' into the existing service design.

See Table 1.3 for a comparison between the traditional and person-centred approaches.

Person-centred planning, however, begins by getting to know the person. An external facilitator assists in establishing a circle of close individuals who ensure that the focus is on the person, and that the person and close individuals control the planning process within, for example, the person's 'home' setting. The external facilitator assists by making records, drawings or graphics and working to establish and promote the vision.

An example of such a collaborative approach can be found in Chapter 7 where Jane Bullock (PCP Facilitator) works with Pat Roberts through this process.

It seems paradoxical that Carl Rogers himself didn't consider his theory available to people with a learning disability. Yet, almost 60 years later we are acknowledging that not only is he the founder of the humanistic person-centred approach for counselling, but that person-centred planning developed out of person-centred therapy (Becker and Pallin, 2001).

As is the case with therapy, the therapist, through offering unconditional positive regard, would allow the person to seek growth. In person-centred planning, although it is not therapy, the facilitator and circle of friends provide an atmosphere of unconditional positive regard whilst assisting the person to work towards their dreams. The attitudes and personal qualities of a facilitator are therefore of paramount importance if person-centred planning is to succeed.

Awareness training is already called for in *Valuing People* (Department of Health, 2002), where five defining ideas of person-centred planning are:

- The person being at the centre of the process
- Listening to and learning from what people want from their lives
- Helping people to think about what they want now and in the future
- Family and friends working together with the person to make this happen
- Reflecting the person's capacities and specifying the level of support required

O'Brien (2004) suggests that this understanding of person-centred planning will generate dissonance among professionals in many service settings, from a perspective of not having an ability to understand an individual's options. An ability to interpret an individual's unique signs in communication is a challenge for person-centred planning.

Bradley (2004, p. 90), emphasises that personal attitudes and practice can facilitate person-centred practice, and of particular importance are:

Table 1.3 Key differences between traditional and person-centred planning approaches. Source: Becker and Pallin (2001); adapted from Bradley *et al.* (1994).

Key question	Traditional planning	Person-centred planning
Who is the person of concern?	The client	The citizen
What is the typical setting?	A group home or day centre	A person's home, workplace or local school
How are services organised?	In a continuum of options	Through a unique array of supports available to the individual
What is the model?	Developmental/behavioural	Ordinary living
What are the services?	Programmes/interventions	Individualised supports
How are services planned?	Individual programme plan based on professional assessments	Through a person-centred plan
Who controls the planning decision?	An interdisciplinary team	The individual or those family or friends closest to the person
What is the planning context?	Team consensus	A person-centred team or circle of support
What is given the highest priority?	Independence/skill development/behaviour management	Self-determination, relationships and valued social roles
What is the objective?	To develop independence and change undesirable behaviours	To support the person to have the lifestyle that they choose in their local community

- Your ability to relate to people and work in partnership
- Your communication skills, especially listening
- Focusing on people's positive features
- Having an open and enquiring mind
- Having a strong commitment to the principles of person-centred planning

Person-centred planning attempts to include and mobilise the individual's family and wider social network, as well as to use resources from the system of statutory services (Mansell and Beadle-Brown, 2004).

This ethos reflects Gerard Egan's model of helping, where as well as working with an individual's self-motivation, the person's social support system is also mobilised so as to work towards individual goals and aspirations, with a greater likelihood of success.

Reservations, however, have also been expressed (Mansell and Beadle-Brown, 2004) about the impact and implementation of not only *Valuing People*, but the process of person-centred planning. These are largely attributed to the varied population of people with a learning disability, which includes severe, profound disability and challenging behaviours. How can PCP be actioned by staff who have difficulties in perceiving the needs of people with such challenging needs? Social isolation in residential settings and in modern society means that communities of support are rather less real in practice, and supportive neighbourhoods are becoming less common.

Services need to demonstrate their use of PCP, for without a clear understanding of what constitutes a valid PCP approach, they are likely to stick rigidly to what is currently described (Isles, 2003).

As a partial answer to these reservations, Towell and Sanderson (2004) suggest that positive change can be achieved through a training and policy focus on enhancing the skills of direct delivery staff so as to make a tangible contribution towards PCP.

Limited research into PCP has been conducted, but a recent evaluation of PCP (Emerson *et al.*, 2005) has focused on the impact of PCP on the life experiences of people with a learning disability, the nature and costs of support, and the personal, contextual and organisational factors which impede the introduction and effectiveness of PCP. The overall results of this study clearly indicated that the introduction of PCP has had a positive benefit on life experiences. For those people who had a plan there was a:

- 52% increase in the size of social networks
- 2.4 times increase in the odds of being in contact with a member of their family
- 40% increase in the level of contact with friends
- 30% increase in the number of community-based activities undertaken in the previous month
- 25% increase in the variety of community-based activities undertaken in the previous month
- 33% increase in the hours per week of scheduled day activities
- 2.8 times increase in the odds of having more choice

In terms of training and education the evaluation report seeks to recommend that the Department of Health, through Strategic Health Authorities (SHAs), should encourage professional social and healthcare staff to work in person-centred ways and have familiarity with PCP. In addition, managers should also have training courses to equip them to use person-centred thinking throughout their work. This is an indicator that, like person-centred therapy, person-centred planning is a quality in attitude, relationships and networks of support.

As McNally (2004) has commented, we are in a climate which is rich in ideology and presentation, but comparatively poor in implementation, and therefore McNally proposes that what is really required is an implementation-based approach, which from a person-centred perspective is clearly required from the existing prevailing evidence.

Conclusion

This chapter has set out to embrace the broad meaning and emphasis of the concept of person-centredness from a psychological, person-centred health conceptualisation through person-centred planning within learning disability services.

Commonalities can be extracted which are seen to be located within the values and attitudes formed within a relationship between a client and a professional, whether in therapy, receipt of healthcare, or the process of person-centred planning.

Current healthcare reforms emphasise that the patient/client is at the heart of practice and that an effective and person-centred partnership between professional and patient/client is an imperative.

Additional education and training for professionals within acute and primary healthcare are indicated if the implementation of a person/patient-centred approach is to be achieved.

From a person-centred nursing perspective, and in particular, in areas where patients suffer from marginalisation, such as dementia care, mental health and learning disability, the focus is on a professionally driven value-based relationship.

The areas of loss of personhood or self-identity as well as client empowerment are where nurses are establishing their loci of practice in an attempt to understand the client's perspective within a wider social and professional network.

Person-centred planning provides challenges for future understanding of valid approaches, which is that PCP facilitator practice revolves around the intricacy of the process of planning with the person.

Finally, implementation barriers have been identified whereby training and education which encompass a value-based approach in thinking and services by professionals must be actualised if true person-centred approaches are to be sustained.

References

Atkinson, D. (2005) Narratives and people with learning disabilities. Chapter 1 in: *Learning Disabilities: A Life-Cycle Approach to Valuing People* (eds. G. Grant, P. Goward, M. Richardson and P. Ramcharan). Open University Press, Berkshire.

Barber, M., Jenkins, R. and Jones, C. (2000) A survivor's group for women who have a learning disability. *British Journal of Developmental Disabilities*. **46-1**(30), 31–41.

Barker, P. (2001) The Tidal Model: developing an empowering, person-centred approach to recovery within psychiatric and mental health nursing. *Journal of Psychiatric and Mental Health Nursing*, **8**, 233–40.

Barr, O. (1997) Care of people with learning disabilities in hospital. *Nursing Standard*, **12**, 49–55.

Barry, C. A., Bradley, C. P., Britten, N., Stevenson, F. A. and Barber, N. (2000) Patient's unvoiced agendas in general practice consultations: qualitative study. *British Medical Journal*, **320**, 1246–50.

Bayliss, P. and Dodwell, C. (2002) Building relationships through drama: The Action Track Project (1). *Research in Drama Education*. **7**(1), 43–60.

Becker, C. and Pallin, R. (2001) *Person-Centred Planning Approaches. A Literature Review. Persons with Developmental Disabilities*. Central Alberta Community Board.

Bradley, A. (2004) *Positive Approaches to Person-Centred Planning*. British Institute of Learning Disabilities Publications, Kidderminster.

Bradley, V., Ashbaugh, J. and Blaney, B. (eds.) (1994) *Creating Individual Supports for People with Developmental Disabilities*. Paul H. Brooks, Baltimore.

Brandon, D. (1989) *Mutual Respect*. Good Impressions, Surbiton.

Brechin, A. (1998) What makes for good care? In *Care Matters: Concepts, Practice and Research in Health and Social Care* (eds. A. Brechin, J. Walmsley, J. Katz and S. Pearce), pp. 170–87. Sage, London.

Brechin, A. and Swain, J. (1988) Professional/client relationships: creating a 'working alliance' with people with learning difficulties. *Disability, Handicap and Society*, **3**(3), 213–26.

Brewster, J. and Ramcharan, P. (2005) Enabling and supporting person-centred approaches. Chapter 24 in: *Learning Disabilities: A Life-Cycle Approach to Valuing People* (eds. G. Grant, P. Goward, M. Richardson and P. Ramcharan). Open University Press, Berkshire.

Bristol Royal Infirmary Inquiry (2001) *Learning From Bristol: The Report of the Public Inquiry into Children's Heart Surgery at the Bristol Royal Infirmary 1984–1995*. Stationery Office, London.

Brodin, J. (1999) Play in children with severe multiple disabilities: play with toys – a review. *International Journal of Disability, Development & Education*, **46**(1), 25–34.

Brown, H., Stein, J. and Turk, V. (1995) The sexual abuse of adults with learning disabilities: report of a second year incidence survey. *Mental Handicap Research*, **8**, 3–24.

Cain, D. J. (1987) Carl R. Rogers: the man, his vision, his impact. *Person-Centred Review*, **2**, 283–8.

Campion, P., Foulkes, J., Neighbour, R. and Tate, P. (2002) Patient centredness in the MRCGP video examination: analysis of large cohort. *British Medical Journal*, **325**, 691–2.

Corey, G. (1991) *Theory and Practice of Counselling and Psychotherapy*, 4th edn. Pacific Grove, CA, Brooks/Cole Publishing Company.

Cramer, D. (1992) *Personality and Psychotherapy, Theory, Practice and Research*. Open University Press, Milton Keynes.

Davies, S., Nolan, M. R., Brown, J. and Wilson, F. (1999) *Dignity on the Ward: Promoting Excellence in the Acute Hospital Care of Older People*. Report for Help the Aged/Orders of St John Care Trust, London.

Department of Health (2000) *The NHS Plan*. Stationery Office, London.

Department of Health (2001a) *National Service Framework for Older People*. HMSO, London.

Department of Health (2001b) *Valuing People: A New Strategy for Learning Disability for the 21st Century*. HMSO, London.

Department of Health (2002) *Planning With People: Towards Person-Centred Approaches*. Department of Health, London.

Dewing, J. (2004) Concerns relating to the application of frameworks to promote person-centredness in nursing with older people. *International Journal of Older People Nursing in Association with Journal of Clinical Nursing*, **13**(3a), 39–44.

Dunn, N (2002) Commentary: patient centred care: timely, but is it practical? *British Medical Journal*, **324**, 651.

Elwyn, G. (2005) Arriving at the postmodern medical consultation. *Primary Care*, **5**(12–13).

Emerson, E., Routledge, M., Robertson, J., Sanderson, H., McIntosh, B., Swift, P., Joyce, T., Oakes, P., Towers, C., Hatton, C., Romeo, R. and Knapp, M. (2005) *An Evaluation Study into Person-Centred Planning*. Lancaster University.

Foster, J. (2005) Learning disability liaison nurses in acute hospitals: is there evidence to support the development of this role. *Learning Disability Practice*, **8**(4), 33–8.

Graham, H. (1986) *The Human Face of Psychology, Humanistic Psychology in its Historical Social and Cultural Context*. Open University Press, Milton Keynes.

Hart, S. (1998) Learning disabled people's experience of general hospitals. *British Journal of Nursing*, **7**, 470–7.

Heibert, B., Wong, B. and Hunter, M. (1982) Affective influences on learning disabled adolescents. *Learning Disability Quarterly*, **5**, 334–43.

Isles, I. (2003) Becoming a learning organization. A precondition for person-centred services to people with learning difficulties. *Journal of Learning Disabilities*, **7**(1), 65–77.

Jonsdottir, H., Litchfield, M. and Pharris, M. D. (2004) The relational core of nursing practice as partnership. *Journal of Advanced Nursing*, **47**(3), 241–50.

Kerr, M., Fraser, D. and Felce, D. (1996) Primary healthcare for people with a learning disability; a keynote review. *British Journal of Learning Disabilities*, **24**, 2–8.

Kitwood, T. and Bredin, K. (1992) A new approach to the evaluation of dementia care. *Journal of Advances in Health and Nursing Care*, **1**(5), 41–60.

Law, J., Bunning, K., Bying, S., Farrelly, S. and Heyman, B. (2005) Making sense in primary care: levelling the playing field for people with communication difficulties. *Disability & Society*, **20**(2), 169–84.

Mansell, J. and Beadle-Brown, J. (2004) Person-centred planning or person-centred action? Policy & practice in intellectual disability services. *Journal of Applied Research in Intellectual Disabilities*, **17**, 1–9.

Markwick, A. and Sage, J. (1997) Self-image and people with learning disabilities. *British Journal of Nursing*, **6**(2), 99–102.

Mearns, D. and Thorne, B. (1988) *Person-Centred Counselling in Action*. Sage, London.

Mencap (1997) *Prescription for Change* (Summary) Mencap Research, London.

Mencap (2004) *Treat Me Right: Better Healthcare for People with a Learning Disability*. Mencap, London.

McNally, S. (2004) *Plus ça change?* Progress achieved in services for people with an intellectual disability in England since the publication of *Valuing People*. *Journal of Learning Disabilities*, **8**(4), 323–9.

National Health Service Executive (1999) *Once A Day*. HMSO, London.

NHS Health Scotland (2004). *Health Needs Assessment Report, People with Learning Disabilities in Scotland*. Glasgow.

Nolan, M. R., Davies, S. and Grant, G. (eds.) (2001) *Working with Older People and their Families: Key Issues in Policy and Practice*. Open University Press, Buckingham.

Nolan, M. R., Davies, S., Brown, J., Keady, J. and Nolan, J. (2002) *Longitudinal Study of the Effectiveness of Educational Preparation to meet the Needs of Older People and Carers: The AGEIN (Advancing Gerontological Education in Nursing) Project*. English National Board for Nursing, Midwifery and Health Visiting, London.

Nolan, M. R., Davies, S., Brown, J., Keady, J. and Nolan, J. (2004) Beyond 'person-centred' care: a new vision for gerontological nursing. *International Journal of Older People Nursing in Association with Journal of Clinical Nursing*, **13**(3a), 45–53.

O'Brien, J. (2004) If person-centred planning did not exist, *Valuing People* would require its invention. *Journal of Applied Research in Intellectual Disabilities*, **17**, 11–15.

O'Brien, J. and Lovett, H. (1992) Finding a way toward everyday lives: the contribution of person-centred planning. In: *A Little Book about Person Centred Planning* (eds. J. O'Brien and C. O. O'Brien), pp 113–32. Inclusion Press, Toronto.

Parse, R. R. (2004) Editorial: person-centred care. *Nursing Science Quarterly*, **17**(3), 193.

Pendleton, D., Schofield, T., Tate, P. and Havelock, P. (1984) *The Consultation: An Approach to Learning and Teaching.* Oxford University Press, Oxford.

Rogers, C. (1957) The necessary and sufficient conditions of therapeutic personality change. *Journal of Consulting Psychology*, **21**, 95–103.

Rogers, C. R. (1959) A theory of therapy, personality, and interpersonal relationships, as developed in the client-centred framework. In: *Psychology: A Study of a Science*, Vol. 3 (ed. S. Koch). *Formulations of the Person and the Social Context*, pp. 184–256. McGraw-Hill, New York.

Rogers, C. R. (1961) *On Becoming a Person: A Therapist's View of Psychotherapy.* Houghton Mifflin, Boston.

Rees, M. (ed.) (1998) *Drawing on Difference: Art Therapy with People Who Have Learning Difficulties.* Routledge, London.

Royal College of Psychiatrists (2004) *Psychotherapy and Learning Disability.* Council Report CR 116. London.

Sanderson, H., Kennedy, J., Richie, P. and Goodwin, G. (1997) *People, Plans & Possibilities: Exploring Person Centred Planning.* SHS Ltd, Edinburgh.

Scottish Executive (2000) *The Same As You? A Review of Services for People with Learning Disabilities.* The Stationery Office, Edinburgh.

Sinason, V. (2002) Treating people with learning disabilities after physical or sexual abuse. *Advances in Psychiatric Treatment*, **8**, 424–32.

Slevin, E. and Sines, D. (1996) Attitudes of nurses in a general hospital towards people with learning disabilities: influences of contact, & graduate-non-graduate status. A comparative study. *Journal of Advanced Nursing*, **24**(6), 1116–26.

Stewart, M. (2001) Towards a global definition of patient centred care. *British Medical Journal*, **322**, 444–5.

Towell, D. and Sanderson, H. (2004) Person-centred planning in its strategic context: reframing the Mansell/Beadle-Brown critique. *Journal of Applied Research in Intellectual Disabilities*, **17**, 17–21.

Waitman, A. and Conboy-Hill, S. (1992) *Psychotherapy & Mental Handicap.* Sage, London.

Wharton, S., Hames, A. and Milner, H. (2005) The accessibility of general NHS services for children with disabilities. *Child Care, Health & Development*, **31**(3), 275–82.

Williams, V. and Robinson, C. (2000) 'Tick this, tick that'. The views of people with learning disabilities on their assessments. *Journal of Learning Disabilities*, **4**(4), 293–305.

Wolfensberger, W. (1972) *The Principle of Normalisation in Human Services.* National Institute on Mental Retardation, Toronto.

Wolfensberger, W. (1983) Social role valorisation: a proposed new term for the principle of normalisation. *Mental Retardation*, **21**(6), 234–9.

CHAPTER 2

The therapeutic relationship

John Aldridge

Introduction

The concept of therapeutic nursing is not new and much has been written on the topic since Peplau (1952) introduced the notion of a therapeutic nursing relationship. However, much of the literature relates to the perspectives of mental health and medical–surgical nursing and does not attempt to deal with the specific and rapidly developing context of learning disability practice. This context is influenced by a range of policy, legal and philosophical issues that strongly influence the way in which we view the nature of services to people with learning disabilities. Not least of these are the changes in service provision that threaten the very existence of learning disability nurses. Over 25 years ago, Levi (1980) warned of 'functional redundancy' in nursing, with many of the more therapeutic aspects of nursing being taken up by specialist therapists. In the case of learning disability practice this leaves us with little more than the custodial 'warehousing' role (Evers, 1981) associated with long stay hospitals. Levine (1973) differentiated between 'supportive nursing', which prevents deterioration in health, and 'therapeutic nursing', which promotes a movement toward health and well-being. Clearly, there is a need for learning disability nurses to demonstrate their therapeutic potential and to show that they have a useful part to play in helping clients in their health, well-being and personal development.

At first sight therapeutic nursing and the therapeutic relationship may seem relatively easy to define, but once we scrape the surface we find a complex range of ideas and concepts that stem from philosophies, ideologies and individual therapies. Sometimes there are difficulties in applying these definitions to our own work. Not least of these difficulties is the relevance of the concept of 'therapy as healing' to learning disability nursing. This begs the question of whether a therapeutic relationship always entails the use of a therapy, or whether there is something more universal and fundamental in therapeutic relationships. It seems important therefore to attempt a workable definition of the therapeutic relationship that has currency within nursing as a whole and specifically within learning disability practice.

Additionally, it seems that therapeutic nursing has two facets. The first of these, and probably the most apparent, is the emotional and interpersonal aspect, which we might call 'therapeutic nursing as an art'. The second is the more logical and objective aspect, which we might call 'therapeutic nursing as a science'. Arguably, there is a synergy between the two that leads to a *gestalt*, and therefore a need to address both aspects if our nursing is to be truly therapeutic in a holistic sense.

This chapter therefore aims to explore the following interconnected elements:

- The policy, legal and philosophical context of therapeutic relationships in learning disabilities.
- An exploration of definitions of the therapeutic relationship and an attempt to develop a definition that has clear application to learning disability practice.
- The therapeutic relationship as an art – emotional and interpersonal aspects.
- The therapeutic relationship as a science – logical and objective aspects.
- How we might evaluate a therapeutic relationship.

The policy, legal and philosophical context of therapeutic relationships in learning disabilities

It is something of a truism that, over the last 25 years, almost every feature of learning disability nursing has changed: where we work with people; what kind of support we offer; who we offer that support to; and most importantly how we offer that support. People with learning disabilities are now much more likely to be living in their parental home, in domestic-style supported living or in their own homes. This has a profound effect on the way that we view our relationship with them. Rather than supporting people in large institutional environments that were predominantly our workplace we are now providing that support in a setting that is predominantly the person's home. The language that we use has also undergone tremendous change. We no longer use the collective nouns 'patients' or 'residents', but we speak about 'clients', 'service users' or even (!) people. We now look back on historical terms such as 'subnormal' and 'mongol' with horror and revulsion – did people really use these words that now seem to belong to an alien world? The implicit subtext of this changed language goes beyond mere political correctness and reflects a deep-seated change in the way we think about and relate to the people we support. We are now providing a *service* to *people*, with all the implications that this would have if they did not have learning disabilities. The fact that we are providing a service means that we are accountable not only to our profession but also to the people for whom the service is provided. This entails a shift in power relationships and empowerment of a group of people who have formally been relatively powerless. However, this power shift is not universal and much work remains to be done. Institutionalisation is determined primarily by interpersonal relationships than by bricks and mortar. Recognition that we are providing a service to people highlights the interpersonal nature of our relationship with them and is a key factor in the true deinstitutionalisation of services. In working therapeutically, we recognise the individuality and personhood of each of our clients and our relationship becomes one of human relatedness, rather than the depersonalised, routine-bound and distanced interactions that characterised institutional approaches (King *et al.*, 1971).

The four key themes of *Valuing People* (Department of Health, 2001a): Rights, Choice, Inclusion and Independence, have immediate relevance to, and underpin the concepts of, therapeutic relationships. Firstly, there is the right of any individual to receive high-quality and effective therapeutic care and to receive that care through a therapeutic relationship with healthcare professionals. Secondly, people have the prerogative to make choices about the nature of therapeutic support. This implies a partnership between the individual and the helper which is enabling and in which there is shared power. Thirdly, therapeutic support will hopefully help the individual to develop independence and a degree of self-sufficiency in their lives. Fourthly, inclusion in the context of therapeutic nursing seems to be about including people in the full range of therapeutic options that would be available to anyone.

Valuing People also places considerable emphasis on person-centred processes. A therapeutic approach is arguably inherently person-centred. Most therapeutic work entails working with the person's issues, from the person's perspective and in ways appropriate to the person. The Department of Health (2001b) defines person-centred planning as

> ... a process for continual listening and learning, focussing on what is important to someone now and in the future, and acting upon this in alliance with their family and friends. This listening is used to understand a person's capacities and choices. Person centred planning is the basis for problem solving and negotiation to mobilise the necessary resources to pursue a person's aspirations.

In speaking about 'listening and learning' and 'acting in alliance', there is much in this definition that directly relates to definitions of therapeutic work and the therapeutic nature of relationships.

Both person-centred processes and therapeutic relationships are underpinned by the concept of partnership, which is emphasised throughout *Valuing People*. Partnership implies a sharing of information, power and decision-making.

Finally, in relation to *Valuing People*, we have the introduction of the concept of Health Facilitation and Health Action Planning. At the personal level, Health Facilitation applies person-centred processes to the individual's health and uses the therapeutic techniques of listening, negotiating and acting-with.

However, these ideological drivers toward therapeutic relationships with service users should be tempered by an awareness of the legal and policy constraints on such relationships. Far from being unhelpful these may act to clarify the parameters of therapeutic relationships with people who have learning disabilities. The United Kingdom Central Council for Nursing and Midwifery (1998) *Guidelines for Mental Health and Learning Disabilities Nursing* [now available through the Nursing and Midwifery Council] note that

> All nurses should be aware of the power imbalance between their role and their clients. Your power and influence must always be directed to meeting the needs of clients and not your own. All clients are to some extent vulnerable to the misuse of power by their carers and by registered nurses.

This comment points to one of the difficulties that we have in establishing truly therapeutic relationships with people who have learning disabilities: that our clients have intellectual impairments to a greater or lesser degree. They may have impaired understanding and a difficulty in exercising balanced partnership because of their need for support in everyday living. The Nursing and

Midwifery Council (2002) take up this point and give guidance on the boundaries of professional relationships. They comment that:

> Boundaries define the limits of behaviour which allow a client and a practitioner to engage safely in a therapeutic caring relationship. These boundaries are based upon trust, respect and the appropriate use of power.

This important issue of the boundaries of therapeutic relationships is one that has exercised mental health and learning disability nurses for a number of years. Many nursing students have been told, 'Don't get involved – maintain a professional distance'. But what is a 'professional distance' and how does one balance this principle against that of developing empathy and intimacy, especially when one's involvement with a client and their family spans many years and a complex range of developing needs? Learning disability nursing is perhaps unique in the extreme duration of professional relationships, which can be lifelong. In such cases the relationship imperceptibly edges toward friendship, as client, family and nurse begin to infuse themselves into each other's lives. Whether or not this is healthy and desirable is a point for debate and it could be argued that it is better to retain a more formal approach to our work and to open and close 'cases' according to need. This is more easily said than done, because of the nature of human relatedness, especially if we attempt to develop empathy and a deeper understanding. Is genuineness and authenticity incompatible with a 'professionally managed' relationship? Peternelj-Taylor (2002) suggests that understanding the power differential within a nurse–client relationship is crucial to building and maintaining professional boundaries and therapeutic integrity.

People with learning disabilities are potentially vulnerable in relationships and this is underlined by considerations of consent and mental capacity. Department of Health (2001c) indicates that, 'before you examine, treat or care for *competent* adults you must obtain their consent' (my emphasis). Clearly, this statement implies that consent is needed for virtually all aspects of care, including any therapeutic activities. The same principles apply to incompetent adults, but there is considerable difficulty here in deciding whether the individual is giving permission for your actions. Absence of dissent does not necessarily indicate assent. No one can give consent on behalf of an incompetent adult, although they may be given treatment if this is in their best interests. The concept of Best Interests has recently been clarified by the Mental Capacity Act (2005), which is accompanied by a Code of Practice. Before undertaking therapeutic activities with a client, we therefore need to consider whether the individual consents to this and whether our involvement is in the person's best interests. The Nursing and Midwifery Council (2002) comment that:

> The relationship between registered nurses and midwives and their clients is a therapeutic caring relationship that must focus solely upon meeting the health or care needs of the client.

So perhaps the questions we need to ask are 'Whose needs does our work serve?' and 'Is the person going to be better off as a result of our involvement?'. How do we know what 'better off' means and how does that relate to the rather nebulous concept of 'duty of care'?

In the relatively small but significant number of cases where care is given under the Mental Health Act, the therapeutic relationship is attempted under what might be called a 'polluted climate' (Jennings, 1997). The Mental Health Act exists specifically to restrict the individual's freedom and to compel them to accept treatment against their wishes. We need to gain the individual's confidence, but at the same time we have the power to override their choices.

Defining the therapeutic relationship and its emotional components

Attempting to define a therapeutic relationship within a phrase or sentence is surprisingly difficult and many authors seem to avoid doing so. Bazley *et al.* (1973) define a therapeutic relationship as 'a human relationship with goals defined by patients' needs'. This short but profound definition raises three important issues that may differentiate a therapeutic relationship from one that is functional and, perhaps, from one that is simply a caring relationship:

1. The relationship is one of human interaction, between at least two people.
2. The relationship is purposeful and goal-directed, rather simply supportive.
3. It is driven by the individual and is person-centred.

The idea of human relatedness implies connection with the person at an interpersonal level and seems to connect strongly with Buber's (1958) differentiation between I-thou and I-it; the subjective and objective ways of relating. We might interpret this concept as meaning that human relationships (I-thou) involve a 'you-and-me' interaction between people who have thoughts and feelings. An I-it relationship is the sort that you might have with inanimate objects such as household items. We do not have to consider their thoughts and feelings and we do not need to try to communicate with them. Institutional ways of working are arguably characterised by I-it relationships. The terms 'conveyor belt care' and 'warehousing' that are associated with institutional practices have direct relevance to the ways in which inanimate objects are stored and moved around in industrial contexts. Clearly, in attempting a therapeutic relationship we need to 'see the person' and try to understand their thoughts and feelings, to communicate and interact in human ways.

Kirby and Slevin (1992) identify a number of interrelated elements of the therapeutic relationship:

- *Authenticity of being*: This relates to being genuine and relating to others as our real self, rather than hiding behind a professional persona – therapeutic use of self. In being authentic, we reveal elements of ourselves to our clients and relate to them in a genuinely human way that stems from who we are. However, Aranda and Street (1999) explore the need to balance 'being authentic' with 'being a chameleon'. Being a chameleon involves adjusting our interactions to the circumstances and to the client. This concept recognises that different clients and families demand different things from us and that a single unified 'authentic' response may not be sufficient or appropriate. This chameleon-like ability to change our approach to suit the surroundings is not necessarily incompatible with genuineness, but may suggest that we reveal different aspects of ourselves to different clients, just as we might with different friends, and that we might make diverse therapeutic use of our selves.
- *Conscience*: This element seems to relate to both consciousness and awareness of our actions and also the moral sense or ethics of what we do. We need to remain aware of and constantly

reflecting on our actions, making judgements about whether these are in the best interests of the individual.

- *Commitment* is not simply about devotion to duty, but is more about our conscious decision to invest ourselves in the relationship, to show loyalty to both the relationship and to the client. This perhaps relates to Rogers' (1951) concept of unconditional positive regard – an acceptance of the client and non-judgemental support. Such a concept relates closely to valuing diversity in clients, whether this is in culture, religion or sexual orientation.

- *Presence* relates to 'being with' and 'being there' with the client and for the client, sharing experiences and communicating at an interpersonal level rather than necessarily with words. Presence involves being present not just in body, but also in spirit and in mind. It means giving the person our attention, listening to them, taking clues from their body language and paralinguistics, showing that we have heard by responding and active listening (Egan, 2004). Freshwater and Stickley (2004) comment that 'it is the emotionally intelligent practitioner that hears the sigh, makes eye contact, communicates understanding and demonstrates human care'. This concept implies a 'tuning in' to the person's being and the subtleties of their communication.

- *Compassion*: *Collins English Dictionary* (1995) defines compassion as 'a feeling of distress and pity for the suffering or misfortune of another, often including the desire to alleviate it'. Compassion therefore involves an emotional response to clients' experiences but also compassionate action as a response to those emotions. Indeed, von Dietze and Orb (2000) comment that compassion 'is more than an emotion, it revolves around the ways we relate to other people and demands that we act'. The authors imply that compassion is close to love and that it blurs the boundaries of professional relationships. It could be argued that an over-compassionate response risks incapacitating the nurse through over-identification with the client. Some objectivity is required so that we can take effective action with the client. This point is taken up by Stickley and Freshwater (2002), who point out that a therapeutic relationship needs to go beyond mere 'care' and that we need to practise the 'art of loving' in a structured way, using the work of Fromm (1957).

- *Empathy*: Price and Archbold (1997) comment that 'Empathy is a commonly used but poorly understood concept. It is difficult to define or measure as it appears to be a multidimensional concept that has not been fully identified'. However, a commonly used definition is that of Rogers (1957), who explained that it is the ability 'to sense the client's private world as if it were your own without ever losing the "as if" quality. Reynolds (2003) offers both an expanded definition and an attempt to measure empathy from the client's viewpoint, using the Reynolds Empathy Scale (Reynolds, 1994) summarised in Table 2.1.

Empathy, then, seems to involve certain core elements that might be described as:

- Active listening and 'tuning in' to the client
- Emotional understanding of the client's world and needs
- Communicating to the client that we understand, without being patronising
- Responding to our understanding of the client's needs without 'taking over'.

Sadly, Reynolds and Scott (2000) suggest that research on the subject reports broadly low levels of empathy in nursing and that this seems consistent across a 40 year time span, although

Table 2.1 Summary of the Reynolds empathy scale.

High empathy items	Low empathy items
Attempts to explore and clarify feelings ■ Active listening ■ Sensitive understanding	Leads, directs and diverts ■ Communication that is not client-focused
Responds to feelings ■ A willingness to 'journey alongside' ■ Trying to 'get inside the client's shoes'	Ignores verbal and non-verbal communication ■ Inability to listen ■ Failing to hear messages ■ Conveying a lack of caringness
Explores personal meaning of feeling ■ Attempting to clarify and investigate clients' expressions of emotion ■ Helping to let emotions flow	Judgemental and opinionated ■ Criticising ■ Lack of respect and acceptance
Responds to feelings and meanings ■ Helping clients to anchor feelings within a context ■ Helping clients move from general to particular and from past to present	Interrupts and seems in a hurry ■ Not giving client time to communicate issues
Provides the patient with direction ■ Helping clients to focus on solutions	Fails to focus on solutions ■ Lack of acceptance of problems ■ Lack of movement toward problem solving
Appropriate voice tone ■ Conveying warmth, commitment and genuine interest	Inappropriate voice tone ■ Sounds curt ■ Sounding unfriendly, hostile

none of the studies that they cite appears to stem from learning disability practice. However, Gardner and Smyly (1997) do comment on the 'absence of good quality relationships for some of our clients' and that there is a need for clients to have someone who will truly listen to them, value and respect them. Although this is an isolated instance, we should not be complacent. The difficulties of developing an empathic relationship with people with severe and profound learning disabilities who lack significant communication are great. We may attempt empathy and think we know what the client's world is like, but this empathic understanding is filtered through our own perceptions, thoughts and experiences. Bahlinger and Walsh (1993) offer a brave attempt to give an account of a person's day through their eyes, though we can by no means be certain that it is a true representation of Tom's thoughts. There is a danger of putting our own thoughts into clients' minds. Kirby (1995) offers the following quotation from Solomon (1991)

> If I want to know what you're thinking right now, all I have to do is care more about what you're thinking than what I'm thinking.... As soon as I care more what you're thinking than what I'm thinking I will give up my thoughts and I will absorb yours, and I will understand you.

Although this approach goes some way toward addressing Reynolds' (1994) concerns, it is not as simple as Solomon suggests. It is not simply a case of suspending our own selves. People's thoughts do not simply flood into our mind by a process of osmosis. There needs to be a communicative interface along which thoughts and emotions can flow. Perhaps we can never know what it is like to have a severe learning disability and to live in supported accommodation – we can only make what we hope are skilful guesses, based on finely tuned sensitivity and communication.

Empowerment

Over the last twenty to thirty years, the learning disability literature has abounded with mentions of empowerment, which is often taken to mean advocacy or self-advocacy. At its simplest level empowerment means giving people power, but this prompts the question, 'power to do what?'. Parsloe and Stevenson (1992) define empowerment as 'people having power to express their needs and to decide how these needs should be met', which has clear relevance for the therapeutic relationship. Empowerment is, however, a rather nebulous concept, and Rappaport (1984) suggests that it is easier to define in its absence, rather than presence. Disempowerment is perhaps more obvious to the observer than empowerment. The US literature uses the term 'self determination' and this might be a more useful concept. Wehmeyer and Berkobien (1991) comment that self-determination 'refers to the attitudes and abilities required to act as the *primary causal agent* in one's life and to make choices regarding one's actions free from undue external influence or interference' (my emphasis). However, we need to be cautious when approaching empowerment. Does this mean that the client is given all of the power and total control, and what does this imply for our relationship with the person? This might be another reason to use the terms 'self-determination' or 'enabling', rather than 'empowerment'. Being the primary causal agent implies having most of the power, but in real life this is usually balanced by a consideration of the needs of others and an understanding of any limitations: otherwise, in empowering one individual there is a risk of disempowering others. In seeking total empowerment of the client in a therapeutic relationship, there is a danger that we may enslave ourselves.

Within the context of a therapeutic relationship empowerment seems to mean enabling the client to take the lead and to exercise control, not necessarily over the relationship itself, but over the focus and nature of the therapeutic work. An enabling and person-centred approach acknowledges that professionals do not always know best, but that their role is to facilitate the client in exploring and making choices that help to move them forward. Person-centred processes used in a therapeutic relationship inherently enable the client by offering choice and control over a number of issues:

- Whom the client has a therapeutic relationship with. The client needs to be able to enter into and withdraw from a therapeutic relationship with people of their choice.
- Where the therapeutic work takes place: choice of venue and surroundings.

- When the therapeutic work happens: the timing of the therapeutic work, how long each session lasts, and how often sessions take place; when to withdraw from the therapeutic relationship; when to close the relationship and move on.
- What the therapeutic work is about: the focus for therapeutic work, the aims and outcomes.
- Why there is a need to undertake therapeutic work: does the therapeutic work address a felt need? Deciding whether the proposed therapeutic work represents a movement toward their own definitions of health and well-being.
- How to undertake therapeutic work: the nature of the therapeutic process, how much to disclose, what to talk about, what kind of therapeutic activities to take part in.

Clearly, enabling, choice and consent are closely allied. If the client is enabled to exercise choice within the therapeutic relationship there is a greater likelihood that they are giving informed consent to the relationship and any therapeutic work that this entails.

Meutzel (1988) offers further insight into the dimensions of a therapeutic encounter between nurse and client and describes three key elements that overlap with one another to form a dynamic whole. The three elements are:

- Reciprocity
- Intimacy
- Partnership

Reciprocity describes the two-way nature of a therapeutic relationship; both client and nurse open up to one another and begin to understand each other, to communicate with one another. We perhaps need to recognise that the nurse and client are both affected by their relationship with one another. The potential benefits and positives will affect both parties, but so too will any possible harms.

The nurse gives of herself to the relationship and brings knowledge, expertise, compassion and commitment. From her work, she may take away a sense of personal accomplishment, professional development, achievement and a sense of having made a positive contribution to another's life. We need also to realise that the client's part of the relationship is not one-sided. One of the primary considerations is that the client should benefit from the therapy and the therapeutic relationship but in return they give of themselves; their trust, their affection and their ability to change us. We are agents of change in our clients' lives, but they are also agents of change in ours (Stuhlmiller, 2003).

Reciprocity seems to relate to the concept of mutuality in nursing: that both the client and nurse enter into a relationship that requires joint investment, effort and action if positive outcomes are to be achieved, and these might be viewed as the mutual costs of the relationship.

Much emphasis is laid on the vulnerability of people with learning disabilities and that they might be harmed by abusive relationships with others (Nursing and Midwifery Council, 2002). However, we sometimes work with people who can behave in very challenging ways. We may be at risk of verbal or physical abuse. In addition to these rather obvious harms there are covert losses. If we attempt therapeutic work that fails to achieve positive outcomes, is it just the client who loses out, or does the nurse lose something too?

The cost–benefit analysis is taken a step further when we realise that in any dyadic relationship one person can benefit while the other loses out. There are a number of possibilities, summarised below:

A Client benefits, nurse harmed	B Both client and nurse benefit
C Neither client nor nurse benefits	D Nurse benefits, client harmed

While position A does not negate the reciprocity of the relationship, it will arguably not be a therapeutic one because, once the nurse realises that she is harmed, she is unlikely to continue to invest herself wholeheartedly.

Position C is clearly a strong indicator for any work to be stopped immediately. If neither person benefits there is little point in continuing. If both are harmed any further work would be unethical.

Position D clearly describes abuse or exploitation of the client and is again unethical.

Position B is arguably the only one that describes a therapeutic relationship. The benefits do not have to be equally shared and it seems likely that the client will often gain more than the nurse. While there are mutual gains, and the client receives more than 50% of that gain, the conditions for a therapeutic relationship are met. We are left, however, with the problem of deciding the minimum share of benefit that is an ethical one. Should the minimum balance be 60–40 or 80–20 in favour of the client, for instance?

Intimacy refers to the closeness of a personal relationship, having access to personal, private or secret things. Nursing inherently entails intimacy at a physical level because it is often characterised by nurses giving physical care and invading individuals' personal space (Hall, 1959) Nurses are often assumed to have a 'licence to touch' areas of clients' bodies that would normally regarded as private (Jourard, 1966) and to assist people with bodily functions that are normally carried out privately and independently. Touch within a nursing context can be used in controlling, functional or therapeutic ways. Therapeutic touch can be intentional or unintentional, but there needs to be some kind of 'healing' effect that results from it (Sayre-Adams and Wright, 2001) for it to be truly therapeutic. However, the concept of intimacy extends beyond touch, closeness and proximity at the physical level. Meutzel (1988) reminds us that, in a therapeutic relationship intimacy describes 'closeness at physical, psychological and spiritual levels'.

Psychological intimacy is defined by Williams (2001) as 'a confiding, trusting relationship in which problems, concerns or worries are shared with another, for the purpose of seeking appropriate solutions'. However, this implies that such intimacy is entered into deliberately and purposefully, whereas psychological or emotional closeness can often result from a bond that grows between the nurse and client imperceptibly as they get to know one another and open up to each other over a period of time. Psychological intimacy is not necessarily easy to achieve unless both parties are willing and able to open up to one another and to communicate concerns and emotions in a reciprocal manner. It seems that there may be a number of prerequisites that must be present to some degree before intimacy can be developed. Some of these are:

- *Sharing time and space.* Arguably, it is impossible to develop intimacy with another individual unless one spends a significant amount of time with them in shared activities. The relationship deepens and develops intimacy over a period of time and is rarely instant. However, time spent together needs to be 'quality time', rather than being task-oriented.
- *Emotional intelligence* (Goleman, 1996), which includes emotional awareness, emotional self-regulation, motivation, empathy and social skills. Cadman and Brewer (2001) argue that

emotional intelligence is an essential skill and a prerequisite for nursing. However, this only fulfils one half of the therapeutic dyad. To develop intimacy with clients we need them to have a degree of emotional intelligence. There is some evidence to suggest that people with learning disabilities may have a specific impairment in the recognition, encoding and expression of emotions (Reed and Clements, 1989; McAlpine *et al.*, 1991; Rojahn *et al.*, 1995) that is not necessarily in line with their intellectual development. Without emotional sharing, there is a possibility that psychological intimacy may be rather one-sided or superficial.

■ *Two-way communication* at a level that enables both parties to understand with some degree of certainty what the other is thinking and feeling. People with learning disabilities frequently have difficulties with communication (Mansell, 1992; Cogher, 2005) but this depends not only on intellectual development, but also on physical impairments and the degree to which helpers facilitate communication in creative ways. There is an imperative here for the nurse to help the client to 'get the message across' in whatever way they can. We need to listen with all our attention and all our skill to the messages that clients are trying to send. True communication is, of course, two-way, and we therefore need to get our message across to the client, again using creative means. This tuning-in to one another is a mutual and reciprocal process whereby each person takes on the roles of sender and receiver.

■ *Acceptance of, and positive regard for each other*. Again, this is a reciprocal process. It is difficult to imagine having an intimate relationship with another person unless one has a degree of liking for them and that liking is returned, at least in part.

Partnership is a concept that implies working together, using shared ideas, shared decision-making, shared aims and shared means of achieving those aims. The concept is close to the ideas of teamwork and co-ownership. Indeed, we might regard the relationship as a 'therapeutic alliance', based on warmth and understanding. Inevitably, a consideration of power enters the discussion. Who is in charge or in control? In the paternalistic ethos that has pervaded learning disability services until recently, it has been the professional who has been firmly in control. The rationale for such an approach has been that people with learning disabilities are child-like and lack the understanding and skills needed to take a directive part in their lives. The professional knows best and directs the context, process and outcomes of any care. This becomes something of a circular argument based on self-fulfilling prophecy. However, the self-advocacy and People First movement successfully demonstrated that, with support, people with learning disabilities are capable of developing the skills to be self-directive and taking the lead in their own lives. In a therapeutic relationship, who is in charge depends on the abilities of the client, the stage of the therapeutic process and the context of the current situation. The power balance is likely to vary, rather than being fixed in favour of either party. In some situations, the therapist may take the lead, while in others it will be the client.

Logical and objective components of therapeutic relationships

Much of the discussion so far has focused on the emotional and interpersonal aspects of the therapeutic relationship, but there is arguably a need to explore the more objective aspects. In this, we return to Buber's (1958) differentiation between I-thou and I-it. The I-it aspect of the relationship

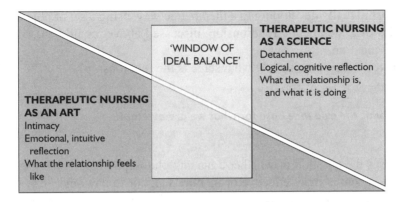

Figure 2.1 The balance between subjectivity and objectivity.

is the objective component – the rational and cognitive aspect of our work. Barker (2003) points out that over-emphasis on the I-it component may lead the nurse to compromise the emotional and compassionate part of her relationship with clients. However, this does not necessarily imply that objectivity is always a bad thing. Indeed, we might argue that, if we lose objectivity, there is a danger that we may blind ourselves to whether our relationship is really a therapeutic one. Clearly, some kind of balance is needed between subjectivity and objectivity in our relationships that avoids either extreme. This is shown in graphical form in Figure 2.1.

There seem to be a number of good reasons to retain at least an element of objectivity in our relationships with clients. Some are discussed below.

Being objective about the relationship and what we are attempting with clients

If the relationship is purposeful and goal-directed, then it follows that we need to be clear about what we are trying to achieve. The goals can be set by, or in partnership with, the client using a person-centred approach, but we still have a responsibility to deliver our part of the bargain. A reflective approach encourages the nurse to think about and take stock of her work. Johns (2000) defines reflection as:

> ... a window through which the practitioner can view and focus self within the context of her own lived experience in ways that enable her to confront, understand and work toward resolving the contradiction within her practice between what is desirable and actual practice.

This implies a need for objective analysis and objective evaluation – what is really happening here, and how well are we doing? Atkins (2000) suggests that one of the skills for reflective practice is critical analysis, in which judgements are made about strengths and weaknesses. Occasionally, then, we need to step back from our work and examine it impartially. The questions we need to ask ourselves are:

- Is the relationship really developing in a therapeutic way, using a set of objective criteria? The characteristics of a therapeutic relationship, discussed above, could be used as the basis for this kind of evaluation.
- Where is the relationship going? At what stage is the relationship?

Being objective about the evidence base for what we are attempting

Kitson (1999) poses the question of whether a nursing philosophy that emphasises the relationship between nurse and client is more effective or morally superior to any other (e.g. problem-based or outcome-based) approach. We could argue that the adoption of an ethos of therapeutic relationships in nursing is something of an act of faith, with little evidence to prove that such relationships are beneficial to clients. The comparative effectiveness of a therapeutic relationship is likely to be difficult to prove by research because of the number of potential confounding variables. However, the work of Reynolds (1994, 2003) suggests a high degree of congruency between what clients value and the parameters of a therapeutic relationship, thus providing evidence that a therapeutic relationship fulfils an expressed need for a kind of nursing that addresses emotional and interpersonal needs.

That said, it might be impossible to divorce the therapeutic relationship from the therapy itself. A therapeutic relationship in itself seems purposeless unless it achieves a therapeutic outcome for the client. What is the point of a therapeutic relationship unless it forms a basis for therapeutic work?

The *Making a Difference* document (Department of Health, 1999) emphasised the need for nurses to base their practice on a robust evidence base, and arguably we have a moral responsibility to clients to offer them therapeutic interventions that are effective – that achieve therapeutic outcomes. This is summarised by Muir Gray (1997) as 'doing the right things right': making sure that we do more good than harm. Pearson and Craig (2002) note that reflective practice is a key component of evidence-based nursing and that, where there is no evidence base for our work, the philosophy of evidence-based nursing should 'stop us in our tracks to reflect on the impact of what we are doing in the name of health, and why'.

This prompts us to consider not only 'Is my relationship a therapeutic one?', but also 'What do I think I'm trying to achieve and how confident am I that the means I am using will achieve that purpose?'.

Although there is a growing evidence base for some aspects of nursing and some interventions, relatively little of this applies to people with learning disabilities. Given the variability of the way in which learning disability affects individuals, we may need to retain a healthy scepticism regarding the likelihood of the success of therapeutic interventions. This is far from saying that we should not attempt therapeutic work in the absence of a robust evidence base. What we need to do is to evaluate objectively the effectiveness of our therapeutic work with each individual client and be ready to accept that some approaches work with some people, rather than using a 'one size fits all' approach. Evidence-based practice is not just about prescribing a particular therapy. Sackett *et al.* (2000) remind us that we need to integrate client preferences and expectations into our decision-making. To this, we might add individual client needs. We need to use a selective approach, so that the therapeutic approach we use with a client is suited to their preferences, but also reflects their personal and unique needs. Selection of a suitable therapeutic mode would be an example of partnership in the therapeutic relationship.

The central question we need to ask here is:

■ How confident am I that the therapeutic mode we have chosen is likely to be effective?

Being objective about the outcomes of our involvement with individuals

The outcomes of care are, to an extent, what vindicate the therapeutic relationship. The end result of the therapeutic process should arguably be the achievement of valued goals that enhance the quality of life of clients and their families. If we accept that our interventions should make a difference, we need to consider what those outcomes should be. Perhaps this is the point at which we need to develop a working definition of 'therapy'. Many definitions of therapy emphasise the concept of healing or the curative function. However, Slevin (1995) suggests that therapy in its broader meaning can mean 'all forms of helping intervention which is [*sic*] related to the treatment of illnesses and/or helping people with problems or difficulties of daily living'. So in short, if our work with a client has been therapeutic, they should be better off as a result. In learning disability practice, therapeutic outcomes seem to fall under a number of different headings:

■ *Physical health outcomes*: the improvement of movement and mobility, improvement of physical health and well-being.
■ *Mental health outcomes*: lowering levels of distress, improving emotional well-being, decreasing disorientation.
■ *Developmental*: work intended to help the client with intellectual, physical, social, language, self-care and personal development, perhaps through a process of teaching.
■ *Palliative or ameliorative*: This kind of therapeutic work can be used in circumstances where the individual's health is static or degenerating and where positive change through therapeutic work or treatment is undesirable or unattainable (The latter word should be used with great reservation). The aim of such work would be to ameliorate or minimise any pain, discomfort or distress using nursing (as opposed to medical) intervention. Any nursing intervention would probably be in conjunction with, rather than instead of, medical treatment.

The questions we need to ask here are:

■ What did we set out to achieve together and are we making progress toward our planned outcomes?
■ Is the relationship achieving its sense of purpose?

The therapeutic relationship as a process

A therapeutic relationship is not an either/or state, but is best seen as a process with a beginning and end. Peplau (1952) was one of the first nurse theorists to write about the nurse–client relationship as a journey. She describes four overlapping stages in this journey as:

- *Orientation*: the client seeks help and the nurse responds to this; they get to know one another and there is a 'coming together' of the nurse and client in a working relationship.
- *Identification*: the client and nurse explore feelings and concerns; the relationship deepens.
- *Exploitation*: the 'working together' phase of the relationship, in which much of the therapeutic work is done. The relationship is literally exploited for its therapeutic potential and the client moves from dependence toward independence.
- *Resolution*: the client and nurse gradually disengage from one another and the client becomes completely independent of the nurse.

Peplau's work was primarily written within the context of American psychiatric nursing in hospital environments in the 1950s and 1960s, where a model of admission – treatment – discharge predominated. Although it may have been difficult to apply this model to learning disability nursing until recently, recent changes in service provision suggest that nursing may be moving from a 'lifetime support' model toward a more traditional health treatment process, albeit one that moves at a relatively slow pace. Peplau's view of the therapeutic relationship, therefore, may begin to have greater currency for learning disability nursing in the 21st century than ever before.

Travelbee (1971) also described nursing as an 'interpersonal process', with an emphasis on human relatedness and human understanding, based on the work of Frankl's (1963) logotherapy. Her work primarily describes the following stages through which the client and nurse progress in order to achieve a therapeutic relationship. Each stage brings the client and nurse closer together.

- *Original encounter*: first impressions of each other.
- *Emerging identities*: each perceives the uniqueness and personal characteristics of the other.
- *Empathy*: sharing in each other's experience and understanding the other.
- *Sympathy*: Travelbee describes this as going beyond empathy (rather the reverse of many definitions), where the nurse makes therapeutic use of self.
- *Rapport*: the full human to human relationship that involves trust and confidence in each other.

One of the main theoretical problems with Travelbee's description of the therapeutic relationship is that is a one-way journey. She fails to comment on what happens once the therapeutic work has been completed and the client and nurse need to move apart, to close the relationship. An additional difficulty with both Peplau and Travelbee is that the relationship as they describe it seems to be rather one-sided. To a degree this is understandable, in that the client is a 'person in need' and the nurse has the power and expertise to address that need. However, more recent empowerment models of the therapeutic relationship (e.g. Barker *et al.*, 2000) and the enabling movement within learning disability practice suggest that a more balanced view of the relationship between client and nurse is needed. We might therefore propose the following model of the therapeutic relationship as a process within learning disability practice that has a beginning, middle and an end.

1. Opening the relationship
   - relationship building
   - sharing time and space
   - getting to know one another

- developing intimacy, empathy, trust
- learning how to communicate with one another
2. Working together in partnership
   - reciprocal use of the relationship
   - sharing ideas and concerns
   - developing shared goals and identifying outcomes
   - joint commitment to achieving goals and outcomes
   - freeing the client from dependency on the nurse
3. Closing the relationship
   - client and nurse increasingly distance themselves from one another, intimacy decreases
   - decreasing time spent together
   - withdrawal and independence
   - each moving on to new relationships

It is important to note that, although the client and nurse need to develop a very close relationship, this does not and should not last forever. Neither client nor nurse own one another and require freedom within the relationship and freedom to close the relationship. It may perhaps be a failing of learning disability nurses in former years to fail to enable the full independence of their clients, to 'let go' and allow clients and families to move on.

Conclusion

We have seen that the therapeutic relationship is not particularly easy to define and may be quite challenging to achieve within learning disability practice. Much of the literature on therapeutic relationships stems from mental health or medical–surgical nursing and assumes that the client has a certain level of ability to reflect upon self, to communicate concerns and to take action upon therapeutic goals. The term 'learning disability' covers an extremely broad range of disabilities and we may need to recognise that the achievement of a therapeutic relationship with clients who have mild to moderate learning disabilities is relatively attainable when compared to the challenges of doing so with people who have profound and complex disabilities. However, we should not be deterred; much valuable work was done by David Brandon (Brandon, 1989, 1991; Brandon and Ridley, 1985) that demonstrated the possibilities of non-verbal therapeutic exploration with people who have severe and profound disabilities.

The essential parameters of a therapeutic relationship may be summarised as follows:

1. *Therapeutic intent*: consciously or unconsciously, both client and nurse need to enter the relationship with the fundamental understanding that it will benefit the client.
2. *Therapeutic processes*: the relationship needs to comply with at least some of the parameters of a therapeutic relationship discussed in this chapter.
3. *Therapeutic outcomes*: It is paramount that the relationship results in some kind of discernible benefit to the client.

There is undeniably an enormous challenge to learning disability practitioners to develop ways of offering a therapeutic relationship to all people with learning disabilities, regardless of their level of ability. Additionally, there is an urgent need to develop a rigorous evidence base, grounded in learning disability practice, that enables us to confidently offer a range of therapies to our clients that are effective and that address their needs. Therapeutic nursing has an important part to play in addressing the key themes of *Valuing People* (Department of Health, 2001a). A therapeutic approach addresses the rights of people to a full range of therapeutic options, enabling independence through a therapeutic relationship and improving choice through partnership and person-centred processes. If the therapeutic work leads to personal development it will arguably enable people to improve their roles and relationships in society and to enable much greater levels of Inclusion.

References

Aranda, S. K. and Street, A. F. (1999) Being authentic and being a chameleon. *Nursing Inquiry*, **6**, 75–82.

Atkins, S. (2000) Developing underlying skills in the move toward reflective practice. In: *Reflective Practice in Nursing*, 2nd edn (eds. S. Burns and C. Bulman). Blackwell, Oxford.

Bahlinger, V. and Walsh, P. (1993) A view from the inside: a day in the life of Tom W. *Mental Handicap*, **21**, 105–8.

Barker, P. (2003) The primacy of caring. In *Psychiatric and Mental Health Nursing: the Craft of Caring* (ed. P. Barker). Arnold, London.

Barker, P., Stevenson, C. and Leamy, M. (2000) The philosophy of empowerment. *Mental Health Nursing*, **20**(9), 8–12.

Bazley, M. C., Cakman, N. C., Kyle, J. H. W. and Thomas, L. B. (1973) *The Nurse and the Psychiatric Patient*. Heinemann, Auckland.

Brandon, D. (1989) *Mutual Respect: Therapeutic Approaches to Working with People Who Have Learning Difficulties*. Good Impressions, Surbiton.

Brandon, D. (1991) Counselling mentally handicapped people. *Nursing Standard*, **6**(7), 32–3.

Brandon, D. and Ridley, J. (1985) *Beginning to Listen*. Campaign for Mental Handicap, London.

Buber, M. (1958) *I and Thou*. Charles Scribner & Sons, New York.

Cadman, C. and Brewer, J. (2001) Emotional intelligence: a vital prerequisite for recruitment in nursing. *Journal of Nursing Management*, **9**, 321–4.

Cogher, L. (2005) Communication and people with learning disabilities. In: *Learning Disability: a Life Cycle Approach to Valuing People* (eds. G. Grant, P. Goward, M. Richardson and P. Ramcharan). Open University Press, Maidenhead.

Collins English Dictionary, 3rd edn (1995) ed. J. Sinclair. HarperCollins, Glasgow.

Department of Health (1999) *Making a Difference: Strengthening the Nursing, Midwifery and Health Visiting Contribution to Health and Healthcare*. Department of Health, London.

Department of Health (2001a) *Valuing People: a New Strategy for the 21st Century*. Department of Health, London.

Department of Health (2001b) *Planning with People: Towards Person-Centred Approaches – Guidance for Implementation Groups*. Department of Health, London.

Department of Health (2001c) *12 Key Points on Consent: the Law in England*. Department of Health, London.

Egan, G. (2004) *The Skilled Helper: A Problem Management and Opportunity Development Approach to Helping*. Wadsworth.

Evers, H. K. (1981) Tender loving care? Patients and nurses in geriatric wards. In: *Recent Advances in Nursing 2: Care of the Ageing* (ed. L. A. Copp). Churchill Livingstone, Edinburgh.

Frankl, V. (1963) *Man's Search for Meaning: an Introduction to Logotherapy*. Washington Square Press, New York.

Freshwater, D. and Stickley, T. (2004) The heart of the art: emotional intelligence in nurse education. *Nursing Inquiry*, **11**(2), 91–8.

Fromm, E. (1957) *The Art of Loving*. HarperCollins, London.

Gardner, A. and Smyly, S. R. (1997) How do we stop 'doing' and start listening: responding to the emotional needs of people with learning disabilities. *British Journal of Learning Disabilities*, **25**, 26–30.

Goleman, D. (1996) *Emotional Intelligence*. Bloomsbury, London.

Hall, E. T. (1959) *The Silent Language*. Doubleday, New York.

Jennings, L. (1997) Trust and relationships in polluting climates, *Mental Health Nursing*, **17**(6), 4–5.

Johns, C. (2000) *Becoming a Reflective Practitioner*. Blackwell, Oxford.

Jourard, S. M. (1966) An exploratory study of body accessibility. *British Journal of Social and Clinical Psychology*, **5**, 221–31.

King, R., Raynes, N. and Tizard, J. (1971) *Patterns of Residential Care*. Routledge & Kegan Paul, London.

Kirby, C. (1995) The therapeutic relationship. In: *Theory and Practice of Nursing* (eds. L. Basford and O. Slevin). Campion, Edinburgh.

Kirby, C. and Slevin, O. (1992) A new curriculum for care. In: *Project 2000: The Teachers Speak* (eds. O. Slevin and M. Buckenham). Campion, Edinburgh.

Kitson, A. (1999) The essence of nursing. *Nursing Standard*, **13**(23), 42–6.

Levi, M. (1980) Functional redundancy and the process of professionalization: the case of registered nurses in the United States. *Journal of Health Politics, Policy and Law*, **5**(2), 333–53.

Levine, M. E. (1973) *Introduction to Clinical Nursing*, 2nd edn. F. A. Davis, Philadelphia.

Mental Capacity Act (2005). HMSO, London. Available online from `http://www.opsi.gov.uk/acts/acts2005/20050009.htm`.

Nursing and Midwifery Council (2002) *Practitioner–Client Relationships and the Prevention of Abuse*. Nursing and Midwifery Council, London.

McAlpine, C., Kendall, K. A. and Singh, N. N. (1991) Recognition of facial expresss of emotion by persons with mental retardation. *American Journal of Mental Retardation*, **96**(1), 29–36.

Mansell, J. (1992) *Services for People with Learning Disabilities and Challenging Behaviour or Mental Health Needs*. HMSO, London.

Meutzel, P. A. (1988) Therapeutic nursing. In: *Primary Nursing. Nursing in the Burford and Oxford Development Units* (ed. A. Pearson). Croom Helm, London.

Muir Gray, J. A. (1997) *Evidence-Based Healthcare: How to Make Health Policy and Management Decisions*. Churchill Livingstone, Edinburgh.

Parsloe, P. and Stevenson, O. (1992) *Community Care and Empowerment*. Joseph Rowntree Foundation, York.

Pearson, M. and Craig, J. V. (2002) Evidence-based practice in nursing. In: *The Evidence-Based Practice Manual for Nurses* (eds. J. V. Craig and R. L. Smyth). Churchill Livingstone, Edinburgh.

Peplau, H. (1952) *Interpersonal Relations in Nursing*. Putnam, New York.

Price, V. and Archbold, J. (1997) What's it all about, empathy? *Nurse Education Today*, **17**, 106–10.

Peternelj-Taylor, C. (2002) Professional boundaries. A matter of therapeutic integrity. *Journal of Psychosocial Nursing and Mental Health Services*, **4**, 22–9.

Rappaport, J. (1984) Studies in empowerment. *Prevention in Human Services*, **3**, 1–7.

Reed, J. and Clements, J. (1989) Assessing the understanding of emotional states in a population of adolescents and young adults with mental handicaps. *Journal of Mental Deficiency Research*, **33**, 229–33.

Reynolds, W. (1994) *The Measurement and Development of Empathy in Nursing*. Ashgate, Aldershot.

Reynolds, W. (2003) Developing Empathy. In: *Psychiatric and Mental Health Nursing: the Craft of Caring* (ed. P. Barker). Arnold, London.

Reynolds, W. and Scott, B. (2000) Do nurses and other professional helpers normally display much empathy? *Journal of Advanced Nursing*, **31**(1), 226–34.

Rogers, C. R. (1951) *Client-Centred Therapy – Its Current Practices, Implications and Theory*. Houghton Mifflin, Boston.

Rogers, C. R. (1957) The necessary and sufficient conditions of therapeutic personality change. *Journal of Consulting Psychology*, **21**, 95–103.

Rojahn, J., Rabold, D. E. and Schneider, F. (1995) Emotion specificity in mental retardation. *American Journal of Mental Retardation*, **99**, 477–86.

Sackett, D. L., Strauss, S. E., Richardson, W. S., Rosenberg, W. and Haynes, R. B. (2000) *Evidence-Based Medicine. How to Practice and Teach EBM*, 2nd edn. Churchill Livingstone, London.

Sayre-Adams, J. and Wright, S. G. (2001) *Therapeutic Touch*, 2nd edn. Churchill Livingstone, Edinburgh.

Slevin, O. (1995) Therapeutic intervention in nursing. In: *Theory and Practice of Nursing* (eds. L. Basford and O. Slevin). Campion, Edinburgh.

Solomon, P. (1991) Paul Solomon speaks on spiritual roots and the journey to wholeness. *Human Potential Magazine*, **16**(3), 28–32.

Stickley, T. and Freshwater, D. (2002) The art of loving and the therapeutic relationship. *Nursing Inquiry*, **9**(4), 250–6.

Stuhlmiller, C. (2003) Nurse–consumer collaboration: go with the Flo! In: *Psychiatric and Mental Health Nursing: the Craft of Caring* (ed. P. Barker). Arnold, London.

Travelbee, J. (1971) *Interpersonal Aspects of Nursing*, 2nd edn. F. A. Davis, Philadelphia.

United Kingdom Central Council for Nursing and Midwifery (1998) *Guidelines for Mental Health and Learning Disabilities Nursing*. UKCC, London. [Now available through the Nursing and Midwifery Council.]

Von Dietze, E. and Orb, A. (2000) Compassionate care: a moral dimension of nursing. *Nursing Inquiry*, **7**, 166–74.

Wehmeyer, M. and Berkobien, R. (1991) Self-determination and self advocacy: a case of mistaken identity. *Frontline*, Summer.

Williams, A. (2001) A literature review on the concept of intimacy in nursing. *Journal of Advanced Nursing*, **33**(5), 660–7.

CHAPTER 3

Interpersonal therapeutic relationships

Cheryl Chessum

Introduction

This chapter aims to guide nurses not only to revisit the importance of the therapeutic relationship, but to consider it in the context of the work role when engaged with clients. Specifically it asks nurses to consider how their basic assumptions and values about both the client and the nature and expectations of work role influence how the nurse undertakes the task of caring for the client. The challenge implicit in this task is summarised by the thoughts of Paley (2004), who comments that in modern organisational life ambiguity, uncertainty and role-conflict are endemic.

In order to facilitate this type of thinking various materials are included to expand the ideas further, but all are relational. The general orientation of the nurse to being a particular style of 'carer' – one of three broad types – is categorised and described to highlight some key differences in the style and is intended to demonstrate that not all nurses operate the same way in care-giving relationships. This is then considered from a practice preparation perspective, suggesting that this orientation should be an explicit organising principle in preparation for employability and job specifications, drawing on the work of Brunklaus (2003) in the Netherlands, which is portrayed both in diagrammatic form and a table to explore the elements with more clarity.

To understand the relevance of the concept of the nurse's orientation fitting the needs of the client two things are explored: one being case vignettes of potential problems and the other a sociological perspective on the different ways of interpreting need described by Bradshaw (1972), showing that there can be a different view of 'need' in the narrative between nurse and client.

In this chapter the therapeutic relationship being considered is that of the nurse–client relationship, although some of the issues will be salient to any personal therapeutic relationship with clients especially in the context of multidisciplinary working or interprofessional, interagency working. The use of the term 'nurse' in this chapter relates principally to Learning Disability Nurses and Mental Health Nurses.

Relatively recent policy initiatives (Department of Health, 2001a, 2001b; Scottish Executive, 2000) and several reports related to the skills and capabilities of the practitioner (Sainsbury Centre for Mental Health, 2004; Skills for Health, 2003) place some considerable emphasis on the nature of the relationship between the client and professional carer. They highlight essential aspects of the skills, attitudes and values underpinning practice by the worker, which should facilitate person-centred approaches to care planning and delivery. These are expected to balance the needs, wishes and wants of the client with the needs of carers and the concerns of the community.

Some of the key influences on the development of person-centred planning include:

- A developing understanding of the rights of people with learning disabilities within society
- The social model of disability
- The transition to 'care in the community'
- Individualised approaches to care planning
- Social exclusion

(adapted from workbook; Bradley, 2004).

There are many groups of people recognised to be at risk of social exclusion and recognition of multiple factors that impact negatively upon their health and well-being. Person-centred planning is characterised by placing the person at the centre of the process, with family members and friends being full partners in the planning process. It comes from a strengths perspective that focuses on the person's capabilities, priorities and support to achieve them. Activity is focused on supporting the person in achieving their goals (which may be firmly linked to their rights in society) and is a continual cycle of learning and listening and action. It is not difficult to see that this can represent a radical shift in the balance of power in some professional relationships as well as highlighting some inherent tensions in perspectives of what is 'needed' from a macro- to a micro-perspective, whether practical or esoteric, which has traditionally been viewed from an 'existing resources' perspective.

Delivering person-centred care has a clear link to the nature and quality of the interpersonal therapeutic relationship between client and worker. To attempt to deliver this type of care the style of the worker needs to embody certain values and beliefs to have a fidelity to the philosophy. Summarised (Bradley, 2004, p. 22) these values are considered to be:

- Individual rights
- The value of every individual
- The rights of every person to independence, self-determination and control over his or her own life
- The right to equality of opportunity
- The recognition of diversity in relation to individual aspirations, gender, sexual orientation, cultural identity, age and religious belief
- The right to social inclusion and freedom from oppression

These become organising principles for the behaviour of workers in their relationships with clients and it is an interesting notion to try to reflect upon what services would look like if this was fully integrated into the philosophy and practice of teams and services. Thus how workers see themselves, the clients and the nature of the work could be critical to the effectiveness and quality of services.

Much has been written about the importance and nature of therapeutic relationships in the literature pertaining to nursing, from early on in the development of psychiatric nursing in particular (Peplau, 1952; Orlando, 1961), to the extent that in some areas of practice the principles have been synthesised into good practice frameworks (Registered Nurses Association of Ontario, 2002). It is considered as a key element in the effectiveness of the outcomes in the helping relationship regardless of the therapeutic model used by the helper with the client, e.g. Transactional Analysis (Berne, 1969), Cognitive Behavioural Therapy (Beck, 1976) or Client-Centred Counselling (Rogers, 1951). Roth and Fonagy (1996) stated that there were 460 recognised models of psychological/talking approaches to helping, all of which involve some form of therapeutic alliance with the client.

However, whilst some interventions can be described as formally organised therapeutic models, not all the comprehensive needs of clients can be described as requiring one structured approach, needing instead an eclectic orientation towards achieving a general goal or themed outcomes. In this chapter this is broadly divided into three areas both for ease of classification and because it reflects ideas on this theme undertaken elsewhere (Brunklaus, 2003), namely treatment with some conclusion or resolution, rehabilitation and recovery or continued care depending on type and severity of disability.

The context for the therapeutic relationship has changed significantly in recent decades, with the government policy leading to a major transition from much of the service delivery to people with a learning disability or mental health problem being relocated from institutions into the community. Since the late 1980s there has been an unprecedented volume of policy in a relatively short period of time, influencing the reform of service models and care delivery, and further changing the landscape of community care with significant implications for practice. The Nursing and Midwifery Council (2002a) viewed itself as having strategic tasks in relation to quality assurance that included establishing the standards of education and training necessary for programmes leading to registration and recordable qualifications.

Expectations of the services and service providers, often delivered as personal services, have continued to grow in complexity. Linked agendas include clinical governance, evidence-based practice, collaborative care planning and partnership working, plus key socio-political issues of social exclusion and service user empowerment. All serve to challenge the practitioner to deliver high-quality care creatively and effectively. The setting for this care spans an eclectic range of residential arrangements, on the spectrum from full-time residential care to total management in the home or clinic. This reflects a wide range of situations in which the giving of care or therapeutic interventions/relationships can be expected to flourish or operate.

Working in community settings has meant that nurses have had to accommodate working in a wide range of settings. Practice has had to be adaptive, flexible and creative, where the cultural rules of the consulting room or ward do not technically apply. A potential problem is that practitioners can always take the old rules with them and replicate a hierarchical relationship in the community, which is easily imposed upon vulnerable clients and families. The opportunity to do something different is lost and the status quo of the power differential and how this is reflected in care delivery is maintained, so that the professional can be psychologically secure in being in a familiar place. In some instances, taking a conscious hierarchical stance is necessary or useful when there is a clinical risk management issue or advocacy is required, but ideally this is picked up and put down mindfully.

A definition or some deconstruction of the phrases 'therapeutic relationship' or 'therapeutic alliance'

'Therapeutic relationship' is a commonly used term, but does everyone have the same understanding of what this means, for whom is the relationship meant to be therapeutic and who is the judge of its success? In order to clarify how this term is best interpreted by nurses, the Registered Nurses Association of Ontario (2002) offers a definition:

> **Therapeutic relationship**: the therapeutic relationship is grounded in an interpersonal process that occurs between the nurse and the client (s). The therapeutic relationship is a purposeful, goal directed relationship that is directed at advancing the best interest and outcome of the client

In this definition the success of the relationship appears to be determined by outcomes chosen by the client rather than by the nurse or provider organisation. Against this definition it is possible to see how mandated relationships present a unique challenge to the construct of a 'therapeutic relationship'. It does, however, convey the principles of being client-centred, collaborative and empowering; a stance that reflects the principles relating to values-based practice (Woodbridge and Fulford, 2004).

For practice to encompass the principles of collaborative care, working in partnership, empowerment, advocacy and person-centred care, based on values which accommodate the diversity, disabilities and personal preferences of the client, the worker has to be able to engage and work therapeutically in a style which makes these principles a reality in practice. The practice may be bounded by constraints outside the worker's control, e.g. codes of conduct, organisational policies and procedures. The concern is that there is an assumption that nurses subscribe to and practice within the construct of 'client autonomy' wherever it is possible and safe to do so, whatever the needs of the client. This is combined with the expectation that the nurse is able, adaptable and flexible when faced with assessing a client's needs to judge the degree of autonomy to be assumed by a client.

In contemporary care the 'therapeutic relationship' may be entangled with case management responsibilities, where distinctions of the different elements pertaining to a nurse's role are blurred. Nurses may be clinical case managers working to a model that demands they are a direct care provider *and* a coordinator or broker of other providers and services, depending upon the model of case management in operation. In some cases it means that the therapeutic relationship is transacted in a relationship where the possibility of contributing to compulsory aspects of care is a reality. The nurse is also engaged in various tasks around the care of the client, needing to have many relationships with others on behalf of the client

In this setting, having only one conceptual framework of who the worker is as a therapeutic agent is an inadequate source of guidance on how to provide care. The multiple roles in clinical case management have been described and formulated into a well-known model of case management by Kanter (1989).

Personal therapeutic style/role

The ability to form a therapeutic relationship is underpinned by several capacities and includes self-awareness and self-knowledge, respect and empathy (Reynolds, 2000) and the ability to manage the limits and boundaries of the professional role (Forchuk *et al.*, 2000). Thus a nurse's personal therapeutic style says something about the nurse, as it incorporates and reflects personal values, beliefs and attitudes about the nature of the client and the work. It has to be integrated into, and is mitigated by, organisational directives (policy and procedures), service models, frameworks for practice, and constraints of resources – human, financial and material.

In training, nurses are influenced by classroom training and educational experiences. Knowledge of models and theories about therapeutic approaches give insight and instruction to 'how the therapist/nurse should be', (i.e. when nurses take on the role of therapist as part of a care plan) and how they should understand the nature of the client and their world, and the therapist's role.

As much of the nurse's training and experience can take place in clinical practice or on placement the nurse is influenced by exposure to, and modelling upon, custom and practice as seen in others. This is a powerful organising dynamic, and can be a great force for good. However, if the custom and practice seen and participated in does not reflect the positive principles of collaborative care, user empowerment, person-centred practices etc., then the nature of the interpersonal therapeutic style risks being adversely affected by this process of the socialisation of the worker into practice. It can lead to practices that are not respectful of the client or their needs or wishes, but are continued because they have been transmitted by the influential culture-carriers in the organisation or care setting. Attitudes to client autonomy can range from beneficent to paternalistic and can significantly impact upon the nature of care-giving and client empowerment (Svedberg and Lützén, 2001). Much has been written about the dynamic of the power differentials in the relationship between doctors, nurses and the client (Hopton, 1997), and these dynamics can be learned and then replicated in the practice context and in the language of the role which places and keeps the client in the least powerful position in the relationship.

In the contemporary lifetime of the nurse–patient relationship the nature of the relationship has changed and has become less formal, paternalistic and distant with the advent of the named nurse concept, primary nurse and care co-ordinator role (McQueen, 2004). The engagement in the therapeutic relationship which develops and can be sustained over time, especially with clients who have complex and long-term care needs is a skilled and demanding task. McQueen (2004) describes how in more recent times management of self in relation of routine exposure to emotional distress in clients and empathic management of a client's distress without undue 'contagion' (Omdahl and O'Donnell, 1999) is considered to be a quality associated with emotional intelligence (Gardiner, 1993; Goleman, 1996). Both interpersonal skills (those that are used between people) and intrapersonal (being self-aware and managing one's self in social situations, including work role) skills are required in nursing relationships. A concern is that therapeutic continuity in clients' lives often fails in community settings for many reasons, but a key factor can be staff turnover.

Work role

The importance of understanding one's own motivation for being in the role, a particular branch of nursing for example, can reveal the perceptions of the role in the wider sense, e.g. 'custodian' or 'helper' are commented upon by Speedy (1999), who asks 'Can we ever have therapeutic alliances with others if we do not know ourselves?'. Furthermore there must be a willingness to understand the client's world from the client's unique experience as well as external factors acting upon it, as we cannot expect ourselves to accurately predict their past experiences or interpretation of the world; this can be described as 'empathy'.

The work tasks of a paid health or social carer are usually summarised in the contractual obligations that are in part included in a job description and accompanied by a person specification. Factors leading an individual to apply for a particular job or role may be many and various. They may include desiring increased experience, more money, more responsibility, career progression, convenience of location or hours or both, availability, wanting a new challenge, unhappiness in previous work role, service needs or relocation. The level of personal preference may be guided by any of the above and may or may not include a level of self-awareness and insight into their own therapeutic orientation. This is where the acquisition of self-knowledge is useful, enabling nurses to differentiate between their own past experiences, desires and values and those of the clients.

The therapeutic orientation/style of the worker to meet the needs of a particular client group is not necessarily a focus of the appointment, more the ability of the person to fulfil the role to the specifications, although personal specifications may well include the ability 'to form therapeutic relationships with clients'.

When a learning disability nurse or mental health nurse elects to actively change their current role or job, they may be reflecting their 'sense of self', i.e. their desire or orientation for more or less autonomy, or a desire to be task-orientated or creative or more collaborative. If the aspirations are not met, then in the gap between expectation and disappointment is the possibility for work-related stress to arise. A study by Peter *et al.* (2004) investigated the 'moral habitability' of a role. It is here we can divide the orientation of the nurse into one of three broad therapeutic styles, in order to reflect upon whether this orientation is best suited to meet the client's needs from a therapeutic perspective.

To begin to classify the different types of care-giving role, Table 3.1 attempts to differentiate and define the aspects of a therapist, carer and rehabilitator. Further on in the chapter an understanding of these terms will assist in analysing a diagram that concerns itself with practice preparation for a range of nursing roles in different healthcare settings.

In the current approaches to preparation for practice in the UK (at both pre- and post-registration levels) a strong emphasis is now placed upon becoming a reflective practitioner. After many years of being proposed, and as a tool for enthusiasts (Schön, 1987) to use to analyse and develop practice, it has now been placed in the mainstream. This is one of the skills required, in conjunction with other undertakings such as training, education and clinical supervision, to continually learn from and refine practice, not only for the benefit of the client but for a much wider community. The quality and reality of some aspects of the preparation in and for practice compared to the assumptions which are made that this happens are strongly challenged by Cook (1999), who critically analyses this in relation to self-awareness and suggests that more scrutiny is required

Table 3.1 The framework of care-giving relationships: therapeutic orientation.

Therapist	Agent of change, assuming role of expert in a particular therapy; disciplined application of models used by a generic therapist with skills in many approaches; someone who views their interventions as broadly 'therapeutic' in whatever they undertake with the client.
Carer	Someone who sees themselves as 'looking after' another or doing things for someone unable to do them for themselves, either permanently or temporarily. Giving care in a timely and appropriate manner, reflecting the expressed needs and wishes of the client and is not disempowering. Undertaking a role which has fluidity – i.e. can decrease and increase, nurturing but not static – so that care can be developmental and progressive too. The perspective can be impeded by conceptualisation of a mother child relationship from psychoanalytic metapsychology: mother = nurse, client = child. Therapeutic care is not necessarily custodial care or control that can be restricting of personal growth and development.
Rehabilitator	A restorative or even developmental process for some clients, suggesting dynamic change over time, which is progressive but determined by the pace and needs of the client. It is of a varied focus depending upon the needs of the client. Essentially empowering for clients who move from less to more independence and autonomy, experiencing personal growth and development in the process. It assumes expectations of change because of the capacity inherent in the client, through support, assistance and encouragement, for example.

in relation to certain basic requirements to fulfil the conditions to be able to make 'therapeutic relationships'.

The proposal is that work or role orientation should become a feature of practice preparation and development, so that individuals would be able to identify through self-awareness and reflection how they understand and construct their therapeutic relationships with others, especially clients. Furthermore then, this orientation is then formed into a conceptual framework which can be understood and utilised when identifying the desirable characteristics of the worker in job specifications and job appointments. Potential benefits include positive outcomes in relation to some aspects of recruitment and retention, where there is a good fit between the work role and the worker who is already orientated to work in the therapeutic style required for the benefit of the client.

The sense of job satisfaction from being able to function and practice within 'one's own skin' may impact on motivation, morale, sickness and absence rates, staff turnover, cohesion with team and improved team-working, and improved client and carer satisfaction, to name a small but significant number of preferred outcomes.

Some simplistic vignettes of a poor fit may include:

- A nurse orientated to being a '**carer**' manages their work with a client by organising services for a client that are too intrusive and overprotective from the clients point of view. The worker is perceived as 'fussy' and 'smothering', not allowing the client personal growth, or to develop and take risks. Much to the '**carer's**' distress, who perceives they are doing their best to look after the client by taking extra care to ensure all needs are met by others, the relationship breaks down and the client becomes angry and frustrated, wanting another worker.
- A nurse orientated to being a '**therapist**' is enthusiastically embracing the opportunity to work with a client whilst undertaking a post-registration course in cognitive behavioural therapy. This work will form part of the evidence of achievement in practice, so the nurse has to take tapes of the sessions in for supervision. It is all going horribly wrong, as the client is not doing the work between sessions and reports they are not making any improvement. The nurse, being a novice, begins to think the client is 'resistant' and complains to the supervisor at their next meeting. The feedback that they are given is that they are not picking up the cues from the client and attending to them, are going too fast for the client and are more focused on meeting their own agenda. The client does not turn up for the next appointment and sends a message to say they do not want any further appointments and have arranged to see a voluntary counsellor.
- A nurse orientated to being a '**rehabilitator**' is working with a client who has been in the service for many years. Originally the client was in a long stay ward but now lives in a small nursing home. The previous key worker has left and the nurse is keen to get involved and motivate the client to do much more with their time, so sets about organising attendance and involvement in various clubs and centres. The manager of the nursing home contacts the team manager, as the client, who is normally happy and well settled, is becoming aggressive and uncooperative with staff and other clients and she is worried about the change in the client's disposition. Having failed to communicate her concerns to the new keyworker, who saw it as a stage of 'change', she felt she had no option but to go to the manager.

In contemporary case management, where models have been imported mainly from America, the frameworks base the management plan on assessment of need. As a conceptual framework an understanding of what 'needs' are is often assumed, i.e. there is a shared, universally understood, meaning to 'needs'. None of the guidance on case management (Department of Health, 1991) offers a framework about defining needs other than broad areas of need and how the perspective of what is needed by the worker and the client can easily be at variance. Bradshaw's (1972) sociological perspective on need suggests that need should be considered at four levels (Table 3.2). This allows a more open scrutiny of whose needs are being met when plans are made and services provided. Caseworkers may well, in complex cases, have to deal with multiple levels of need and be better orientated to responding to some than others. For example, some nurses may be more comfortable with task orientation in case work than with creativity and uncertainty; or with structure and prescribed stages; or with close/intimate but professional relationships with clients that are exploratory and uncertain by nature.

To illustrate this see Table 3.3, adapted from Fish and Twinn (1997), which highlights some aspects that they identify in their book which could be considered within the framework of therapeutic relationships where the professional nursing role can operate at two ends of a spectrum. One occurs where the nurse views themself as a technician or operative and is more rule-bound; another arises when responsiveness and creativity, which are less rule-bound, are more attractive

Table 3.2 Bradshaw's (1972) sociological perspective on need.

Type of need	Explanation of how this may be seen in practice or in services.
Normative	Expert or professional opinion of what is needed by individuals, families or communities, sometimes based on evidence/research, i.e. population-based interventions, sometimes underpinned by a 'capacity to benefit' belief.
Expressed	What clients, families or communities state they want or what professionals state is needed on behalf of others, often expressed as a resource – respite, nursing care beds, daycare places for example – artificially restricted or expanded by social and educational background or expectations.
Comparative	What is needed in one area is seen to be needed in a similar area or situation.
Felt	Wants, wishes and desires of clients, families or communities not always articulated because it is not thought to be available nor expressed as a consensus view.

Table 3.3 Two ends of the spectrum of nursing roles.

Rational technical	Professional artistry
Adheres to laws, rules, routines, prescriptions for set problems	Allows for interpretation of frameworks, and the exercising of individual judgment in complex cases
Pre-set routines and procedures to be rehearsed and learned in preparation for case work	Knowledge emerges from practice-generated wisdom and understanding from case work
Requires training	Requires education
Applying skills to the client as taught	Selecting skills to fit need of client
Change is imposed from the outside	Creativity and innovation comes from within
Quality is most concerned with what is easily measurable	Quality comes from deeper insight re values, priorities, actions
Technical expertise is paramount	Professional judgment is important
Professional activities can be mastered	Professional activity can have elements of mystery in its holistic state

features of the work role. This is not a value judgement about one being superior or preferential; indeed, both styles are important depending upon context. What is relevant is that both the role and the style of the nurse are complementary. This is for the benefit and satisfaction of the client and the quality of the delivery of care.

The therapeutic relationship as a tool

The therapeutic relationship evolved as a concept in psychotherapy but has spread from the confines of a controlled therapeutic environment to reflect, in the UK and other countries like USA, Canada, New Zealand and Australia for example, an outreach model of community care. It is seen as a fundamental flexible tool in all aspects of care delivery.

On occasion it can function as the acceptable face of limited or less than attractive public health or social care services, with nurses brokering their personal therapeutic skills to keep people engaged in services that otherwise can have little in the way of what the client really wants or needs. Alternatively, it can be used to translate the codes (systems and language) of the organisation into something palatable or understandable by the client (Blount, 1998)

Barriers to the therapeutic relationship have been identified at several levels, not least the historical neglect and stigma of the client group, sub-standard education for paid carers and outdated ideas about care (Speedy, 1999).

Therapeutic intimacy

Therapeutic intimacy reflects the ability and willingness of the worker to use communication and other skills to develop a deep understanding of the client's internal world – thoughts, feelings, perceptions, wishes, beliefs and opinions, for example, often set in the context of life experiences to date. This understanding, knowledge and insight are the means by which the worker forms a bridge to others (agencies, clinicians, providers) in the external world, trying to facilitate or participate in the delivery of appropriate care and services.

This 'active transitional participant' role in a client's life is the basis of a therapeutic relationship, and is not exclusive to meetings in professionals' offices or premises but also occurs where the client is located, especially where the client is intellectually or emotionally impaired. It is a role described by Winnicott (1964) when acting as a social worker with evacuated children. In people with intellectual and communication impairments or children, language-based engagement may not be suitable or sufficient as a standalone approach, and more concrete practical, physical or social activities may be the key to engagement.

In providing care in a community-based setting more than one professional may be involved, but those at the top of the hierarchy (i.e. doctors) may well spend the least time with the client and be the most remote and least intimate, having to base their decisions on the findings of the intimate relationships of others as well as on objective clinical questioning and examination.

The balance between intimacy and the boundaries of a professional relationship is a challenge to be met by the personal and professional development of the nurse, as well as a team member, where there is support to be both close and then distant from the personal relationship. The challenge is to balance the need for some distance and to be able to establish a therapeutic relationship. The conditions for emotional language-based intimacy need to reflect the security of the transient partnership, notably a willingness for closeness and sharing of experience of some sort, where trust allows vulnerability to be revealed but respected and contained in the relationship (Meutzel, 1988).

Some forms of intimacy are not elective either on the part of the nurse or the client, and this is most obvious in the clients need for hands-on basic nursing care, where self care, either permanently or temporarily, places both parties in the position of intimacy. The opportunity to make this aversive or acceptable, as a form of therapeutic care-giving which is received as such, is strongly influenced by the values, beliefs and approach of the nurse.

Preparation for orientation to the work role

The work of Okko Brunklaus, (working as part of a team in Avans Academy of Health and Nursing, Breda, Netherlands) has drawn upon and synthesised the work of many eminent writers in interpersonal therapeutic styles and skills into training for mental health nurses who take post-registration courses in preparing to become Social Psychiatric Nurses (SPNs) (equivalent to Community Psychiatric Nurses in the UK). The training is delivered in a higher education establishment. It has developed into a framework to help nurses trained predominantly in institutional settings to prepare to work in the context of community care settings.

Figure 3.1 describes eight possible ways to approach the therapeutic role (in bold outside the octagon). Inside the diagram, left to right, following two of four compass points is the proposed orientation of the nurse (person orientated or procedure orientated) and how this will influence the style of the therapeutic relationship as defined in bold outside the diagram. The remaining two compass points indicate a spectrum of self-awareness relating to personal competencies and deficiencies that will also influence the therapeutic style of the nurse and what interactions and interventions they are likely to be oriented towards.

The framework identifies eight interpersonal orientations to 'helping', which can be understood by examining each interpersonal orientation against two fundamental factors: agency and communion. Table 3.4 offers an explanation of the terms to assist in interpreting the diagram.

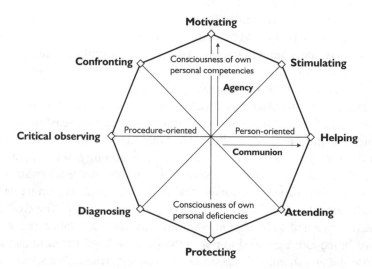

Figure 3.1 The interpersonal circumplex: eight modes to be of help.

Table 3.4 Agency and communion.

Agency	Self/autonomy – own ability tempered by deficits
Communion	Social self – need for support tempered by need for control over one's own life and how one's own self/deficits constrain choices/autonomy

These differentiate between different tensions in the client and the environment, and these tensions then indicate what type of therapeutic relationship with the carer may be most beneficial.

It is these two factors which underpin the way people organise their lives and relate to their environment and as such 'create their own niche' (Brunklaus, 2003). The personal makeup of the individual plays a substantial role in the creation of the 'niche'. Relating this to nursing, he goes on to explain that the predominant interpersonal style of a helping professional will mirror his personal *milieu* of feeling and affect, so in dealing with the problems with others nurses are simultaneously dealing with their own inner world, and this will act upon and influence their behaviour with clients. The experience of working interpersonally with clients and then how the nurse experiences themselves and the client, both cognitively and affectively, will also be influenced by the nurse's inner world. This concept may be understood from a psychodynamic perspective that is not necessarily at the forefront of contemporary practice, but which may still have much to contribute to a reflective framework for practice in nursing.

Table 3.5 expands further on the factors identified in Figure 3.1 to allow for a more detailed analysis of the concept contained within the diagram.

Table 3.5 Therapeutic styles.

Dominant interpersonal therapeutic style	Potential competencies of nurse	Potential deficits of nurse
Therapy and treatment-oriented (therapist)	Problem centred/focused Skills in diagnosing and problem identification Autonomy enhancing for client Use of tools/instruments	Risk of neglecting clients frame of reference Failure to listen accurately to clients Emotional distance from client
Rehabilitation and recovery-oriented (coaching/rehabilitator)	Relationship building Being there with the client Inducing hope Listening Stimulation and guidance	Giving premature or unwanted advice Going too fast for pace of the client Over-optimistic about what can be achieved and how fast
Caring-oriented (carer)	Health protection, promotion and prevention Being with the client – contact Listening Attending to the clients' needs personally	Lack structure Indecisiveness Over-protectiveness

A key point therefore is the idea that to be prepared for a professional helping role in the community, self-knowledge and self-awareness of your dominant helping style, which may have either positive or negative effects on the desired outcomes of the client, is important. The setting, however, seems irrelevant.

From an employer's point of view there is the question of whether or not it would be useful to identify specific core aspects of a person's dominant interpersonal therapeutic style when recruiting to posts, especially if the service model or team focuses on one dominant approach to care or need, e.g.

■ Continuing care for severely impaired individuals
■ Psychological therapies
■ Recovery and rehabilitation from serious illness or disability
■ Short-term crises or problems

In a mixed care economy how do employers, leaders and managers get the clinical teams balanced for a useful or complementary mix of interpersonal therapeutic styles without considering this as a personal specification? Some individual nurses may well possess sufficient interpersonal flexibility to change their interpersonal style so that they can work across a wide range of needs effectively, and they may indeed prefer a mixed caseload. However, some may have a more unidimensional dominant orientation in their therapeutic style, and in these cases the match of nurse to role is more important for the client's sake.

Figure 3.2 is a suggested pathway for the interface between employers and educational bodies.

Critical questions to consider and reflect upon

1. How much do we know ourselves in relation to how that influences our relationship with clients?
2. To what degree should education raise awareness of 'self' so that we can make more informed, conscious decisions about our work role – where we should or should not be for the client's sake?
3. Is it reasonable or even ethical, as Cook (1999) questions, to use education and training to tamper with people's selfhood in order to improve the ability/skills to develop interpersonal therapeutic relationships?
4. How much should we be expected to mould, shape or manipulate our inner world for the client's sake?
5. How much should nurses' employers insist upon 'knowing' about a person in order to place them in the work role to which they are best oriented for the benefit of the client?
6. What balance should there be to the intrusion upon the person by the agency/organisation on behalf of the client?

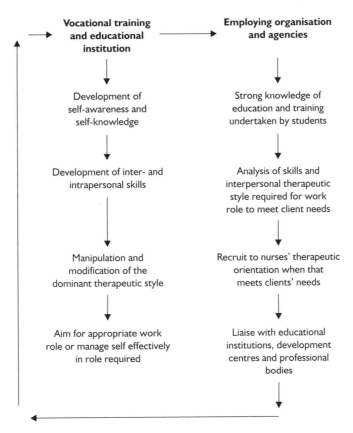

Figure 3.2 A suggested pathway for the interface between employers and educational bodies.

Conclusion and summary

This chapter has looked at what can be considered old issues or topics, i.e. therapeutic relationships and styles, but has tried to locate them in contemporary practice issues. We are now in an era where frameworks for practice and services in the UK (e.g. National Service Frameworks (Department of Health, 1999), *The Capable Practitioner* (Sainsbury Centre for Mental Health, 2001), National Occupational Standards for Mental Health (Skills for Health, 2003), *Ten Essential Shared Capabilities* (Department of Health, 2004), *Requirements for Pre-registration Nursing Programmes* (Nursing and Midwifery Council, 2002b)) all seek to standardise the service and shape the practitioner for the client's benefit.

In this context we need to reflect upon whether all the necessary dimensions have truly been considered in an effort to deliver the vision of the characteristics and skills required to develop the nurse of the future. By considering seriously the work role orientation of nurses an important contribution could be made to securing effective care delivery in conjunction with education and skills training requirements laid down in the above-mentioned guidance and in future recommendations and requirements for programmes, leading to registerable nursing qualifications. The challenge is to integrate all these into programmes of education and to see that there is consistency in practice elements of training and lifelong learning. It will almost certainly demand a review of the delivery of some aspects of training to increase the awareness in self-awareness.

References

Beck, A. T. (1976) *Cognitive Therapy for Emotional Disorders*. International Universities Press.

Berne, E. (1969) *Games People Play*. Penguin, London.

Bradley, A. (2004) *Positive Approaches to Person-Centred Planning*. British Institute for Learning Disabilities, Kidderminster.

Blount, A. (ed.) (1998) *Integrated Primary Care: The Future of Medical and Mental Health Collaboration*, p. 24. Norton, London.

Bradshaw, J. (1972) The concept of social need. *New Society*, **19**, 640–3.

Brunklaus, O. (2003) Personal communication and presentation adapted from *Yourself as the Instrument: The Nursing Relations Circle as a Guide* – unpublished work, used with kind permission. Avans Academy of Health and Nursing, Breda, Netherlands.

Cook, S. H. (1999) The self in self awareness. *Journal of Advanced Nursing*, **29**(6), 1292–9.

Department of Health (1991) *Care Management and Assessment: Practitioner's Guide*. HMSO, London.

Department of Health (1999) *National Service Frameworks for Mental Health*. Department of Health, London.

Department of Health (2001a) *National Service Frameworks for Older Adults*. Department of Health, London.

Department of Health (2001b) *Valuing People: A New Strategy for Learning Disability for the 21st Century*. Department of Health, London.

Department of Health (2004) *The Ten Essential Shared Capabilities: A Framework for the Whole of the Mental Health Workforce*. Department of Health, London.

Fish, D. and Twinn, S. (1997) *Quality Clinical Supervision in the Health Care Professions: Principled Approaches to Practice*. Butterworth-Heinemann, Oxford.

Gardiner, H. (1993) *Multiple Intelligences: The Theory in Practice*. Basic Books, New York.

Goleman, D. (1996) *Emotional Intelligence: Why it Can Matter More Than I.Q.* Bloomsbury, London.

Forchuk, C., Westwell, J., Martin, M., Bamber-Azzapardi, W., Kosterewa-Tolman, D. and Hux, M. (2000) The developing nurse–client relationship: nurses' perspectives. *Journal of the American Psychiatric Nurses Association*, **1**(6), 3–10.

Hopton, J. (1997) Towards a critical theory of mental health nursing. *Journal of Advanced Nursing*, **25**(3), 492–500.

Kanter, J. (1989) Clinical case management: definition, principles, components. *Hospital and Community Psychiatry*, **40**(4), 361–8.

Muetzel, P. A. (1988) Therapeutic nursing. In: *Primary Nursing in the Burford and Oxford Nursing Development Units* (ed. A. Pearson). Chapman & Hall, London.

McQueen, A. (2004) Emotional intelligence in nursing work. *Journal of Advanced Nursing*, **47**(1), 101–8.

Nursing and Midwifery Council (2002a) *Practitioner–Client Relationships and the Prevention of Abuse*. Nursing and Midwifery Council, London.

Nursing and Midwifery Council (2002b) *Requirements for Pre- registration Nursing Programmes*. Nursing and Midwifery Council, London.

Omdahl, B. L. and O'Donnell, C. (1999) Emotional contagion, empathic concern and communicative responsiveness affecting nurses stress and occupational commitment. *Journal of Advanced Nursing*, **29**(6), 1351–9.

Orlando, I. J. (1961) *The Dynamic Nurse–Patient Relationship: Function, Processes and Principles*. Putnam, New York.

Paley, J. (2004) Commentary: The discourse of moral suffering. *Journal of Advanced Nursing*, **47**(4), 356–67.

Peplau, H. E. (1952) *Interpersonal Relations in Nursing*. G. P. Putnam and Sons, New York.

Peter, E. H., Macfarlane A. V. and O'Brien-Pallas L. L. (2004) Analysis of the moral habitability of the nursing work environment. *Journal of Advanced Nursing*, **47**(4), 356–67.

Registered Nurses Association of Ontario (2002) *Establishing Therapeutic Relationships*. Registered Nurses Association of Ontario, Toronto.

Reynolds, W. (2000) *The Measurement and Development of Empathy in Nursing*. Ashgate Publishing, Aldershot.

Rogers, C. R. (1951) *Client-Centred Therapy: Its Current Practice, Implications and Theory*. Houghton Mifflin, Boston.

Roth, A. and Fonagy, P. (1996) *What Works For Whom? A Critical Review of Psychotherapy Research*. Guildford Press, New York.

Sainsbury Centre for Mental Health (2001) *The Capable Practitioner. Report produced for the for the National Service Framework For Mental Health Workforce Action Team*. Sainsbury Centre for Mental Health, London.

Schön, D. A. (1987) *Educating the Reflective Practitioner: Toward A New Design for Teaching the Professions*. Jossey Bass, San Francisco.

Scottish Executive (2000) *The Same As You: A review of services for People with Learning Disabilities*. The Stationery Office: Edinburgh.

Skills for Health (2003) *National Occupational Standards for Mental Health*. Skills for Health, Bristol.

Speedy, S. (1999) The therapeutic alliance. In *Advanced Practice in Mental Health Nursing* (eds. M. Clinton and S. Nelson), Chapter 4. Blackwell Science, Oxford.

Svedberg, B. and Lützén, K. (2001) Psychiatric nurses' attitudes towards patient autonomy in depot clinics. *Journal of Advanced Nursing*, **35**(4), 607–15.

Winnicott, C. (1964) *Child Care and Social Work*. Codicote Press, Hertfordshire.

Woodbridge, K. and Fulford, W. (2004) *Whose Values?: A Workbook for Values Based Practice*. Sainsbury Centre for Mental Health, London.

PART 2

Understanding and applying strategies

CHAPTER 4

Practical ways of involving users in everyday planning

Mark Gray

This chapter is very much the ignition system of the person-centred process for people with profound and complex needs. It dovetails neatly into the concept of 'life story work' explored elsewhere in this book.

Life stories concentrate on the need for a person with profound disabilities to have a sense of identity with his or her carers, but also creates the foundations of a 'self', albeit mainly established by third party means (Hewitt, 2000).

Person-centred plans that are 'service priority'-generated often appear to lose the sense of the person that they are about, and life stories are essential in maintaining a sense of the person's identity in the planning process, particularly if the individuals' ability to advocate for themselves is very limited. The establishment of 'Identity' is seen as the starting point for the process of self-advocacy and determination (Lee-Foster and Moorhead, 1996).

I hope therefore that this chapter will provide you with a sound practical framework for your future working practice. In it we shall explore the landscape that profound disability exists in via 'Zoning Theory' (Bradley *et al.*, 1993).

'Why should I bother with the terrain?' you might ask. 'If it's person-centred, surely the disabling conditions are not relevant?' It's a bit like gardening without understanding the soil's pH. On the face of it, it looks unimportant, but when your expensive plants start to die you realise, often too late, why you should have taken some time to looking at the landscape first.

How often have you seen programmes and staff resources tied up on a hopeful mission destined for failure? Usually such missions are started out of a strong sense of passionate belief in enabling someone, but in the aftermath of the plan's demise the idea is often written off with 'We've tried all that before' syndrome.

Don't get me wrong – this chapter is not the magic formula. It's a tried and tested approach that works, but it's not a quick fix either: the two case studies presented are taken over four- and sixteen-year implementation spans. This may be a bit of a worry if you're only using this approach to comply with *Valuing People* (Department of Health, 2001), which is time limited (at the time of writing) to 2006. I guess here, therefore, is my first key point:

A person-centred plan is for life, not just for the short-term goal.

Returning to the landscape and setting the scene we can plan our route over the next few pages, beginning with zoning theory (Bradley *et al.*, 1993, 2000).

Mark Gray

Zoning theory

Zoning theory was first devised in 1993 as part of the RNIB certificate in multiple disability programme. It was revised in 2000 and has been revised further for this book. It is based on the following knowledge of profound disability used by RNIB multiple disability services:

- Approximately 1 in 3 people with learning difficulties could be registered blind or partially sighted (RNIB, 1999).
- 79% of people with profound or multiple disabilities are likely to have a severe congenital or cortical visual impairment (Department Of Health Social Services Inspectorate, 1995).
- Approximately 1 in 4 of the entire population of people with learning difficulties experience some degree of severe or profound hearing loss (Change, 1991).

The impact of sensory impairment on a person with a learning difficulty will have profound implications for communication, mobility and self-help skills. The greater the degree of learning difficulty the greater the impact of the sensory impairment on these areas. Therefore, if we are looking to involve people with profound learning difficulties in person-centred approaches we need to consider the practicalities involved and we cannot ignore the major impact that a sensory or even a dual sensory impairment will have on how we select, identify and teach simple communication methods that give individuals a real say in their lives. This is where the principles of zoning apply.

First, imagine yourself laid on the floor like a starfish. Now take away all of your sight and your hearing, and remove everything you have ever learned, including your thoughts, memories and powers of communication. You may have severe physical disabilities that restrict your ability to move and that alter your physical shape.

You will probably be aware of smells, pressure, textures where your skin is contact with a chair or carpet, and the feeling of your clothes, although you have no concept of what they are or of the things you can feel around you.

You will be aware of random touches from people who lift you and move you and you will be aware of temperature, movement, tastes, bodily signals, hunger, toilet needs etc.

You make groaning or squealing noises that we associate with these states of being.

Someone in this primeval soup of random experiences would be considered as being in Zone One.

Returning to our previous experience, we can now hear sounds that are low, loud or that vibrate close to us, and we are aware of colours and moving objects, although they are not easy to focus on. What limited movement we have now motivates us to reach and grab at these objects. Although our hand and arm movements may be severely restricted, we may be able to explore their possibilities for taste and smell (sensory integration). We can now discriminate some of these tactile experiences by the addition of colour and possibly smells, and we are aware of basic routines.

This person would be considered as being in Zone Two.

In Zone Three we are able to focus on people, faces and objects that are close up. We are aware of events in the distance and our hearing range is extended, although limited to around a couple of metres for everyday speech. We may recognise words that have a regular association with an object or person in a familiar routine and these may also be indicated by physical gestures or formal signs which we are now able to copy in order to control events. We may even be able to use some ourselves.

We are less reliant on touch and feel for information, but are very aware of taste and smells. However, our limited communication ability does mean that there are periods of frustration in our exchanges with others.

In these first three zones I have tried to convey a picture of what life may be like for someone who has both intellectual and sensory impairments, and have given a view of the restrictions that are imposed by physical shape, and the ability to locate by sound, touch and vision the world that happens around us.

There are another three zones, but I wish to concentrate primarily on the first three for the purposes of this chapter, as these are the areas where most of our client group will spend much of their lives.

The remaining zones are Zone Four, where the user has a specialist communication system in which his or her supporters need training (BSL/Makaton/Rebus etc.); Zone Five, in which the individual requires an aid to communication that does not require the receiver to be trained, such as an interpreter, glasses, hearing aid or speech communicator, without which the communicator is struggling to speak or listen; and Zone Six, which is where no aids or support are required. Given that most care workers are in Zones Five and Six it is important that we adapt our communication methods accordingly.

Having established what the zones are, the next stage for us when involving people in communication is establishing, through assessment, which zone the person is in. This will aid us in our chosen communication method. At this stage the services of a speech and language therapist who specialises in early communication would be useful. A functional assessment of vision and hearing is also required in order to establish which sensory method will be the one to be utilised as the main means of communication.

Most people in Zones One and Two will respond primarily to touch, but the brief rules of thumb are:

- **Zone 1**: Touch, smell, taste, movement, respiration rate, muscle tone
- **Zone 2**: Touch, smell, taste, movement, respiration, muscle tone, reach, light and colour awareness, loud or low close sound responses
- **Zone 3**: Improved vision, sound and reach and grasp, and less reliance on muscle tone, touch, smell, taste etc.

Establishing the communication zone

The assessment process should be based on the client's responses to stimuli placed near to them with set properties relating to touch, smell, taste, sound etc. A good starting point is a variant of the Manchester Affective Communication Assessment, which gives the assessor space to record a range of responses: from head movement to trunk movements, respiration rate, posture, sounds and gestures the individual makes in response to different sensory stimuli. This enables us to locate the response and send signals of the individual's choice or ability.

At this point we need to agree that our definition of communication is that of a shared experience. My favourite definition is that of Helen Bradley's (1991) in her *Assessing Communication Together* publication for APLD:

Communication is the exchange of information by any means possible.

This statement implies that there is a sender, a receiver and an exchange of messages. Therefore both parties need to be able to participate and utilise the method of exchange between them. The fact that she also includes the phrase 'by any means possible' is also important, because often the means of communication is limited and informal, sometimes being unrecognised and missed completely.

By observing these early communication responses of movement, gesture, and sounds we can piece together the exchange mechanism for our communication responses.

The next part of the landscape we need to explore is that of how early communication develops between young babies and their parents. What is the process that conditions these primitive sound and body responses and enables us to become the communicators that we are? This area is the subject of a lot of further research, but in the context of the multiply disabled client group we need to look at the work of practitioners such as Phoebe Caldwell, Dave Hewitt and Melanie Nind, and in particular the theory of Intensive Interaction.

Intensive interaction

Intensive interaction is based on observations of parent–child communication responses before the age of six months. It was first noted and applied as a theory in the work of the late Gary Ephraim from The Harperbury Hospital School, where it was known and implemented as 'Augmented Mothering' during the mid-1980s. The first use of the new term and the process is recorded in *Access to Communication* (Nind and Hewitt, 1995). A further useful variation of this methodology for deafblind people can be found in *Co-Creating Communication* (Nafstad and Rodbroe, 1999).

Essentially, the process requires the co-communicator or parent to mimic the chosen expressive communication of the communicator, who usually takes the lead. This can be done by any means available to the individual. The process usually involves copying a noise or gesture and mimicking the response back, evoking laughter and another response.

These early games develop basic skills of:

- Looking
- Listening
- Awareness of another person/object
- Sharing and turn-taking episodes (sometimes called conversations)
- Endings

Where the person is deafblind or in Zone One, the co-communicator takes the lead and builds up from a passive response.

Looking and listening may not be skills that are developed, but awareness of another person, sharing tactile routines (or other responses) and turn taking, (similar to those in a sighted hearing model) are.

The main criticism of the intensive interaction approach is that it does not advocate going beyond making the initial very rewarding conversations. However, using the following real life case studies of Lydia and Simon I will attempt to show you how zoning theory and intensive interaction were used effectively to enable both Simon and Lydia to develop their basic communication skills, utilising their own unique methods to basic decisions about their lives.

Case study 1: Simon

Simon is 29 years old at the time of writing. He is the only child of a single parent mother living in Glasgow. He is totally blind and deaf and was believed at the time of my involvement to have a profound learning disability. He has cerebral palsy which has resulted in him having quadriplegia. In addition he has a hypotonic muscle tone (floppy) in all four limbs which renders him incapable of independent movement for reach, grasp or sign.

His blindness means he cannot eye point or understand or use the concept of controlled blinking, and his deafness means he is unable to hear or understand the mode of speech. He does not make sounds or use speech. He is fed and dressed by a range of home carers who support his mother, who does everything for him.

Simon clearly fits the model of a Zone One candidate for his communication ability and level.

My first meeting with Simon and his mother was in a special needs day centre, where he attended part-time.

The first session was very much an observation of the interactions between Simon, his mother and support staff. The conclusion of my initial observations was that Simon's communication was completely one way – things happened to Simon as a result of routine or intermittent happenings where things were done to him.

If we are to follow the Helen Bradley quotation from earlier we can observe that Simon's behaviour is for the most part totally passive. Therefore this communication is telling us of his profound difficulties. However, observation shows us that he does have very subtle fundamental behaviours, which he shares with others.

He appears to be aware of touch and smell, and he is able to breathe. He is unable to use touch as an exploration tool or to hold objects, but he can use the pressure and feel of touch to discriminate. Smell is very much subjective, but is linked to rooms, places and people. It is possible that he will be able to discriminate between them.

This leaves respiration as the only active response he can control and that others can share and possibly condition his responses.

Holding that series of statements there for a moment, I need to digress briefly to another sphere of work that influenced my decisions in the development of Simon's eventual communication plan. Several years earlier I had been working with two friends of mine who collaborated on a book called *Aromatherapy and Massage for People with Learning Difficulties* (Sanderson *et al.*, 1991). In the course of their work I was introduced to the concept of 'centering', which is about sharing the space with the person you are about to massage. If you hold a person that you are about to massage, and you are both sitting or lying comfortably and both parties are totally relaxed, it is possible that you will both share and experience the same breathing/respiratory rate as you concentrate on the person you are with.

I decided that this was the starting point for Simon and his mother to develop his communication system. It fulfilled the criterion of a shared two-way communication and it was a behaviour that could be conditioned to the series of tactile prompts that happened in Simon's everyday life.

At first, and quite understandably, Simon's mother was a little apprehensive about my suggestion, so for the first session I suggested we use the multi-sensory room, which had a series of soft lights and music to help her, if not Simon, relax.

The three of us lay in a row on the floor either side of Simon, placing our arms across his chest and his across ours. (Now you may understand why I champion Helen Bradley's phrase literally, as this was the most bizarre communication session I had ever set up.) After 20 minutes in the room, however, the three of us were breathing in perfect rhythm. Simon's mother was also profoundly moved by the experience and I think that this greatly influenced the success of the next stages.

So let us summarise our progress. We have identified the zone that Simon communicates in and we have identified a methodology of receiving and sending messages (breathing and touch).

After the initial session I asked Simon's mother to repeat these sessions at home and in our next session both of them were so adept that they reached the centering stage within five to six minutes of starting.

With myself now observing the process I was able to ask the mother to vary her breathing using a short deep breath, which on cue she did. I placed a straw on Simon's lips, which he began to suck on. I then withdrew the straw after Simon had taken a small sip of drink and they began the centering process again, until a repeat of the breathing routine was requested and the straw routine was again carried out.

Once again I asked Simon's mother to repeat the routine at home within the next fortnight to their next session. On their return to the next session Simon's mother had already informed me by phone that Simon had made the deep breath movement independently and that she had given him a drink. Indeed, Simon did just that at the start of the session before we'd started, so I was happy that he had understood the link.

Over the next few months we introduced a different textured straw that was associated with tea and another regulated breath pattern.

Simon has now five basic requests, which have developed over a period of five years:

■ Squash
■ Tea
■ Toilet
■ Food
■ Outside

We will return to Simon at the end of the chapter when we look at the link between basic responses and the use of information technology and switching.

Case study 2: Lydia

Lydia's story is not dissimilar to that of Simon, except she was the first of my two case studies and in fact was part of the inspiration for my conditioned communication approach with Simon several years later. My involvement with Lydia stretches back to my earliest work in this field, over 20 years ago. Sadly she has since passed on, but her story is a legacy which continues to benefit many long after her death.

Lydia was born with cerebral palsy. She had a spastic quadriplegia, although she did have limited use of her right arm, which she could raise above her head in a flexed position. She was severely partially sighted, only able to discriminate bright objects or colours close to her, and was partially deaf. She presented as having severe/profound learning difficulties.

Lydia had lived in a long-stay hospital (where I first met her incidentally as a student) in her childhood and moved to a succession of small group homes of various sizes as a young adult.

Applying zoning theory it is clear that Lydia is Zone Two because of her use of vision and hearing, albeit limited. She also has limited use of her right arm.

Like Simon her world was essentially passive and things happened to her rather than her having control of things around her. She was able to make basic sounds which corresponded with her body shape to indicate if she was happy or upset.

When I first met her, and for many years afterwards, Lydia had been made to raise her closed right hand to her mouth before receiving a drink – an approximation of a Zone Three/Four activity (Makaton and speech). Needless to say she never mastered the sign or the speech several years later.

At this point, however, I was in a position to change things, and suggested that perhaps the obvious thing was that because she could not hold a cup or even see the action of a cup she would not understand it. As she used a straw to drink with, this seemed the most obvious item to represent a drink with. The problem for me was that we, the staff, had control of the straw. So the communication, although better, was still essentially one-way.

If we placed the straw on her lip she would anticipate the drink, so we knew immediately that she understood its texture and placement. The challenge was to find a way that she could she use it independently. It was the idea of placement that in fact led to a solution. If you placed a straw to a lip it was obvious it had been learnt as a matter of routine. What if the straw could be placed elsewhere where Lydia could get to it?

She spent most of her day in a specialist Everest-Jennings upright chair with a large plastic grey tray around her midriff. Her right elbow rested on the tray most of the time and it seemed obvious that as this was the elbow which moved that the straw should be placed on the tray where she could locate it with her elbow.

This was agreed with the team, and at the start of every drink session we placed Lydia's elbow onto the straw on the tray. Within 24 hours of this routine starting she had mastered it and kept asking for drinks!

At first this was still a cause for celebration. However, it was only later, when related problems arose, that we realised that communication is a Pandora's box. First, Lydia became more incontinent as a result of requesting drinks and the reinforcement by the staff, and she was being toileted around 10–15 times a day. It was becoming clear that she thought that the straw sign not only meant 'drink' but also 'give me attention'.

So two more strategies were implemented. On every trip to the toilet Lydia was made to feel the toilet door handle as part of the routine, and we introduced a second straw for hot drink. The second straw was a difficult choice, as it meant a hot drink had to be constantly on tap. Lydia would experiment in her learning by trying out the different textures, so we limited the touches on the straws to just single sips. At the end of the first fortnight she had mastered both signs.

It was then that a case conference about her had been called and she was wheeled into the room with a range of professionals. Her key worker and her mother were also present. We were going to introduce the 'door handle' concept, It was displayed and placed on her tray, and while we continued to talk Lydia moved the handle off the tray. It was replaced and she did it again. Her key worker took her to the toilet, and from that day she was able to ask to go to the toilet and no longer required incontinence pads during the day.

After the conference many staff stopped having a hot drink readily on tap. They would go to the kitchen when Lydia placed her elbow on the appropriate straw and make the drink. It was here that a vital issue about people in Zones One and Two was realised.

On return from the kitchen several minutes later with the drink, Lydia would often appear distressed and would be biting her hand. The drink would be given to her, thus intermittently reinforcing hand biting as the new way of obtaining a drink. As the situation grew worse we had to examine the whole process again, and as part of that process it was realised that deafblind or totally blind service users have no concept of time passing or of activities taking place beyond their range of hearing or immediate sense of touch. So although Lydia understood that she had made her sign, she could not see that it was being responded too, and because she was only taught instant gratification she had no idea of process (time) either.

It was then decided to re-teach the original programme, backward chaining each step using just Lydia's elbow as the reference point. The process for a cup of tea took over a year to implement, but later, once Lydia was in the kitchen waiting for the kettle to boil, she would happily wait in the knowledge that her drink was coming.

From this we learn that staff consistency and patience are vital and that the observations we make are often based on sighted hearing models because that is what we assume people to be like. Frequently this is not the case given the statistics I gave you at the start of the chapter.

Lydia went on to learning over 30 different activity symbols and nearly the same number of place and people symbols in her later years, Because of the bulkiness of the system, as she grew more adept with it we had to alter the initial system, limiting it to just three textures, which indicated separate symbol strips that she would then request and participate in dialogues with.

Both Lydia and Simon are prime examples of how people with profound intellectual disability can be assisted to develop their own choices and opinions within their lifestyles and show clearly how the theoretical models produced are applied to practice.

Assistive information technology

As I mentioned earlier, Simon's story continues, and here I want to introduce the concept of assistive information technologies to help someone who is essentially in Zone one of communication transfer their skills to participate equally with those in Zones Five and Six.

Simon's communication method, as with all people who have profound and multiple learning difficulties, has developed painfully slowly, and the main issue that his mother had was that of the frequent changeover of staff, so much so that she was unable to keep up with explaining his simple system to all the home helps and carers that Simon interacts with.

Taking her comments on board, I spoke with a colleague of mine who is involved in special needs switch access and I explored the use of a modified 'blow switch' and portable switch controller for Simon to try using his breathing response. With a little modification to his chair and with the help of his physiotherapist and occupational therapist we were able to get Simon to breathe into the switch when he wished to ask for drinks etc.

The controller has been attached to a small sound sampler/playback device that contains the following phrases in a Glaswegian accent:

- 'Please can ye get me a cup o' tea?'
- 'Cannae have drink of squash please?'
- 'Cannae go outside?'
- 'Cannae go to the toilet?'

Simon is of course unaware of the sounds made by his switch and sampler device combination, but it makes it easier for him to be reinforced by other people without the need for constant training and retraining. His key worker and his mother are trained in maintaining the batteries in the switch controller and the sampler and new phrases are still continuing to be worked upon.

Communication passports

In conclusion, to involve people in their lifestyles and person-centred plans means involving them at some point in making some, if only limited, decisions in their everyday lives, and a fundamental part of the person-centred plan should include their life story, which says who they are and how they got here, and gives them an identity to the outside world.

A communication passport states clearly how to respond to the individual and what communication he or she uses in a range of situations, from being at home to going to the doctor or shopping.

Finally, the method needs people who are prepared to be in the process for the long run and not for the short term run of its current heightened awareness through *Valuing People*.

References

Bradley, H. (1991) *Assessing Communication Together*. Training Package. APLD Publications, Nottingham.

Bradley, H., Gray, M. J., Parker., M. and Snow, B. (1993) *Developing Communication and Motivation in People with Multiple Disabilities*. RNIB Certificate in Multiple Disabilities course book, Vol. 6. RNIB, London.

Bradley, H., Gray, M. J., Parker, M. and Snow, B. (2000) *Developing Communication and Motivation in People with Multiple Disabilities*. RNIB 'Changing Lives' course book, Module 4, Unit 2. RNIB, London.

Change (1991) *Agenda for Change*. Committee for the Multi-Handicapped Blind and South East Thames Regional Health Authority, London.

Department of Health (2001) *Valuing People: a Strategy for People with a Learning Disability for the 21st Century*. HMSO, London.

Department of Health Social Services Inspectorate (1995) *Planning for Life: Developing Community Services for People with Multiple Difficulties*. HMSO, London.

Harrison, J., Price, S. and Sanderson, H. (1995) *Aromatherapy and Massage for People with Learning Difficulties*. Hands on Publications, Birmingham.

Hewitt, H. (2000) People not subjects: a life story approach to issues concerning people with profound learning disabilities. *British Journal of Nursing*, **9**(2), 90–5.

Lee-Foster, A. and Moorhead, D. (1996) *Do the Rights Thing*. SENSE Publications, London.

Nafstad, A. and Rodbroe, I. (1999) *Co-Creating Communication*. Forglaget Nord Press, Denmark.

Nind, M. and Hewett, D. (1995) *Access to Communication*. David Fulton Publishers, London.

RNIB (1999) *Right to Sight. Access to Eye Care for Adults with Learning Difficulties*. Resource pack. RNIB, London.

CHAPTER 5

The use of touch in learning disability nursing

Eve Gale

The greatest poverty is not to live in a physical world
Wallace Stevens (1879–1955)

This chapter addresses the use of touch in the care of people with a severe learning disability. Two basic beliefs underlie it. The first is that, although touch is a vitally important part of learning disability nursing, most touch used by nurses is 'functional' rather than 'expressive' or 'therapeutic'. That is, people are frequently touched when some physical action is being performed on them, such as being bathed or dressed, but are more rarely hugged, stroked or massaged. A further distinction between these different 'types' of touch is that whereas 'functional' touch is demand-led by the physical needs of the patient for washing, feeding and so on, 'expressive' and 'therapeutic' touch are more concerned with the psychological needs of an individual.

The second belief is that being touched is conducive to psychological health; that people, especially people with a severe learning disability, who are touched more often in a caring or therapeutic manner, will enjoy a greater quality of life.

The nature of touch

Touch is an integral part of human life; we are touched and touch others all through our lives. Touch is one of the five senses used to gain knowledge about our surroundings and to transmit interpersonal attitudes and emotions, ranging from affection to aggression (Le May, 1986). Touch can be interpreted as the acknowledgement of a person's presence, a display of love, an act of aggression, a desire for comfort or a feeling of physical closeness (Gale and Hegarty, 2000). How one person interprets the touch of another depends upon each person's cultural background, the nature of the relationship and each individual's feelings at that time.

Touch has been described as the first and most fundamental and powerful form of communication (Barnett, 1972) and is thought to be essential to human development. It has been described as a basic human need which becomes important during gestation (Montagu, 1971) and continues to remain a fundamental component of communication throughout life. It can convey a myriad of positive and negative messages between people (Le May, 1986). Even in its most primitive mode touch can frequently 'reach' a person when nothing else will. Physical contact provides crucial physiological information about the environment, with the skin functioning in the regulation of internal homeostasis (Kertay and Reviere, 1998). Touch, however, goes beyond simple physical contact, as it can also induce emotions and enhance emotional contact between human beings. In humans the skin has acquired significance beyond physiology and has taken on social and psychological functions (Masters, 1987).

Touch enables a child to form secure bonds with others and acts as a primary form of communication and learning. Deprivation of early tactile experiences may compromise a child's future learning as well as its capacity for more tactile communication (Frank, 1957). After childhood and into adulthood the role of touch changes, becoming less a means of communication as alternative verbal and non-verbal skills are developed. Touch then becomes reserved for use in special, permitted occasions. The use and acceptance of touch on these occasions depends on a wide range of attitudes and practices specific to various cultural and personal characteristics.

In some cultures touch appears to be an essential part of everyday life, while in others it is discouraged. For example, people of Anglo-Saxon origin, the English and German in particular, are relatively non-tactile. Cultures such as Latin, Russian and Jewish are highly tactile (Jourard, 1966; Montagu, 1971).

Gender can also influence acceptance of touch. Jourard (1966) studied the use of touch by American students and found marked sex differences in the students' use of touch. Females were touched more by parents, same-sex friends and opposite-sex friends than males. Henley (1973) proposed that touching behaviour is also affected by status, where actively touching a person is indicative of a higher status, whereas 'cuddling' is indicative of a lower or submissive status.

Under what conditions does a person permit another person to touch him or her? According to Pratt and Mason (1981), we permit the touch of another in one of three ways. Firstly, through the acceptance of touch-inclusive roles, for example when visiting the health practitioner, the hairdresser or the tailor. Secondly, although not entirely distinct from the first, touch is permitted through a personal or individual sanction of the touching activity. Here it matters who the person is and whether the person is liked, rather than the role they may have. The third category of permitted touching is that considered to have occurred by accident.

Bowlby (1969) suggested that touch was also important in situations of danger, incapacity and sickness and in these situations the necessity for security, rest and comfort may increase an adult's need for touch. Barnett (1972) and Goodykoontz (1979) concur with this view, suggesting that becoming a patient may produce a greater need for touch. If people who have become patients require a greater need for touch, the people primarily responsible for giving that touch will be nurses.

Touch in nursing

It has been accepted that physical touch is an essential and universal component of nursing care and that nurses touch within the caring perspective (Routasalo and Isola, 1996; Verity, 1996; Kezuka, 1997; Edwards, 1998).

Watson (1975) defined the role of touch in nursing as an intentional physical contact between two or more individuals. Watson divided this type of touch into two categories: 'instrumental' and 'expressive'. 'Instrumental' touch was a deliberate physical contact needed to perform a nursing task. 'Expressive' touch was a spontaneous act which is not perceived necessarily as an essential part of nursing, e.g. holding a patient's hand to reassure them. Watson believed that some patients were deprived of expressive touch, particularly if they were impaired, dependent or elderly. The act of nursing relies on caring and one of the major components of caring is comfort. Nurses in the process of caring use physical touch as the main behavioural mode to provide comfort to patients (Lange-Albert and Shott, 1994).

Caring is a process and an art that requires commitment, knowledge and continual practice and encompasses a feeling of dedication to another (Leininger, 1981). This same definition could be applied to touch. To touch another person implies a commitment on the person touching (there is a reason for touching). Equally, knowledge of how to touch is required if that touching is to be effective for the individual. A nurse who touches to benefit her patient could be seen to be dedicated to that person.

Caring and touch are complex, intricate and subjective. Noddings (1984) suggests that both caring and touch need to be fully understood to enable carers to be better equipped to deal with pain and conflict that caring sometimes induces. An ethic of nursing care is that people should be treated as individuals with different needs, with a recognition that one of these needs may be to be touched. Natural caring is an attitude that exists between individuals in certain relationships. Touch used within that relationship might be a significant way to convey the attitude of caring. Hegarty and Gale (1996) believe that touch is important in the caring relationship by helping to provide a loving relationship.

The use of touch with people who have a learning disabilities

Watson (1975) suggested that there are patients, such as people with an altered body image, people who have lowered self-esteem or who are dependent, anxious or dying, who would actively benefit from communication through touch. The author believes that people with a severe learning disability would also benefit from communication through touch. For people with a severe learning disability touch may be experienced in mainly functional ways, such as in feeding or bathing, which may be perceived as affirming and supportive, but may also be felt as somewhat coarse and manipulating (Gale, 2002). For such people touch that has a more therapeutic focus may be rare. This may be because of a natural reluctance of people to relate adequately to those who are 'different' from the socially acceptable norm. Gale and Hegarty (2000) explored the use of touch with adults with severe to profound learning disabilities in a non-participant, observational study of the work routines of carers in three different residential care settings. The results showed that clients received more 'functional' touch (purposeful touching to help with everyday functions) than 'expressive' or 'therapeutic' touch. 'Expressive' touch is the act of touching a person spontaneously with emotional intent to express feelings; 'therapeutic' touch aims to benefit the person either physically or psychologically. Clients reacted with more positive non-verbal responses when expressive or therapeutic touch was used, whereas functional touch elicited negative responses such as aggression and inhibition.

The medium of communication between therapist and client in many therapy approaches is verbal. For example, in the client-centred therapy of Carl Rogers (1951, 1961) clients are encouraged to share their feelings and thoughts with the therapist, who takes a non-directive but encouraging stance. Major difficulties with people who have a severe learning disability is that they may have few or limited verbal skills and are therefore potentially debarred from such therapy. Non-verbal ways of developing a therapeutic relationship are required. Important among these is touch and other information conveyed through tactile or kinaesthetic sensory pathways.

For individuals who have severe and profound learning disabilities, touch may be the clearest way they have, by receiving information from people around them, of understanding their world. Farrah (1971) describes situations when any person may need touch to help them understand their world, for example:

■ When a person is depressed or anxious and fails to respond to verbal communication.
■ When a person needs encouragement to take a difficult step.
■ When a person is fearful or needs to 'reach out' in periods of stress.
■ When a person needs assurance of their acceptability.
■ When a person is unconscious, in pain, terminally ill or dying.
■ When a person is rejected or lonely.

All of these situations are equally appropriate to a person with a severe learning disability and can be seen as vitally important aspects of their lives.

Touch can be used as an effective therapeutic intervention. Its use with people with a severe learning disability can be recognised as being both appropriate and valued. I will now describe three media where touch can be used in a therapeutic way. This will be illustrated through evidence-based practice and my own work in this area.

Massage

Massage, an extension of touch, can be used as an effective therapeutic intervention. Its use with people with a learning disability can be recognised as being both an appropriate and valued way of offering touch. This approach does not have to be complicated to be effective: for example, a simple hand massage can provide valuable physical contact.

I was approached by staff of a residential unit to see if massage could help one of the residents (Ms K) who had a severe learning disability and severe behavioural problems, which at times included aggressive behaviour, self-injurious behaviour, damaging property and stripping her clothing. There were 12 sessions of therapy conducted in a quiet room. The massage component lasted between 10 and 25 minutes. I visited Ms K for six sessions before beginning any massage and measurements of her pulse and respiration rates were taken during these sessions to provide a baseline. At the beginning of the session Ms K was a little suspicious of being touched in any way. The only physical contact that she found acceptable was for me to hold her hand to apply nail varnish. There was no change in her pulse and respiration rates before and at the end of these sessions.

I massaged Ms K's head, neck and shoulders using stroking techniques. I used small circular movements with the tips of my fingers and the heel of my hand. The strokes varied between using both light and strong pressure. I would then sit by Ms K and massage her hands and lower arms. Ms K was not asked to remove any clothing for these sessions and no massage oil was used other than a little hand cream when massaging her hands. Once Ms K allowed the massage to take place there was a remarkable change in her attitude, physical appearance and pulse and respiration rates. From an apparent dislike of being touched she began to ask for a massage; she would visibly relax and sometimes went to sleep during these sessions. Her pulse rate before each session of therapy varied between 80 and 91 beats per minute and her respiration rate was between 20 and 28. After the massage pulse rates dropped to between 61 and 77 and respiration rates to between 18 and 22 per minute.

The most notable change in Ms K's behaviour was reported by staff: Ms K had become more sociable and would now start up a conversation with staff. The instances of problem behaviours decreased, ranging from 15 to zero during the intervention period of 6 months. Strikingly, there was a marked increase in social activities with Ms K being taken out into the community. Prior to the massage sessions she was rarely taken out because of her marked behaviour problems. I believe that the results demonstrate that a comparatively short period of structured therapy, using touch as a therapeutic medium (i.e. massage) can have a powerful effect for a client with severe learning disabilities.

Cohen (1987) reports on the work of a nurse working with a person with a learning disability who uses foot massage as a therapeutic intervention. Cohen describes her working with the tips of her fingers using feather-like circular movements, intuitively sensing where her hands need to move. A further example details her building a particularly intimate rapport with a 24-year-old man who has a learning disability who is also deaf and blind. For the first few weeks on the ward she did not touch the man, allowing time for him to absorb her presence. Now, having developed an acute awareness of her touch and smell, he is always able to show her exactly where he wants to be touched. He pulls her hand down to his foot and rolls his head, smiling with each stroke. Profoundly absorbed, he smiles and laughs when his hands are massaged. It is reported that not only has this treatment increased the client's communication skills and concentration span, but he is also reported as being very relaxed and happy with this kind of physical contact.

Harrison and Ruddle (1995), occupational therapists and aromatherapists, also give examples of how touch can be used as a therapeutic intervention for people with a learning disability. Harrison and Ruddle's paper details work completed with Tom, a very hyperactive man whose concentration lasted not much more than a few seconds. In the study, Tom's key worker decided to try using massage as a way of relaxing and making contact with him. She rubbed relaxing massage oil onto her hands and let Tom smell and touch her hands. Occasionally he would let her brush the back of his hands with her hands before running off. Tom gradually learned to enjoy massage, letting the key worker massage his hands more fully and then allowing his back to be massaged. This massage provided him with a firm foundation from which he could go on to enjoy other experiences and activities.

Another client detailed in the study is Clare, who has dual sensory impairment and severe learning disability. After living in a large hospital for many years, she moved to a new home. It had been difficult to explain to Clare why she was leaving familiar surroundings and people for a completely strange environment. On arrival she seemed very upset, confused and frightened. She started pulling out her hair, and cried and was unable to sleep at night. Harrison showed the staff how to perform hand and foot massage with Clare. The staff found Clare responded very well and would fall asleep after a session of massage. Over time, Clare began to settle into her new environment and became more relaxed. The staff found that massage was an excellent way for them to make contact with Clare, to reassure her and begin to develop a more trusting relationship.

Gray (1990), a massage therapist, reports working with a young woman who has a severe learning disability and who displayed extreme disruptive and severe self-injurious behaviour. The woman responded to regular foot massage, initially only for ten minutes, but gradually she allowed the therapist to massage her feet, lower legs, arms and back for 20–30 minutes. It was reported that the client's self-injurious behaviour reduced, and that she was less tense, smiled and was more sociable.

Sanderson and Carter (1994) have also used massage as an intervention for challenging behaviour. The client in this case study was a 28-year-old lady with profound learning disability and visual impairment who was described as having challenging behaviour because she regularly picked and scratched her left forearm. The client was introduced to aromatherapy with the aim of helping her to relax. The authors also used interactive massage which encompassed the principles of Gentle Teaching (McGee, 1985). Gentle Teaching emphasises the development of relationships and provides a sequence through which a person may develop. McGee states that as a child learns to accept touch and develop non-verbal communication skills he or she begins the 'resist' stage of touch. The child then progresses through the 'tolerate', 'cooperate passively', 'enjoy', 'respond cooperatively', and 'lead' and 'imitate' stages until finally there is initiation of touch by the client themselves.

During the first session with the client, three different relaxing essential oils on smelling strips were brought near to the client's nose in turn. She ignored two of them and moved closer to smell the third, lavender, repeatedly. This response prompted the therapist to choose lavender to make up into massage oil. The following four sessions only lasted 30 seconds, as the client would only accept massage oil lightly wiped on her hands, before she pulled away. Sanderson and Carter believe this to be the 'resist' stage in the interactive sequence. Over two months the length of the weekly sessions was extended to three minutes and by the end of the second month the client would bring her hands near to her face to smell the oil. From this 'tolerate' stage, she began to 'cooperate passively' and allowed the therapist to turn her hands gently over and stroke the palms. During this time the client would smile slightly when touched and actually appeared to enjoy the experience.

After three months of weekly sessions the client began to 'respond cooperatively' and offered each hand in turn for massage. By now the sessions were lasting 20 minutes. The arm that the client usually scratched and pinched seemed less inflamed, and she even began to make circular movements with her right hand on her arm. This represented the 'imitate' stage in the sequence. The whole process of this intervention took two years, but eventually the client began to initiate massage sessions by giving the bottle of oil to the therapist when she wanted a massage.

Reflexology

Reflexology is the use of a sophisticated system of touch, usually on the feet but sometimes on the hands, in which the areas being massaged are thought to correspond to a map of the whole body (Tiran, 2002). It is a non-invasive, cost-effective therapy requiring no equipment yet producing powerful responses in recipients. It has an advantage over body massage in that only the feet need to be accessible, thus eliminating the need to undress. It can be performed in any setting and does not require a separate treatment room if the person prefers to remain with others. This can have particular benefits for people with learning disability living in residential accommodation who may be disturbed by others entering the room inadvertently.

The use of reflexology may help to improve general health, revitalising people physically, emotionally and spiritually and help to enhance quality of life (Gale, 2002). The effects of immobility for those people with a physical as well as a learning disability who are confined to a wheelchair may be relieved by reflexology through the circulatory improvements that are thought to occur (Dryden *et al.*, 1999). Hand reflexology may be necessary for someone with major lower limb impairments to improve movement and aid with independence. Stimulation of the area of the feet corresponding to the excretory processes may help to reduce constipation arising from immobility, and this may decrease the use of regular laxatives (Joyce and Richardson, 1997). People with a severe learning disability who display self-injurious behaviour or aggressive behaviour may find that reflexology can relieve symptoms of anxiety and stress by inducing deep relaxation (Griffiths, 2001). The relaxation effects, aiding sleep of increased quality and duration, may reduce the need for night sedation. The sense of relaxation may engender an appreciation of sensual pleasure that may be denied to people with a learning disability, enhancing their subconscious sense of self-worth and possibly decreasing challenging behaviours. Regular reflexology provides something to which they can look forward and an additional activity in a life where variety may be limited (Gale, 2002).

Snoezelen

In recent years a growing body of knowledge has accumulated showing that certain children with learning disabilities can benefit from additional sensory input (Ayres, 1979; Hutchinson, 1991; Sharpton and West, 1992). One of the treatment approaches available to this population is the provision of sensory stimulation by means of 'Snoezelen' (the word is derived from the Dutch words for 'doze' and 'smell'). Snoezelen is a concept that believes that people with a profound learning disability interact with the environment primarily through the sensory and motor modalities of sight, hearing, touch, smell and taste (Cunningham *et al.*, 1991). The method involves the use of a specially adapted sensory room together with an 'enabling' non-directive approach to therapy (Hutchinson, 1991; cited in Shapiro *et al.*, 1997). This stimulation invokes environmental manipulation to effect internal change in the person, decreasing maladaptive behaviours, reducing stress and producing more adaptive behaviour (King, 1993). Touch, usually in the form of non-invasive contact by holding or stroking the hands and feet, is a popular therapy used in the Snoezelen environment. It has the potential to relieve stress and anxiety. Using touch in the Snoezelen room may also foster a therapeutic relationship through enhanced communication, thus empowering the client and enabling them to feel respected and valued (Gale, 2002).

Many Snoezelen and therapy rooms also utilise aromatherapy oils to stimulate the sense of smell and develop an affinity to particular pleasant aromas (Armstrong and Heidingsfield, 2000). This may be a situation in which a combination of touch in the form of foot or hand massage with aromatherapy could work synergistically to the benefit of the client.

A study by Shapiro *et al.* (1997) attempted to determine the short-term efficacy of the Snoezelen in the management of children with severe or moderate learning disabilities who exhibit maladaptive behaviours. The method they adopted was an open, controlled, crossover design. Twenty children (5–10 years old) received treatment in both the Snoezelen (study treatment) and 'play-room' (control treatment) over four time periods. During treatment their behaviour was recorded by means of written observations and video. The children's heart rate was also monitored by means of a portable electrocardiogram recorder.

The results of the study showed that children in the Snoezelen showed a significantly greater decrease in the mean number of stereotypic behaviours (1.6 in the Snoezelen versus 4.2 in the play-room), a significantly greater increase in adaptive behaviours (5.0 in the Snoezelen versus 3. 3 in the playroom). There was also a significantly greater mean absolute percentage change in heart rate in the Snoezelen. The researchers concluded that the Snoezelen is an effective therapeutic setting for short-term reduction of self-stimulating behaviours and facilitating adaptive behaviours in children with moderate to severe learning disabilities. Long-term effects, however, still need to be studied.

The use of touch with autistic children

The use of touch as a therapeutic intervention may also be beneficial for autistic children. A study conducted by Field *et al.* in 1997 investigated the effects of 'touch therapy' on three problems commonly associated with autism including inattentiveness (off-task behaviour), touch aversion and withdrawal. The participants of the study were 22 autistic children, average age 4.5 years, and were from middle socio-economic status families. They were randomly assigned to a touch therapy or a touch control group. The children assigned to the touch therapy group received touch therapy from a volunteer student for 15 minutes per day, two days per week for a period of four weeks (eight therapy sessions). The children were fully clothed (except for the removal of shoes and socks), and their body was rubbed using moderate pressure and smooth stroking movements on each of the following areas: head/neck, arms/hands, torso and legs/feet. These stroking move-ments included downward strokes, circular movements with fingertips, rubbing and kneading soft tissue areas of the body, all similar to Swedish massage techniques (Arnould-Taylor, 1982). For the children assigned to the touch control group a volunteer student sat with the child on her lap with her arms around the child and engaged in a game selecting different colour/form/shape toys. The control group sessions were also held for 15 minutes per day, two days per week.

In the results of the study it emerged that touch aversion and off-task behaviours decreased in both groups. Stereotypic behaviours decreased in both groups but significantly more in the touch therapy group. Significant changes occurred for the touch therapy group, including increases in attention, social behaviour and initiating behaviour.

Guidelines for the use of touch as a therapeutic intervention

The following guidelines relate equally to the care of people other than those with learning disa-bilities, but can be applied specifically to this client group and are suggestions for good practice.

- The practitioner must be adequately and appropriately trained.
- Touch, offered as a therapeutic intervention, should be structured into individual care plans.
- The client must be offered a choice, presented in a way which they are able to understand, in order that they can give consent to receiving touch in as informed a way as possible.
- The needs of the client should be taken into account, as individual aspects such as mood or behaviour changes may influence the therapeutic intervention.
- The caregiver is motivated to touch on the basis of the client's needs.
- When giving touch to a client the practitioner practices according to a framework for touching that has been established through education and experience.
- The setting for the touch therapy should be conducive to a therapeutic environment and all aspects of the client's health, safety and any risk factors should be addressed.
- Not all clients will be receptive to touch as a therapeutic intervention and it is important to identify those for whom this therapy may not be appropriate.
- Verbal and non-verbal cues must be recognised and interpreted correctly.
- Comprehensive records of the touch therapy intervention must be maintained.

Conclusion

Touch has many meanings. It can be interpreted as the acknowledgement of a person's presence, a display of love, an act of aggression, a desire for comfort or a feeling of physical closeness. How one person interprets the touch of another depends upon each person's cultural background, the nature of the relationship and each individual's feelings at the time.

Touch used as a therapeutic intervention has potentially much to offer carers and their clients. Touch provides a valuable therapeutic tool that may affect the person physically, emotionally and spiritually, enhancing their self-esteem and effecting changes in their overall health and well-being. The care given when using touch becomes a sharing and empowering process in which both the carer and the client benefit as a relationship develops and communication is enhanced.

The studies discussed in this chapter all claim that the work has been vital to their client. It was reported that these clients increased their communication skills and concentration span, and that the clients seemed very relaxed and happy. The treatments were also reported to have had some success in reducing incidents of challenging behaviour.

The quality of touch that a person receives will often give clearer non-verbal cues as to the true feelings of the person offering touch than any accompanying vocalisations. The non-verbal messages we convey through touch and the quality of touch that a person receives are very important and can affect the quality of relationships with others and perhaps affect their overall quality of life.

References

Armstrong, F. and Heidingsfeld, V. (2000) Aromatherapy for deaf and deaf blind people living in residential accommodation. *Complementary Therapies in Nursing and Midwifery*, **6**, 180–8.

Arnould-Taylor, W. E. (1991) *The Principles and Practice of Physical Therapy.* Stanley Thomas, London.

Ayres, J. A. (1979) *Sensory Integration and the Child.* Western Psychological Services, Los Angeles.

Barnett, K. A. (1972) A survey of the current utilisation of touch by health team personnel with hospitalised patients. *International Journal of Nursing Studies*, **9**, 195–209.

Bowlby, J. (1969) *Attachment.* International Psychoanalytical Library, Vol. 1. Hogarth, London.

Cunningham, C. C., Hutchinson, R. and Kewin, J. (1991) *Recreation for People with Profound and Severe Learning Disabilities: The Whittington Hall Snoezelen Project.* North Derbyshire Health Authority, Chesterfield.

Cohen, N. (1987) Massage is the message. *Nursing Times*, **83**(19), 19–20.

Dryden, S., Holden, S. and Mackereth, P. (1999) 'Just the ticket'; the findings of a pilot complementary therapy service (part 11). *Complementary Therapies in Nursing and Midwifery*, **5**(1), 15–18.

Edwards, S. C. (1998) An anthropological interpretation of nurses and patients' perceptions of the use of space and touch. *Journal of Advanced Nursing.* **28**, 809–17.

Farrah, S. (1971) The nurse the patient and touch. In: *Current Concepts in Clinical Nursing* (ed. M. Duffey, F. H. Anderson, B. S. Bergerson, M. Lohr and M. H. Rose). Mosby, St Louis.

Field, T., Lasko, D., Mundy, P., Henteleff, T., Kabat, S., Talpins, S. and Dowling, M. (1997) Brief report: autistic children's attentiveness and responsivity improve after touch therapy. *Journal of Autism and Developmental Disorders*, **27**(3), 333–8.

Frank, L. (1957) Tactile communication. *Genetic Psychology Monographs*, **56**, 209–55.

Gale, E. (2002) Advocating the use of reflexology for people with a learning disability. In: *Clinical Reflexology: A Guide for Health Professionals* (eds. P. A. Mackereth and D. Tiran). Churchill Livingstone, Edinburgh.

Gale, E. and Hegarty, J. R. (2000) The use of touch in caring for people with learning disability. *British Journal of Developmental Disabilities*, **46**(2), 97–108.

Gray, N. (1990) Healing by the laying on of hands. *The Independent*, 2 January.

Griffiths, P. (2001) Reflexology. In *The Nurse's Handbook of Complementary Therapies*, 2nd edn (ed. D. Rankin-Box). Harcourt Publishers, London.

Goodykoontz, L. (1979) Touch: attitudes and practice. *Nursing Forum*, **18**(10), 4–17.

Harrison, J. and Ruddle, J. (1995) An introduction to aromatherapy for people with learning disabilities. *British Journal of Learning Disabilities*, **23**(1), 37–40.

Hegarty, J. R. and Gale, E. (1996) Touch as a therapeutic medium for people with challenging behaviours. *British Journal of Learning Disabilities*, **24**, 26–31.

Henley, N. M. (1973) The politics of touch. In *Radical Psychology* (ed. P. Brown). Harper and Row, New York.

Hutchinson, R. (1991) Sensory environments and experience. Some ideas for application. In: *Sensation and Disability* (eds. R. Hutchinson and J. Keewin). Rompa, London.

Jourard, S. M. (1966) An exploratory study of body accessibility. *British Journal of Social and Clinical Psychology*, **5**, 221–31.

Joyce, M. and Richardson, R. (1997) Reflexology can help MS. *International Journal of Alternative and Complementary Medicine*, July, 10–12.

Kertay, L. and Reviere, S. L. (1998) Touch in context. In: *Touch in Psychotherapy* (eds. E. W. L. Smith, P. R. Clance and S. Imes). Guilford Press, New York.

Kezuka, E. (1997) The role of touch in facilitated communication. *Journal of Autism and Developmental Disorders*, **27**, 571–93.

King. B. H. (1993) Self-injury by people with mental retardation: a compulsive behaviour hypothesis. *American Journal of Mental Retardation*, **98**, 93–112.

Lange-Alberts, M. E. and Shott, S. (1984) Nutritional intake. Use of touch and verbal cuing. *Journal of Gerontological Nursing*, **8**(3), 152–5.

Leininger, M. M. (1981) *Caring: An Essential Human Need*. Wiley, New York.

Le May, A. (1986) The human connection. *Nursing Times*, 19 November, pp. 28–30.

Masters, R. (1987) The psyche and the skin. In: *Touch in Psychotherapy* (eds. E. W. L. Smith, P. R. Clance and S. Imes). Guilford Press, New York.

McGee, J. J. (1985) Gentle teaching. *Mental Handicap in New Zealand*, **9**, 13–24.

Montagu, A. (1971) *Touching: The Human Significance of the Skin*. Columbia University Press, New York.

Noddings, N. (1984) *Caring: A Feminist Approach to Ethics and Moral Education*. University of California Press.

Pratt, J. W. and Mason, A. (1981) *The Caring Touch*. London: Hayden.

Routasalo, P. and Isola, A. (1996) The right to touch and be touched. *Nursing Ethics*, **3**(2), 165–76.

Rogers, C. R. (1951) *Client Centred Therapy*. Constable, London.

Sanderson, H. and Carter, A. (1994) Healing hands. *Nursing Times*, 16 March, p. 11.

Shapiro, M., Parush, S., Green, M. and Roth, D. (1997). The efficacy of the 'Snoezelen' in the management of children with mental retardation who exhibit maladaptive behaviours. *British Journal of Developmental Disabilities*, **43**(2), 85.

Sharpton, W. R. and West, M. D. (1992). Profound and severe retardation. In *Developmental Disabilities: A Handbook for Best Practice* (eds. P. J. McLaughlin and P. Weham). Butterworth-Heinemann, London.

Tiran, D. (2002) *Clinical Reflexology: A Guide for Health Professionals*. Churchill Livingstone, Edinburgh.

Verity, S. (1996) Communicating with sedated ventilated patients in intensive care: focusing on the use of touch. *Intensive and Critical Care Nursing*, **12**, 354–8.

Watson, W. H. (1975) The meaning of touch. *Geriatric Nursing Journal of Communication*, **25**(3), 104–12.

CHAPTER 6

Multi-sensory environments

Sarah Newman

The aim of this chapter is to show some of the benefits that a multi-sensory environment (MSE) may have and also how using one provides a tool for the professional to use to build therapeutic relationships with people with profound to severe learning disabilities. The theory of MSE first came to my attention as a student nurse when I was greatly enthused by the concept. Over the years I, like many others, had concerns about the purpose of such rooms, especially with the growing emphasis on evidence-based practice (Kay, 1995; Nursing and Midwifery Council, 2002; Slevin and McClelland, 1999; Thurtle and Wyatt, 1999) and suggestions that MSEs were being used merely as a dumping ground (Ayer, 1998; Whittaker, 1992). However, I remained enthusiastic about the potential that MSEs might have. Presently I work in an NHS-run children's short-term care unit as a staff nurse. The team have worked hard to raise money to develop a conservatory into a multi-sensory environment, which has been a great success. It provides firstly a great asset to the unit that the children and staff love and benefit from, and secondly a facility that has allowed my own theories to develop and has alleviated some of my concerns.

This chapter will give a history of MSEs, what they can offer and the different ways in which they can be used. I will conclude with the benefits of using an MSE and how they aid in building a therapeutic relationship with individuals. The examples used in this chapter are based on adults and children who have severe to profound learning disabilities, physical disabilities and health-care needs. All are based on my observations during my own practice.

It is felt that some terminology will need to be clarified; the content of this chapter is aimed at supporting the professional. This implies those working in health, social care and education as well as carers and families who are often expert about their loved one's life and all that goes on in it.

Before venturing forward in to the realm of MSEs it is first vital that we understand what the senses are. Most people are aware that we have the five senses of sight, sound, taste, touch and smell, but in the world of MSEs there is often a sixth sense added: that of movement. This is because our senses are those which we use to perceive, and many of the individuals that use the MSE are either wheelchair users or have physical disabilities that limit their movement, therefore reducing their perception of movement and the sensation of moving. It is important that the professional enable individuals to experience the sensation of movement during the MSE sessions equally to the other senses. (Pinkney, 2002).

It should be noted at this point that the use of aromatherapy oils is not encouraged in conjunction with MSEs as with massage, unless a professionally certified person is present or has been consulted.

The history of the MSE

Multi-sensory environments (MSEs) first began as a collection of rooms described as a 'Sensory Cafeteria', designed to be a place where the senses could be stimulated and choices could made, with a discotheque feel to them (Cleland and Clark, 1966). MSEs were developed from this first concept and have been around since the late 1970s. The concept was further developed in Holland. It is commonly known as a 'Snoezelen Environment', a name developed by its founders Hulsegge and Verheul (1987). This name was given as it roughly translates into 'smell' and 'doze'. It was hoped that this might conjure up the lazy relaxed feeling that a Snoezelen or MSE was capable of producing and was not at all scientific, nor was it intended to sound scientific in its origins. The word 'Snoezelen' is now a registered trademark of Rompa, one of the commercial suppliers of equipment and devices for MSEs.

Hogg and Cavet (1995) define MSEs as 'a collection of devices that offer sensory stimulation, some of which have been specially designed for people with severe or profound and multiple disabilities'. Around the same time similar approaches were also being developed, such as white rooms and black rooms (Doble *et al.*, 1992; Potenski, 1993) both of which were very closely linked to the Snoezelen approach.

Whilst these new approaches to providing meaningful activities were being developed, some professionals were arguing that these were not normal activities and that it had been specially designed; therefore was it appropriate and should people with learning disabilities be participating in it? This goes against the theory of normalisation (Wolfensberger, 1972). It was not an activity everyone in society could access. In essence, individuals were able to be in a world of their own, not integrating into the community and the rest of society.

Many professionals working with people with learning disabilities remained enthusiastic and continued to introduce MSEs to schools and day centres. For many professionals it seemed at last that there was a meaningful activity that was designed for people with profound learning disabilities. One of the main difficulties that faced professionals was the ability to provide an activity that was deemed age-appropriate. MSEs had the answer: a non-age-specific activity that was accessible to all individuals with profound to severe learning disabilities.

As the concept developed, the notion of multisensory training was being incorporated into the school curriculum. The experience could vary from one or two pieces of equipment, through home-made areas using foils, fabrics and shakers, to a complex purpose-built room. Pinkney (1998) suggests that the MSE enables a unique individually tailored sensory therapy that is non-directive, therefore allowing the individual more control over the session (Pinkney 2001):

A Multi-Sensory Environment is designed to stimulate the primary senses of touch, taste, sight, sound smell without the need for intellectual activity. Trust and relaxation are encouraged via non-directive therapy. The idea of Multi-Sensory Environment encompasses a sensory therapy which is unique to each individual.

Originally there was no other purpose than to offer an experience that was an appropriate leisure activity. There were no expectations of success or failure and no demands made of the individual. However, over the years it appears that the notion of an MSE as a therapy has had to develop to justify its existence. The idea of the MSE as being therapeutic, activating the brain and stimulating the senses, gave a rationale for using them amongst professionals; this is supported by Kewin (1994). This helped to counter the 'normalisation argument'. The concept of what an MSE is has not changed much over the years and the principles and theory have remained the fundamental basis for the use of MSEs. It should be relaxing and fun without any pressure to be successful.

In more recent times the use of MSEs has become more widespread and can now be found in maternity units, elderly people's homes, social education centres, children's play areas in restaurants and crèches; in fact almost anywhere. Many retail outlets now sell products that appear to be based on MSE designs, especially in lighting and use of textured fabrics, and there is increasing popularity of new era music and room fragrances, and even the use of massage cushions. For the first time the culture of people with learning disabilities has given something to the rest of society that they have embraced, and therefore it has become normal and accepted by all.

MSEs can be simple or complex and can be in any room or area. Multisensory experiences can be incorporated into bath time, cooking or even going out for a walk. Our everyday environment is loaded with sensory experiences. However, these can often be confusing for people with severe learning disabilities. The world of a person with learning disabilities is often too rich in stimuli and therefore chaotic, or threatens to become chaotic (Hutchinson, 1994). An MSE offers the opportunity to have a defined area, where breaking things down and simplifying experiences can be achieved, enabling the individual the opportunity to focus on one sense at a time and allowing the individual time to make sense of the stimulus being received. For some individuals with severe learning disabilities that can be as simple as a glowing light, developing recognition for something and showing it through a change in facial expression.

Why use a MSE?

The purpose of an MSE has long been debated and what started out as providing an accessible leisure activity for people with profound learning disabilities and sensory deficits, fulfilling the right that everyone should be able to access suitable leisure opportunities (Hagger and Hutchinson, 1991) has turned in to a multifunctional facility used worldwide (Pinkney, 2001). There have been several studies indicating potential benefits when used as a therapy to reduce maladaptive behaviours (Hutchinson and Haggar, 1994; Shapiro *et al.*, 1997; Cuvo *et al.*, 2001), as pain relief (Schofield and Davis, 2000; Schofield, 2002), to enhance communication (Lindsay *et al.*, 2001), and for therapeutic relationship building (Kewin, 1994; Terry and Hong, 1998). They have also been used to counter the effects of dementia (Moffat *et al.*, 1993; Hope, 1997) and even as relaxation areas in maternity units (Ayres, 1994) to mention but a few. MSEs are perhaps still most commonly used with individuals with severe to profound learning and physical disabilities.

Before MSEs were developed, people with profound learning disabilities were expected to participate in 'normal' activities which may have had little or no meaning to them. Day centres and schools would often focus on a classroom style setting with large groups and focusing much of the day around art and craft. Many individuals found such activities confusing and meaningless (Vlaskamp *et al.*, 2003). Although it is recognised that any activity that offers a social experience is beneficial and is often fun, there have always been those individuals who didn't seem able to be reached and remained pretty much unchanged, no matter what activity they were involved in.

The MSE offers an opportunity for an individual to spend quality one-to-one time with professionals. Kewin (1994) suggests that often one-to-one time is based around attending to personal hygiene needs, which doesn't allow the professional a chance to develop a relationship with the individual and it wasn't until the use of MSEs that the personality of individuals began to be recognised. Professionals began to recognise that individuals were interesting people in their own right and had quite definite personalities, enabling a more therapeutic relationship to form.

MSEs also allow individuals the opportunity to be alone, with equipment that is designed to be accessible to their cognitive level and giving them the chance to be in control of their environment, operating cause and effect switches that can change speeds, volumes and lighting (Thompson and Martin, 1994). Specific pieces of equipment have been designed to operate by noise or movement, enabling individuals with minimal abilities to control their milieu. This, for some individuals, is the first time in their lives that they have been in control. It offers a great sense of achievement and in some cases the notion that 'what they do will have an effect on their surroundings' provides an invaluable sense of self-worth. There have been many anecdotal accounts of people showing reduction in aggressive behaviours and even smiles where none had been observed before. The development of skills has been observed in some schools and teachers felt that these skills might be generalised and used in other areas (Ayer, 1998); being able to operate a switch can open up a world of opportunities.

It is believed that the MSE has the potential to be beneficial in many ways. The list below summarises the aims that it is hoped will be achieved by the individual using a MSE.

1. Provide a stimulating environment that heightens awareness through developing the individual's own senses.
2. Develop relationships between the professional and individual.
3. Development of the individual's perceptual skills.
4. Provide an interesting atmosphere that encourages participants to explore their environment.
5. Improve hand–eye coordination and other skills.
6. Develop the individual's awareness of cause and effect.
7. Assist in the development of communication skills.
8. Increase independence, enabling the individual to access the equipment.
9. Provide an enjoyable leisure activity that is meaningful to the individual.
10. Offer a secure setting to allow the individual mental and physical relaxation.

It is not intended that all of these aims should be met by all the individuals that use an MSE, as that would imply expectations and pressure, and this would oppose one of its fundamental goals. These are merely broad aims that could occur if the individual wishes and if the professional structures the time and the MSE towards achieving specific aims.

How to use the MSE

We have already discussed how the MSE can have many functions (Hutchinson and Haggar, 1994; Shapiro *et al.*, 1997; Cuvo *et al.*, 2001; Schofield and Davis, 2000; Schofield, 2002; Lindsay *et al.*, 2001; Kewin, 1994; Terry and Hong, 1998; Moffat *et al.*, 1993; Hope, 1997; Ayres, 1994) and with many different individual groups. When working with individuals who have severe profound learning and physical disabilities and in some instances sensory deficits that there are three main ways in which a MSE might be used:

1. A group leisure opportunity
2. To provide sensory experience (e.g. a woodland experience)
3. To enable the development of an individual's senses and independence on a one-to-one basis, using an assessment tool

Hong (2004) identifies the above three and names these the 'Dutch movement', 'atmospherics and theme rooms' and 'interactive room'. There may also be other ways of using an MSE with many additional benefits; however, these three will be focused on in more detail.

When designing an MSE it is important to consider the users and the ways in which you intend to use the MSE. Many companies offer free design advice which will take both of these into consideration. It isn't always necessary to spend a large amount of money (Laurent, 1992), as a few small pieces of equipment in a room can be enough to be effective. In this section the term 'session' will be used to describe the period of time in the MSE. One commonly asked question is how long should a session be? This depends on the type of activity.

How long a session should be?

■ *Group leisure*

If using the MSE for group leisure, a duration of about 45 minutes to 1 hour was suggested by Kewin (1994). If the group is responding well and there are no time constraints then a longer period is feasible, up to 2 hours. Ashby *et al.* (1995) suggest that people with profound learning disabilities often have a shorter concentration span than the average person; this is thought to be around 20 minutes (University of Bristol, 2005). Therefore change, variety and choice should be encouraged regularly by the professional to maintain interest.

■ *Sensory experience*

A whole morning or afternoon could be based around a sensory experience. If plenty of opportunity and variety are offered it may even develop across a whole day, incorporating other areas in the building/facility, not just within the MSE.

■ *Assessment*

Short periods are more beneficial, particularly when using the room on a one-to-one basis. When carrying out a developmental assessment, about 15–30 minutes (Kewin, 1994) should be long enough. It should be taken into consideration that an assessment might be hard work for the individual and therefore tiring.

Pinkney (2002) suggests that the length of time spent in the MSE should be modified to meet the individual's needs; it is thought that some individuals may find it frightening at first, as it is new and unlike anything that has been experienced before. Therefore they are unaware of what is about to occur. Several exposures to the environment should be tried before deciding that the individual doesn't like it or isn't responding. When starting a session in the MSE, one of the most fundamental aspects to remember is that the equipment alone will not work: it is the therapist that makes it work (Pinkney, 1998) through having appropriate training and knowledge.

Group leisure

In this instance the work within the MSE is with a larger group of individuals. The initial setup of the room is controlled by the professionals. Each session can be structured to cater for the group of individuals that are about to enter the MSE. The atmosphere that is initially created and the first impression can determine the way that a session may be run.

When working with a group there is less scope for individual preferences, as there may be conflicting tastes and not every one will be able to have their own choices. therefore it is fairer to let the professional initially set up the MSE. The session can be tailored to the group that is about to enter according to age, gender, and whether it is to be a lively invigorating session or a calmer more relaxed session. Depending on what is desired, any combination of these can be used. Some examples of room setups can be found in Box 6.1. The way in which the MSE is set up will depict these differences. The individual will recognise the differences through the stimulation that the senses receive from the different equipment used. For example, sound is very influential. Children's nursery rhymes may not be appropriate for older individuals and modern pop music is less relaxing than calm ethereal music.

It should be noted that not everyone enjoys the same music, and what might be relaxing for one person may be really irritating for another. Initially it is a case of trial and error until a suitable balance is found. White (1999) documents that listening to music which has 60 or less beats per minute is generally considered relaxing. This is due to it being slower than the average adult heart beat of 72 beats per minute (Weller, 2005). Lighting, when used as bright, flashing defined shapes is invigorating. When used as glowing, slow-changing pastel colours it can be relaxing. Equipment such as a projection lamp can tailor the MSE to a particular group of individuals. There is a wide range of discs available: cartoon style for younger children; liquid ones that constantly change, suitable for teenagers or for relaxing; and discs with birds or nostalgic pictures for older individuals.

The individuals should be assisted to enter the room and should be in a comfortable position. For some this will be lying on a mat or sitting in a beanbag. Once the individuals are in the room they will take control, exploring their environment and controlling it through switches, buttons, movement, noise, pressure pads and light beams. For some individuals the ability to explore is limited by physical disabilities and it is therefore the responsibility of the professionals (Kewin, 1994) to assist them by bringing them different pieces of equipment, and offering new sensations, experiences and variety on a frequent basis. The professional should observe for preferences either through non-verbal expressions or vocalisation and then encourage and enable participation in these preferences.

The purpose of a group leisure activity would be to enable a group of individuals to enjoy an activity that they are able to fully participate in, that is meaningful to them with no expectations, where they feel at ease from social pressures and where they can form relationships with their peers and professionals. (Hong, 2004; Hulsegge and Verheul, 1987; Pagliano, 1999).

Box 6.1

Younger children group: leisure experience

Sound
Disney CD
Music for children CD
Vibration mat
Singing nursery rhymes

Sight
Projection discs:
    Teddy bears picnic
    Dino
    Countryside
Fibre optic lights
Bubble tubes

Touch
Toys, jelly, messy play, beanbag, water, touch nursery rhymes, vibrating mat

Taste
Jelly sweets
Chocolates
Crisps

Smell
Lavender

Movement
Passive movement
Gentle massage
Roly poly

Older children experience

Sound
Chart music
Radio

Sight
Liquid projection disc

Touch
Massage
Touch beanbag
Ball pool

Taste
Sweets
Chocolates
Crisps

Smell
Perfumes/aftershaves

Movement
Vibrating mat
Passive movement
Dancing

Stimulating experience

Sound
Zulu heartbeat CD
Thunderstorms CD
Pop music

Sight
Mirror ball
Liquid projection disc
Fibre optic lights
Milky Way mat

Touch
Spiky ball
Interactive toys
Wall panels

Taste
Fizzy (Space dust), fizzy pop drinks
Citrus drinks

Smell
Citrus

Movement
Tickling, rocking, peddling

Relaxing experience

Sound
Pachelbel, Calm ocean sounds CD

Music for children
Body music
Dolphins and whales CD
Sight
Liquid, clouds, Avalon dawn
Seasons dawn projection discs
Touch
Gentle hand and foot rub
Taste
Chocolates
Honey

Smell
Lavender, chamomile, peach room fragrances
Movement
Passive movement
Slow rocking and swaying
Vibrating mat on slow and low setting

Sensory experience

The idea of a sensory experience session is to create, stimulate or heighten the senses received during an experience. These sessions are often based on a theme: ideal for topic work in schools, but also great fun in other settings. We may ask 'Why not just allow the individual the real experience?' (Cavet, 1994). This is encouraged where possible, but for some individuals this can be too confusing and chaotic (Hutchinson and Haggar, 1994; Vlaskamp *et al.*, 2003). By developing a themed session the sensations and sensory input that might be gained can be experienced individually, slowly and at the individual's own rate, allowing the individual to absorb the experience and interpret each aspect separately through each of the senses.

In some settings it may be possible to make it a theme for a day, incorporating elements of the theme into all that is done throughout the day: a meal that represents the theme, a movie that is appropriate to the theme, and at bath time toiletries that again tie in with the theme. It is a good idea to have the theme planned out on paper, providing a list of tools and equipment that might be required to create the sensory experience. Box 6.2 provides some examples of the themes and the type of equipment that might be used to create them. Sensory experiences can be carried out as a group or on a one-to-one basis.

Assessment

The use of the MSE has long been debated (Slevin and McClelland, 1999) and has developed over the years, changing from only being recognised as a leisure pursuit to an increasingly used therapy. This has largely come about with the need to justify its existence (Kay, 1995; Nursing and Midwifery Council, 2002; Thurtle and Wyatt, 1999). The MSE has arguably been shown to assist in the development of skills from social to sensory and also aid the development of independence skills (Ayer, 1998; Houghton *et al.*, 1998; Lancioni *et al.*, 2002; Lindsay *et al.*, 2001; Long and Haig, 1992; Mitchell and Van der Gaag, 2002; Thompson and Martin, 1994).

Box 6.2

Woodland experience

Sound
English country dawn CD
Woodland nightfall CD
Bird sounds
Sight
Forest projection disc
Seasons woods projection disc
Touch
Crunchy paper or dry leaves
Crinkle panel on beanbag
Feathers
Concurs
Acorns
Taste
Honey
Berry jams
Smell
Pine tree scent box
Movement
Arms up stretched and swaying like a
tree

Rainforest experience

Sound
Spirit of the rainforest CD
Jungle CD
Rain shaker
Sight
Butterflies projection disc
Touch
Wet leaves
Tickle games, e.g. Incey Wincey spider
Feathers
Rubber bugs
Taste
Mango juice
Melon
Smell
Pineapple scent box
Pine scent box
Movement
Arms up stretched and swaying like a
tree
Finger tapping massage to simulate rain

A walk in the country experience

Sound
English country dawn CD
Sight
Avalon dawn projection Disc
Countryside (cartoon style) projection
disc
Touch
Artificial grass
Feathers
Leaves
Taste
Berry jams
Apple juice
Smell
Spring fresh
Floral
Movement
Walking motion with legs

Ghost experience

Sound
Ghosts CD
Copying sounds, e.g. Ooooo, Aaaaaah
Sight
Mirror ball
Black light

Touch
  Velour fabric on beanbag
  Cotton wool
  Ice
Taste
  Lime jelly
  Pumpkin pie
Smell
  Musk
Movement
  Wobbly
  Shaky and shivery

Space experience

Sound
  Millennium CD
  Alien encounter CD
  White noise (vibrating mat)
Sight
  Space ritual projection disc
  Milky Way mat
  Star net
  Laser light
Touch
  Tin foil
  Cold/hot
  Metallic
Taste
  Fizzy (Space dust)
  Fizzy pop
Smell
  Firework scent
Movement
  Fast swinging movements, arms out flying

Night experience

Sound
  Woodland nightfall CD
  Even wolves dream CD

Sight
  Space ritual projection disc
  Milky Way mat
  Star net
  Fireworks
Touch
  Velour fabric on beanbag
  Silky panel on beanbag
Taste
  Moon cheese and star milk
  Hot chocolate
  Milky Way and Galaxy chocolate
Smell
  Lavender
  Firework scent
Movement
  Slow rocking
  Gentle massage, soft stroking

Weather experience

Sound
  Thunderstorms CD
Sight
  Clouds projection disc
  Mirror ball
Touch
  Water
  Cotton wool to simulate clouds
  Hot/cold
  Wind from fan
Taste
  Ice, water
  Candy floss
Smell
  Musty
  Musk
  Cut grass
Movement
  Finger tapping massage to simulate rain
  Wind from fan
  Small parachute to create billowing wind

Around the world experience	Ocean experience
Sound	**Sound**
Compilation CD	Pachelbel, calm ocean sounds CD
Music from different countries	Dolphins and whales CD
Sight	Running water
World or clouds projection disc	**Sight**
Touch	Deep projection disc
Balls	Bubble tubes
Taste	**Touch**
Food from around the world, e.g. Indian,	Water
Chinese, Turkish delight, Greek yogurt	Pebbles
Fruits	Sand
Smell	**Taste**
Smells from around the world, e.g.	Salt
Curry powder, Chinese spices, josh	Ocean sticks
sticks, rose water	Fish paste
Movement	**Smell**
Walking motion	Sea scent
Circulate motions with arms	Dried seaweed
	Movement
	Rolling to simulate waves

It is important to establish firstly what it is that the individual is to develop; this can be established by assessing the individual and identifying an area of need. This is often determined initially by a lack of response, identifying a lack of skill, inappropriate behaviours or a sensory deficit. Box 6.3 gives an example of the type of assessment tool that might be used.

Once the initial assessment has been carried out, a session plan can be drawn up. An example can be seen in Box 6.4. It is recommended that a sensory assessment is completed each time the individual enters the MSE and evaluated on a regular basis.

The time-scale for individual evaluation will vary depending on the rate at which progress takes place. For some this could be monthly, while for others it could be weekly. We should also evaluate if it is felt that no progress has been made. It may be that the assessment needs repeating, as the individual may have had a change in needs and preferences. The frequency of evaluation will also vary depending on how frequently the individual is exposed to the MSE. In a school or day centre it may be daily, and therefore there will be a lot of information being collected. Over time it is hoped that a positive response will develop.

To enable the individuals that use MSE to develop it is paramount to success that the skills that are to be learned are broken down in to the simplest form. For example, in assessing sight, at first glance the eyes may appear physically healthy yet the individual has never appeared to see any thing. Moralda and Jeffery (2001) document a mother's delight when her child first experienced the MSE and a bunch of fibre optic lights were held in front of her and she began to smile.

Box 6.3 Assessment tool

Name: Age:
First assessment date:
Known sensory deficits:

This is an initial assessment to ascertain areas and equipment that might be used to aid an individual to develop their social or sensory skills and/or to aid the development of independence skills. For others it is an assessment of equipment that will provide a suitable experience that offers a leisure opportunity that suits the individual's needs and abilities, enabling them to access a facility that is meaningful to them. Equipment should be assessed one piece at a time and with a minimum of exterior influences. The assessment must take place on a one-to-one basis.

The individual should be helped to feel comfortable, safe, relaxed and without pressure. It is important to remember that not all individuals enjoy the multisensory environment.
The aim of the assessment is to provide a session that is tailored to each individual's developing skills, focusing on equipment that will assist in developing these, or an opportunity based on preferences. From this a personalised plan can be developed, e.g. working with specific pieces of equipment in a session to develop skills or with several pieces to provide a pleasurable environment based on choice.

Fill in the assessment on the next page using the following guidelines.

Guidelines

Equipment being used: Enter the name of the piece of equipment that the individual is being exposed to.

Duration of interest: There may be individuals that show no interest and indicate the desire to use another piece of equipment. This is fine, and encourages independence. This should be recorded. The average attention span is 20 minutes, in an adult of average intellectual ability. It is likely that it could be much less for the individuals we are exposing to the MSE.

Reaction: This can be visual, tactile, facial expression or a sound. It may be a change in behaviour, e.g. became content, relaxed or excited. Some individuals' reactions may be as small as a quick glance; this may be a starting block to development and is very important.

Support needed: Did the individuals need assistance in order to access the equipment, e.g. support to sit, hand over hand or position required?

Comments: Your opinion on how the piece of equipment could/does benefit the individuals.

Through monitoring the sessions any progress in the individual's response can be observed. It may be that the individual may not require the development of their senses, or they may need the opportunity to develop relationship building, the ability to relax, or the opportunity to be stimulated and invigorated. This assessment tool may be used and adapted to meet all of these requirements and others not listed.

Sensory assessment

Name:

Equipment being used	Date	Duration of interest	Reaction	Support needed	By whom or what	Comments

Evaluation of assessment

Name:

In this section information is gathered from the sensory assessment and goals are set. From this an individual session plan can be drawn up. The following sessions should also be assessed using the sensory assessment form so as to identify any developments or changes in preferences.

Comment on the pieces of equipment the individual responded to most				
Comment on the pieces of equipment the individual responded to least				
Identify areas that you, the professional, believe the individual would benefit from developing				
Set an objective, i.e. the purpose of this is to enable the individual to...				
Set a goal, i.e. the individual will be able to... within ... sessions/weeks				

Box 6.4 Sensory experience personal session planner

Child's name:

Date:

Review date:

Equipment	Duration	Support needed	Comments

This was the first time she had shown that she was actually seeing something. The very nature of a learning disability means that the individual was born with or acquired at an early age a brain injury or deficiency, and therefore the brain is not functioning normally. The signal received through the eye may be jumbled and the brain is unable to make sense of the signal it is receiving. The individual may not be able to understand the benefits of using their eyes until it is broken down into the simplest form.

Through exposing the individual to light in a pleasurable environment the ability to track the light may develop. It is thought that this may be done through the development of new neurological pathways which convert the signal that the eyes receive into a recognised message that the brain relates to (Pagliano, 1999). The eye then follows the light. This may be as much as the individual is able to achieve, or they may go on to give eye contact or even have the ability to see an object they desire and reach for it. The motivation is the sensation that the individual receives from which pleasure is gained. In other cases it may be the development of hearing, the confidence to touch or the opportunity to smile and relax.

When developing the senses it is essential that there are no disruptions in the concentration of the individual, as this will distract them and they may be reluctant to start again (Pagliano, 1999).

Box 6.5 provides a list of equipment that might typically be found in an MSE and a quick look-up chart to see the sense that is most likely to be stimulated when using that piece of equipment.

Box 6.5 List of equipment and possible uses

Activity board
Made up of many different items, which are either visual or tactile, set in the walls, this allows the individuals and professionals to interact with each other. Some individuals will sit and investigate, touching, feeling, pushing and hitting. Professionals can then use this board to help the individuals with their hand–eye coordination using hand over hand pointing and asking questions, e.g. about the shape, sounds or feel of the different items. This piece is good for aiding communication.

Aromatherapy diffuser
This piece of equipment should only be used by a qualified member of staff who has been sufficiently trained, as some of the oils used could have an adverse effect on the individual. Smell is one of the most powerful senses we have. The aromatic fragrances given out by the oils fill the room, creating a relaxing or stimulating environment (combining this with simple foot or hand massage can provide you with a basis for communication and for building relationships of trust with your individual).

Beanbags/musical beanbag
Beanbags scattered about the room provide a safe environment for some of our more vulnerable individuals. They are filled with special granules that form to the body shape,

allowing the individual to relax and take in the atmosphere of the room. They also create a great sound if you scratch them or tap them gently.

The musical beanbag has sounds that penetrate through the bag and are picked up through the body, creating various sensations and sounds. This is very good for people with little or no hearing ability as it creates an inner body noise.

Bubble tubes and padded seating area
These are both visual and tactile and they can be relaxing or stimulating, depending on the speed they are set on. They offer a diffused light that creates a visual experience as the bubbles rise and the colour changes. The padded area round the tubes allows individuals to sit or lie down among them, put their face or hands up against the tubes, or wrap themselves around them. The individual is able to gain a tactile sensation as the tubes gently vibrate, giving off a low bass noise.

Ceiling hangings
These are fun to look at, and some are interactive in that they can be reached and pulled, allowing cause and effect. These are more effective with non-visually impaired individuals.

Fibre optic curtains and sprays
The sprays give both a tactile and visual experience. As the light moves down the spray it continually changes colour. The spray is soft and flexible and allows the individual to pick up one strand or groups of strands and wrap them around their hands or body, to run their fingers though them, or to put them close to the face and peer closely into the light. These are very beneficial for people who are partially sighted, particularly when used for tracking.

Hanging curtains placed in the entrance give a visual and tactile experience as individuals walk through them. Individuals must be observed closely with these as they have a tendency to put them in their mouth. Although no electricity flows through them, they are filled with optical fibres, which are very sharp.

Light net
This is a great visual experience which can be stimulating or relaxing, depending on speed setting. For individuals that lie on the mats this is great.

Loose accessories
Within the room there can be a wide range of smaller loose objects. These can be used on their own or in conjunction with the rest of the room and are suitable for a wide range of individuals. They will both stimulate and have a therapeutic effect on whoever is using them. Handheld vibrating massagers create a gentle tingling sensation on the body, and the spiky rubber ring gives a different sensation when given to visually impaired individuals. It will stimulate them to explore it, running their fingers over it and placing it on their face to experience the sensation it creates. It's good to experiment with the accessories to find which suits your individual.

Milky Way carpet

When used by itself this can be a very stimulating experience. Soft and warm to touch, the shimmering effect can be relaxing as the individual sits on the floor, beanbags or soft areas, watching the dots changing colour and twinkling. This is ideal to encourage movement, crawling and reaching.

Mirror ball

Gives a perception of space as the light from the projector hits it, sending hundreds of beams of coloured light around the room, changing colour as they go. Following the contours of the room and the bending beams of light as they make their way around the room can be very stimulating. It is very effective when used by itself or with soft mellow music, and it is also safe for people with epilepsy.

   In some cases individuals and staff have experienced a feeling of motion sickness, so observe closely.

Mirror hexagon

This is great for individuals lying on the floor, enabling them to see their own reflection, or with fibre optic lights draped over it to enhance the effect.

Music stereo system

The stereo is a major piece of equipment when creating a mood in the room. The choice of music can be very influential and can range from lively pop music and nursery rhymes to relaxing sounds of the sea, dawn chorus or rainforest. Some CDs will, when played, bring the individuals' breathing into line with the music, therefore creating a feeling of safety and tranquillity.

Neon box

This is a particularly good for using on a wheelchair with a tray, bringing the activity closer to the individual. This has a built in ultraviolet (UV) light. When switched on the loose objects in the box glow very brightly.

Neon light/mirrored panel

The UV light has a very stimulating visual effect which is also reflected in the mirror. Individuals can sit very close to it, holding the individual coloured strands, which give out a very bright neon light. The strands are pliable and can be held by the individuals, who can run their fingers through them. Good for both visual and non-visual individuals.

Projector (wall lighting)

The projector, in conjunction with the range of music that we have, produces a constantly moving pattern or whole images which are reflected onto the walls. Depending on the music you use, this could either stimulate or relax the individual.

Reflexology and massage

Only a trained and qualified person should undertake this activity. The effect that this treatment can have is often very beneficial and therapeutic. The different oils and the ways that they are applied to the body will have differing effects. Some individuals would benefit from increased circulation, while others may find it calming. This is very good for both visual and non-visual individuals. Basic hand and foot rubbing using just baby oil is as effective as massage oil. It is essential before starting that you find out whether the individual has any circulation problems or skin problems; if so, seek medical advice.

Scent box

This is a good way of arousing the sense of smell and has a wide range of fragrances, some of which are very strong scents. The pot should be held under the nose but about 15 cm away and then wafted from side to side.

Vibrating massage bed

This versatile mattress can give both enjoyment and sensual experiences to those with sight and hearing problems. The control panel allows either the individuals or staff to set the pulse/speed etc. The control panel also allows you to work on those parts of the body which may need stimulating, especially if the individual has poor mobility. The vibrating mat can also stimulate hearing, as it has a low-frequency bass note that runs through the whole body.

Water mattress

This is good for movement, enabling the individual to have the sensation of being in water without getting wet. The individual gains the ability to feel changes in body pressure and to experience a floating sensation. Also, the sound of swishing water can be heard.

Quick lookup table

Item	Sound	Sight	Touch	Taste	Smell	Movement
Activity board		✓	✓			✓
Aromatherapy diffuser					✓	
Beanbags	✓		✓			✓
Bubble tubes and padded seating area	✓	✓	✓			
Ceiling hangings		✓	✓			✓
Fibre optic curtains and sprays		✓	✓			✓
Light net		✓				
Loose accessories	✓	✓	✓			✓

Item	Sound	Sight	Touch	Taste	Smell	Movement
Milky Way carpet		✓	✓			✓
Mirror ball		✓				
Mirror hexagon		✓				
Musical beanbag	✓		✓			
Music stereo system	✓					
Neon box		✓	✓			✓
Neon light/mirrored panel		✓	✓			✓
Projector (wall lighting)		✓				
Reflexology and massage			✓		✓	✓
Scent box					✓	
Vibrating massage bed	✓		✓			✓
Water mattress	✓					✓

Conclusion

Despite all my efforts over the years I am aware that the MSE is occasionally used as a 'dumping ground' for individuals. However, it is my belief that this is often due to shortage of staff, lack of funding and lack of professionals with adequate training and knowledge. Professionals are often aware that this is what they are doing; many justify this by the fact that the individual is spending time in a safe environment and that they are able to access a milieu that they understand. Often they are sharing the experience as a group and are able to influence the environment themselves. This helps us to feel comfortable with the fact that we are giving them the opportunity to spend time with peers and develop socially; to be independent and not pressured to achieve goals, the way that Hulsegge and Verheul (1987) intended it to be used.

This is not, however, an excuse, and when possible the professionals should participate in the MSE, providing variety and change for those who can't achieve this themselves. Specific session times should be identified and carried out to get the full use out of the MSE.

The development of the MSE has come a long way over the years and this evolution must continue for the MSE movement to reach its full potential. It is still felt by many that there needs to be more relevant research (Ashby *et al.*, 1995; Hong 2004; Pinkney 2002; Schofield, 2002; Thurtle and Wyatt, 1999; Vlaskamp *et al.*, 2003; Whittaker, 1992) to continue to justify its use with people with severe to profound learning disabilities and other groups. The process of continuing research will enable professionals to share their findings, and consequently the individuals using them will continue to benefit. It is through this enthusiasm that the MSE will continue to prove its worth.

The case study in Box 6.6 outlines one example of an individual who has benefited from exposure to an MSE. In brief, this is a little boy who was thought to be unable to see very much at all and who will now locate and reach for objects he desires. This is an amazing accomplishment and illustrates that despite having a severe learning disability, the ability to learn is still there, albeit a little slower. Through using the assessment tool, areas of need were identified, a session plan established and evaluation completed. This in turn enabled the professional to provide stimulation at the right level, allowing the individual to develop new skills. Often there are too many variables to attribute this development solely to the use of the MSE, especially if the individual has input from other areas and therapies. However, it is felt that the MSE most definitely has aspects that contribute and that are beneficial.

Hong (2004) discusses the recent innovations of making the MSE mobile, as does Pagliano (1999), who goes on further to talk about increased integration and how having a portable MSE will facilitate the classroom of the future to cater for all the pupils' needs. MSEs historically take up quite a large area, which is not always feasible. Mobile/portable MSEs have great scope for use, for instance on hospital wards, by community workers, and in individuals' homes. The list is endless. The main benefit is that equipment can be stored away when not in use. The way in which MSEs are to be used continues to develop. With the publication of assessment tools the potential as a therapy is also being developed. Put the two together and a community-based multisensory professional who carries out an assessment and development programme using a portable MSE is born. What a wonderful idea! This role would break down some of the stigma currently held about MSEs and they would comply more with current theories and policies: the Community Care Act (Department of Health, 1990), normalisation (Wolfensberger, 1972), and the principle of inclusion and the person-centred approach (Department of Health, 2001).

Schofield (2002) talks of nurses as being 'enablers of patient potential'. This is particularly relevant for any professional using an MSE, working alongside the individual, sharing the experience and both working towards the same goal; a therapeutic relationship that enables individuals to fulfil their identified needs.

Box 6.6 Case study

Background

For the purpose of this case study the individual will be named James. He is an eight-year-old boy who attends a short-term care unit for one overnight stay every two weeks for three nights and one other day at a weekend. He has quadriplegic cerebral palsy, global developmental delay, epilepsy, constipation and poor vision. He attends a special needs school every day. He lives at home with his mum and stepdad, and has two sisters: one younger and one older. James has been attending the unit since he was 18 months old. At this time he also used to attend the Child Development Centre. James would become quite tearful and often the cause would not be known. It was hoped that exposure to the MSE would have a positive effect on reducing his tearful episodes and develop the use of his sight.

Initial assessment

In the beginning James used to attend mostly for day care, as he was pre-school age. Some structure to his day visits was required and the MSE was thought to be suitable. It was identified that James had visual impairment and unexplained tearful periods. James was exposed to bubble tubes, the fibre optic lights and the star net. The initial assessments were carried out and James showed a definite reaction to the bubble tubes and the fibre optic light strands.

Planned session

James was to be enabled to use the optic fibre lights. He needed support to sit in a beanbag and the professional would clump a handful of lights together and move them from left to right close to his eyes. This was to be done for a period of 5 minutes. He was also to be exposed to the bubble tubes to allow him time to relax and control his own visual input.

Outcome

At first James showed little interest in the fibre optic lights, but over the weeks he began to smile and then he started to follow the movement of the lights. When James was helped to lie between the bubble tubes he would frequently stop crying and he started to laugh. He would bring his hands up above his face and would appear to be looking at them or the light behind them caused by the bubble tubes.

Since this work began James has started to attend school full-time, and his package of short-term care has altered. James still becomes upset on occasions with no known cause, although this is less frequent now. If he is helped to use the MSE he will nearly always calm down and become more content. His parents appreciate the benefits he gets from the MSE and have incorporated several pieces of equipment into his bedroom at home, especially the bubble tube, which remains a firm favourite. In more recent years the professionals that work with James have noted that he will now appear to be reaching for an object that he desires – for instance a toy when lying on the floor – and occasionally gives a fleeting glance that seems to be direct eye contact, especially when singing to him or playing tickle games. In spite of having known James for a long time, it is still difficult to interpret just how much of his environment he is able to make sense of. However, it would seem that there has been some development in his sight and an activity identified that he enjoys that reduces his tearful episodes. It is felt by all who know him that the MSE has played a big part in that.

References

Ashby, M., William, L. R., Pitcaithly, D., Broxholme, S. and Geelen, N. (1995) Snoezelen: its effects on concentration and responsiveness in people with profound multiple handicaps. *British Journal of Occupational Therapy*, **58**(7), 303–7.

Ayer, S. (1998) Use of multi-sensory rooms for children with profound and multiple learning disabilities, *Journal of Learning Disabilities for Nursing, Health and Social Care*, **2**(2), 89–97.

Ayres, M. (1994) Learning difficulties a multi-sensory experience. *Access by Design*, **64**, 9–11.

Cavet, J. (1994) Multisensory environments Snoezelen – your questions answered. *Community Living*, **7**(3), 26.

Cleland, C. C. and Clark, C. M. (1966) Sensory deprivation and aberrant behaviour among idiots. *American Journal of Mental Deficiency*, **71**, 213–393.

Cuvo, A. J., May, M. E. and Post, T. M. (2001) Effects of living room, Snoezelen room, and outdoor activities on stereotypic behaviour and engagement by adults with profound mental retardations. *Research in Developmental Disabilities*, **22**(3), 183–204.

Department of Health (1990) *NHS and Community Care Act*. Department of Health, London.

Department of Health (2001) *Valuing People: A New Strategy for Learning Disability for the 21st Century*. Department of Health, London.

Doble, D., Goldie, C. and Kewell, C. (1992) The white approach. *Nursing Times*, **88**(40), 36–7.

Hagger, L. E. and Hutchinson, R. B. (1991) Snoezelen: an approach to the provision of a leisure resource for people with profound and multiple handicaps. *Mental Handicap*. **19**, 51–5.

Hogg, J. H. and Cavet, J. (1995) *Making Leisure Provision for People with Profound Learning and Multiple Disabilities*. Chapman & Hall, London.

Hong, C. S. (2004) Helping children with learning disabilities. Making sense of multisensory environments. *Journal of Family Healthcare*, **14**(2), 35–8.

Hope, K. (1997) Using multisensory environments with older people with dementia. *Journal of Advanced Nursing*, **25**, 780–5.

Houghton, S., Douglas, G., Brigg, J., Langsford, S., Powell, L., West, J., Chapman, A. and Kellner, R. (1998) An empirical evaluation of an interactive multi-sensory environment for children with disability. *Journal of Intellectual and Developmental Disability*, **23**(4), 267–78.

Hulsegge, J. and Verheul, A. (1987) *Snoezelen: Another World*. Rompa, UK.

Hutchinson, R. (1994) Sensory environments and experiences – some ideas for application. In: *Sensations and Disability* (eds. R. Hutchinson and J. Kewin). Rompa, London.

Hutchinson, R. B. and Haggar, L. (1994) The development and evaluation of a Snoezelen leisure resource for people with severe multiple disability. In: *Sensations and Disability* (eds. R. Hutchinson and J. Kewin). Rompa, London.

Kay, B. (1995) Grasping the research nettle in learning disabilities nursing. *British Journal of Nursing*, **4**(2), 96–8.

Kewin, J. (1994) Snoezelen – the reason and the method. In: *Sensations and Disability* (eds. R. Hutchinson and J. Kewin). Rompa, London.

Lancioni, G., Cuvo, A. and O'Reilly, M. (2002) Snoezelen: an overview of research with people with developmental disabilities and dementia. *Disability and Rehabilitation.* **24**(4), 175–84.

Laurent, S. (1992) Atmospherics. A low cost, effective sensory environment, introducing an innovative group massage technique. *Information Exchange*, **36**(19).

Lindsay, W., Black, E., Broxholme, S., Pitcaithly, D. and Hornsby, N. (2001) Effects of four therapy procedures on communication in people with profound intellectual disabilities. *Journal of Applied Research in Intellectual Disabilities*, **14**, 110–19.

Long, A. and Haig, L. (1992) How do clients benefit from Snoezelen? An exploratory study. *British Journal of Occupational Therapy*, **55**(3), 103–6.

Mitchell, J. and Van der Gaag, A. (2002) Through the eye of the Cyclops: evaluating a multi-sensory intervention programme for people with complex disabilities. *British Journal of Learning Disabilities*, **30**, 159–65.

Moffat, N., Barker, P. and Pinkney, L. (1993) *Snoezelen: An Experience for People with Dementia.* Rompa, London.

Moralda, C. and Jeffery, G. (2001). *Snoezelen Backgrounder.* Thames Valley District School Board. Available from `http://www.tvdsb.on.ca/news/2001/backgrounder.pdf#search='mora lda%20snoezelen'`; accessed on 20 July 2005.

Nursing and Midwifery Council (2002) *Code of Professional Conduct.* Nursing and Midwifery Council, London.

Pagliano, P. (1999) *Multisensory Environments.* David Fulton Publishers, London.

Pinkney, L. (1998) Exploring the myth of multisensory environments. *British Journal of Occupational Therapy*, **61**(8).

Pinkney, L. (2001) *Sensory Therapy.* Available from `http://www.sohp.soton.ac.uk/neuro/SEN-SORY.htm`. Accessed on 4 February 2005.

Pinkney, L. (2002) Investigations into the value of multisensory environments. *Nursing and Residential Care*, **5**(2), 63–7.

Potenski, D. (1993) Use of black light as visual stimulation for people with profound mental retardation and multiple handicaps. *Mental Retardation*, **31**(2), 111–15.

Schofield, P. (2002) Evaluating Snoezelen for relaxation within chronic pain management. *British Journal of Nursing*, **11**(12), 812–21.

Schofield, P. and Davis, B. (2000) Sensory stimulation (Snoezelen) versus relaxation: a potential strategy for the management of chronic pain. *Disability and Rehabilitation*, **22**(15), 675–82.

Shapiro, M., Parush, S., Green, M. and Roth, D. (1997) The efficacy of the 'Snoezelen' in the management of children with mental retardation who exhibit maladaptive behaviours. *British Journal of Developmental Disabilities*, **43**(85), 140–55.

Slevin, E. and McClelland, A. (1999) Multisensory environments: are they therapeutic? A single-subject evaluation of the clinical effectiveness of a multisensory environment. *Journal of Clinical Nursing.* **8**(1), 48–56.

Terry, P. A. and Hong, C. S. (1998) People with learning disabilities and multi-sensory environments. *British Journal of Therapy and Rehabilitation*, **5**(12), 630–3.

Thompson, S. B. N. and Martin, S. (1994) Making sense of multisensory rooms for people with learning disabilities. *British Journal of Occupational Therapy*, **57**(9).

Thurtle, V. and Wyatt, L. (1999) Multisensory environments and evidence-based practice. Evidence-based practice. *British Journal of Community Nursing*, **4**(9).

University of Bristol (2005) *Information services document pptt00-t2. Planning and presenting with PowerPoint*. Practical workbook. Available from http://www.bris.ac.uk/is/selfhelp/documentation/ppt00-t2/ppt00-t2. Accessed on 1 July 2005.

Vlaskamp, C., Geeter, K. I. D., Huijsmans, L. M. and Smit, I. H. (2003) Passive activities: the effectiveness of multisensory environments on the level of activity of the individuals with profound multiple disabilities. *Journal of Applied Research in Intellectual Disabilities*, **16**, 135–43.

Weller, B. F. (2005) *Baillière's Nurses Dictionary for Nurses and Healthcare Workers*, 24th edn. Elsevier, Edinburgh.

White, J. M. (1999) Effects of relaxing music on cardiac autonomic balance and anxiety after acute myocardial infarction. *American Journal of Critical Care*, **8**(4).

Whittaker, J. (1992) Can anyone help me understand the logic of Snoezelen?, asks Joe Whittaker. *Community Living*. **6**(2), 15.

Wolfensberger, W. (1972) *The Principle of Normalisation in Human Services*. National Institute of Mental Retardation, Toronto.

PART 3

Psychological therapies

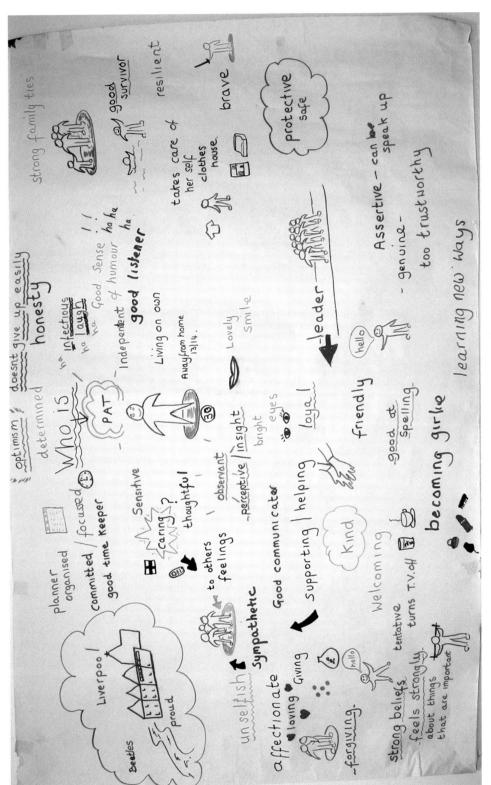

Plate 7.1 Who is Pat?

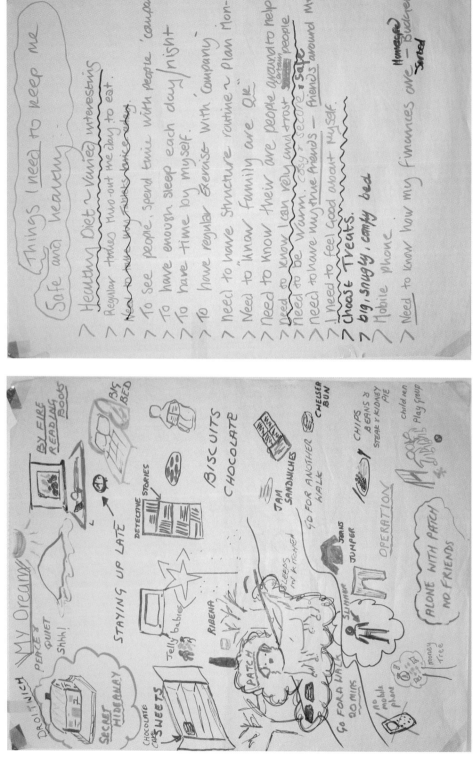

Plate 7.3 Things I need to keep me safe.

Plate 7.2 Pat's dream.

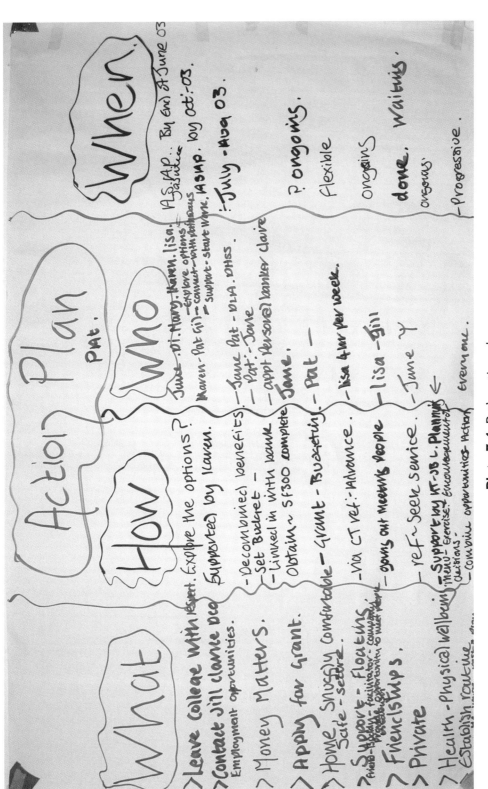

Plate 7.4 Pat's action plan.

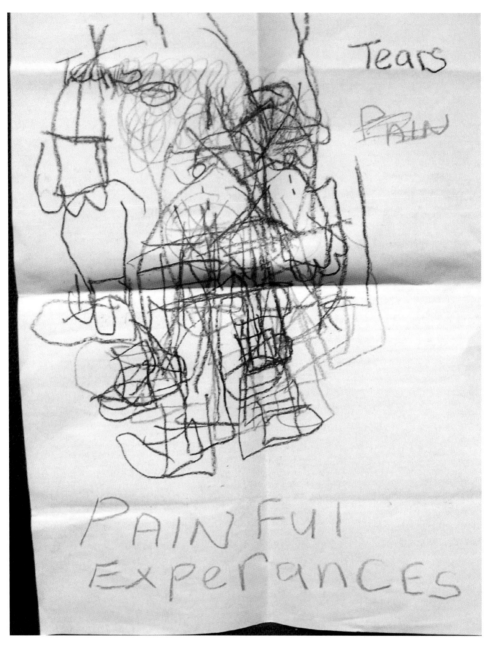

Plate 11.1 Scott's picture.

CHAPTER 7

'Trust the process' – a person-centred life plan unfolds

Jane Bullock and Pat Roberts

Since the advent of *Valuing People* (Department of Health, 2001), the core principles of civil rights, inclusion, independence and choice have been acknowledged, leading to a greater recognition of the rights and dignity of people with a learning disability. Person-centred planning within this piece of social policy reform places the person with learning disabilities at the core. The focus and intention are to empower and thereby enable individuals to participate in community living inclusively, and not make them reliant on what services or resources are available within a given locality.

Person-centred approaches, person-centredness, being person-centred and person-centred planning appear to punctuate every article, report and policy reform. Some service workers and managers may be heard to retort, with regard to person-centred planning, 'Same song, different tune', perhaps making analogies with Individual Programme Planning and other methods of assessment and care approaches. This of course is a fatal mistake, as the value base and ideology behind person-centred planning are lost behind these false assumptions.

This chapter is a joint and largely reflective account between us as co-authors. Jane is a person-centred facilitator, and Pat's person-centred plan is being developed. Its aims are to jointly explore both our experiences of 'person-centred planning'. This will be facilitated by Jane adopting Gibbs (1988) model of reflection, which has purposely been selected because it allows us to describe the process through six reflective stages so as to explore Pat's experiences throughout her plan.

The model further assists us in deepening our awareness and broadening our knowledge, gaining insight into the process and, more importantly, into what intrinsically Pat needs to enable her to take steps toward inclusion and interdependence.

Person-centred planning is an integrated approach using various styles of planning, pictorially as well as with the written word – colours are also important, bringing the plan to life and energising it.

Whilst this chapter recognises the different styles of planning that exist, such as Making Action Plans (Map); Planning Alternative Tomorrows with Hope (Path); and Essential Lifestyle planning, Pat's plan is generally based on a Map style. However, as it has progressed it has taken on a life of its own.

The reflective cycle is adopted to explore boundaries and concerns between us as a developing process. Gerard Egan's (1994) model of Helping is specifically adopted by Jane, underpinning the interpersonal skilled process of person-centred planning from a facilitator's perspective. Here, the model espouses self-determination, and it can be viewed as a catalyst, a process for empowering individuals. The model also assists in embracing and furthering attempts in understanding Pat's interdependency with people within her natural and social environment.

Themes will be identified throughout the chapter, with clear identification between theory and practice.

'Trust the process' will sound familiar to most planners. Person-centred plans are multi-dimensional, focusing on the individual as a whole person, and sit comfortably within such definitions of health as espoused by the World Health Organization (1946): 'A state of complete physical, mental and social wellbeing, not merely the absence of disease'.

Whilst Pat has consented and contributed to this chapter, she has declined for her nightmares to be published.

Background

Pat (Patricia, also known as Patsy) was born in Liverpool on 12 May 1972. She was known to social services neo-natally. Some extracts from her early years reports have been anonymously included.

> *The family background was undesirable and deprived. Patsy witnessed and experienced parental violence. In 1975 she was a subject of a care order.*

Patsy had a total of six foster carers between 1975 and 1978.

> *Concern was expressed over Patsy's emotional health, she gives nothing to a situation and gains no comfort from situations. Patsy gets her only comfort from her sibling and her sibling needs the protective bond with Patsy and so we could never contemplate separating them.*

Patsy was in a culture of care when environments were such that they represented models of institutional containment and rigidity, and if the bell rang and you did not get in line in the playground, the consequences tended to be a very negative experience.

> *Patricia remains a deeply depressed little girl, entirely negative in her functioning and unable to obtain comfort from anyone.*

Generalised statements labelled Pat with little or no mention of therapy, structured play, activities or medication, love, warmth or security.

> *Patsy generally takes no pride in her appearance and is generally negative in her functioning.*

Patsy's behaviour is abominable, Patricia demands constant attention from adults.

Patsy was clearly very angry at the position she had now found herself in, confused and frightened. She also felt very bad about herself.

Patsy remains a very unhappy and disturbed girl. Her speech is immature and she is generally disliked by staff and residents alike.

Pat tells me the highlight of her week was when the dustbin men came to collect the rubbish. They used to bring all the kids presents that other kids had thrown away. 'I loved it'.

Pat and her sibling were successfully fostered and later adopted in 1978. Much can be learnt from these two children and how complex they were. Post adoption reports read:

Patsy has clearly benefited from this family, gaining in self-confidence having a much improved self image, caring about how she looks.

Patsy is able to show warmth and affection and enthusiasm towards others.

Patsy's speech has developed significantly and she is full of enthusiasm for all her school activities.

Her adoptive parents (who will remain anonymous) report:

She has been very rewarding to care for and is much less attention seeking. She enjoys all kinds of family activities.

We must both pause here – Pat's life significantly changed, but she has requested, out of respect for her adoptive parents, that it remain private. She does say, however, that she felt loved by her adoptive parents throughout the good and bad times every family has.

Within psychology the most pervasive view concerning long-term development has been that early experiences predetermine the individual's future. Bowlby (1951), for example, claimed that good mothering was almost useless if delayed beyond two and a half years, in that prolonged deprivation of maternal care might have grave and far-reaching effects on the child's character and subsequently the whole of his or her future life. He believed that the infant–mother bond or infant–mother-substitute bond is different from all other relationships. Changes in this relationship from one to another during the first three or four years, in his theory, result in emotional problems.

Sigmund Freud, in his psychoanalytic theory, according to Hjelle and Ziegler (1981), is based on two premises: the genetic approach, which emphasises that adult personality is shaped by numerous types of childhood experience, and that a certain amount of sexual energy (or libido) is in existence at birth and subsequently follows through a series of psychosexual stages which are rooted in the instinctual processes of the individual organism. According to Freud's theory there are four universal stages of psychosexual development which are decisive for the formation of personality: oral, anal, phallic and genital.

For the purposes of this chapter the oral and anal stages will be discussed briefly for the purpose of providing reference points for Freud's theory of psychosexual development.

The oral stage: birth to 12–18 months

During this first year, infants are naturally dependent upon others for survival. The mouth is the dominant body structure for nourishment and pleasure gratification. Freud's theory asserts that it is at this stage that the infant establishes trust, dependence, independence and reliance in relation to other people.

If problems occur at this stage – for example the mother's absence, delay in gratification or lack of sensitivity – the child's experiences are negative.

In adult life this link between food, love and security can manifest itself through exploitation and domination of others. The person may continually seek approval at the expense of everything else. They may also exhibit pessimism and be argumentative and sarcastic. Eating disorders, alcohol or drug dependency may also coexist, which stem from aggressive impulses associated with this phase.

The anal stage: age 1–3

Freud claimed that all later forms of self-control and mastery have their origin in the anal stage. During the anal stage and the second and third years of life, libidinal energy shifts from the mouth to the anal region.

It is at this stage that toilet training by parents is critical. That, is, if parents are too harsh, children may have a tendency to hold back – in adult life personality traits such as cleanliness, punctuality and stinginess are observed. Conversely, if parents insist on regular bowel movements and consistently overindulge in praise for so doing, an adult fixated at this stage would demonstrate traits of cruelty and spread disorder and hostility.

Such theories as those of Bowlby or Freud can lead to a negative view of where the person is at developmentally, and interfere with possible positive interventions which are creative and promote growth potentials within the person, particularly from professionals who operate from an abnormal pathology perspective.

Extracts from the early reports on Pat mirror this negative focus on adverse behaviour development, and yet do not acknowledge that therapy or positive interventions might assist her.

However, studies which have focused upon adverse family histories (Skeels, 1966) and experiences of adoption and deprivation (Clarke and Clarke, 1976; Rutter *et al.*, 1998) have concluded that children faced with adversity and subsequent successful adoption can and do catch up cognitively, and that mental health also can be restored

Personality development can be viewed more positively in terms of self concept development, which in turn depends on the individual's interaction with other people and the environment (Rogers, 1961).

Carl Rogers (1902–1987), whose name is synonymous with person-centred theory, believed that the individual's innate tendency was to move in the direction of growth, maturity and positive change. It is this, the very essence and magnitude founded in humanistic psychology, that is at the core of person-centred planning.

Pat was a single mother at the age of 25. After being admitted to a mother and baby unit she was discharged to be cared for in an ordinary home, under the umbrella of social services to observe and monitor her parenting skills and her ability to cope with this huge change in her role. For one of the first times in her life she was the one doing the caring and not being cared for. Eventually the baby was fostered and later adopted. This was an extremely difficult and emotionally traumatic time for Pat. Her trust in herself and support services was extremely low – in fact, it was non-existent. Pat to this day still has an aggravated thought process of knowing that having her baby adopted was the right thing to do, but regularly grieves for her loss.

Pat nowadays views herself as labelled as having a learning disability, and she is dependent on services for guidance, especially decision making. She seeks out several people's approval, which at times causes confusion and frequently panics her in sheer frustration, leaving her feeling frustrated and isolated. One of Pat's coping strategies has, in the past, been to cut herself. Pat says this relieves the pain. It was on this basis, together with Pat, that her person-centred plan began incorporating new associations and experiences. Labels and language such as 'empowerment' and 'can do', and the concept of interdependence, were introduced and are still being nurtured, building on Pat's strengths today.

Person-centred planning puts the person at the epicentre of the plan. Friends, family and significant others participate strongly, focusing on what I call 'subjective positivity' incorporating 'total respect'. One of the key principles of person-centred planning is about getting someone a life, not a service (see Appendix 1). 'All means all' upholds 'the values of inclusion' (see Appendix 2) by way of transactions and interactions during the whole process. A humanistic approach emphasises the innate potential that every person is believed to possess. Its roots are firmly akin to Maslow's (1970) theory of human motivation, believing in a hierarchy of needs from the basic biological ones to the more complex psychological motivations. He believed that basic needs, such as physiological needs, the need for safety and a need for belongingness, had to be satisfied in order for the person to view the next level as important. Therefore unfulfilled needs will dominate a person's actions and inhibit their motives.

Pat's experience of services is that of an expert, although her perceptions vary. On one of our first meetings there was an overt sulkiness and Pat proudly told me: 'You lot have interfered with my life always. Some of you I bloody hated and others I liked but got too close to so I played it up. It's different for you, it's your job. Have they told you? Have they told you about me? I will test you, you won't like me then, you will leave'.

Pat was living alone and studying at college. She'd enrolled in a catering course and was in her second year. The course became problematic. Pat was coping by causing chaos, which had an impact on Pat's mental health; all areas of Pat's life were affected. Change needed to happen, so person-centred planning was an obvious way forward. Pat was introduced to my partner, Di Perry, and a 'getting to know you' took place. Pat was at the centre of arranging the plan from the onset. We opened the planning with 'Who is Pat?' (see Plate 7.1).

'Who is Pat?' focuses on drawing out the person's identity and builds positively on that identity. For Pat this experience was totally illuminating. We incorporated 'What are her gifts, strengths and talents?'. By recognising these the concept of 'can do' emerges strongly, along with interdependence.

Pat's nightmares, although done, are not included and she wishes them to remain private. Pat did give permission to disclose 'They are all bad things that happened to me. I don't want them to happen again'.

The dream (Plate 7.2) is a critical point of the planning process. Its purpose is to allow the person to dream, to imagine 'What would my life look like if I had all these important things – objects, people, animals and places around me? What is it that intrinsically motivates me to move forward? How far am I from this?' and obviously 'What do I need to do to get there?', which forms the basis for the action plan. This was a totally euphoric part of the planning process we all enjoyed, with no boundaries, no limits and no restrictions.

To keep Pat healthy and safe we have 'The things I need' (see Plate 7.3). This information is non-negotiable: it's all individualised and very important to the individual to enable, not disable. It should incorporate psychological needs, but if excluded it could have a major impact on individuals. It should reflect allergies, medication or dietary requirements, and equipment. It should also incorporate risks to individuals. It provides consistency to the individual when supported in various areas by different people.

Gathering all this valuable information is both exhausting and rewarding. Themes are identified as the information is analysed. What makes sense and what doesn't are checked back with the person. The action plan (see Plate 7.4) metamorphoses from the information quite uniquely. It was at this point, right at the end, that I understood the saying 'Trust the Process'. 'What', 'How', 'Who' and 'When' are the very simple headings and are by no means new, but it does unite the circle of support in keeping focused and taking ownership and being creative.

The reflective cycle

On reflection of our shared experiences of person-centred planning, Gibbs (1988) model (see Figure 7.1), has been selected due to the models logical sequence in allowing us to describe and draw out experiences, deepening our awareness and ultimately building on our understanding and perception of ourselves and others.

As we progress through this six-stage cycle of reflection Pat's subjective account will introduce our discussion.

Description – What happened?

It was hard going and interesting. I got to choose who came to the meetings and I had them at home in my flat. I arranged my invites and got them typed – posh. I cleaned my flat and got some nice biscuits for everyone. J and Di came and put loads of paper around my walls. I liked the colours Di used and her pictures are funny. I couldn't believe all that was about me. It took a long time.

The planning commenced. Pat was excitably nervous and took pride in preparing for the meetings: her flat was immaculate. From the start, person-centred planning was explained to Pat and she

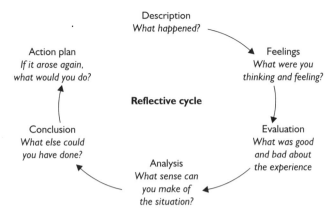

Figure 7.1 The reflective cycle (Gibbs, 1988).

took an active interest, although at times I felt she was overwhelmed. Thankfully this only happened twice. As a planner this was challenging to manage and I found it particularly supportive witnessing the relief on Pat's face as we all progressed.

Egan's (1994) three-stage model of counselling, also known as The Skilled Helper, is essentially humanistic and underpins person-centred planning. The model is also transtheoretical, which means that Egan embraces the foundation of person-centred theory in the formulation and development of establishing an empathic and unconditional relationship. Egan also embraces other theorists' approaches and techniques, such as from cognitive behaviour therapy, transactional analysis and rational emotive therapy. These are melded together to assist the helper and client to move through the three stages so as to move towards their goals and aspirations and is based upon the person's own self-motivation.

Stage 1 – The present scenario

Stage 1 is concerned with reviewing the person's current scenario and uses the skills of listening, paraphrasing and reflecting. Empathic approaches elucidate, summarise and clarify their current scenario. Challenging the person's blind spots on how they view themselves is also a part of this process.

Stage 1 is where we helped Pat focus on more details as she told her story (see Plate 7.1). A picture developed – Pat's nightmares (withheld as explained earlier) did, however, contribute enormously to Stage 2 – Development of a new or preferred scenario. This stage is all about establishing what the future could look like for Pat.

'Who is Pat?' and 'What is her dream?' (see Plate 7.2) enabled the plan to evolve.

Feelings – What were you thinking and feeling?

Mixed up to begin with, scared what people were going to say and if no one bothered to turn up. I was scared how I was going to react when people were horrible, negative about me, I don't like this it makes me feel low. When people are horrible about me it's a mixture it makes me feel I want to do something – hit out, hurt myself. It makes me feel depressed when people are horrible about me.

As the plan went on I felt better. 'Who is Pat?' Made me feel better because I learnt people liked me, liked Pat. Pat is a nice person – it helped me see behind my mask, scary.

My nightmares made me feel unsettled. It made me feel exposed talking about scary things in my past. I liked being in control. I loved that, people had to listen what I had to say. I liked people listening to what I had to say, it was all about me. I liked being treated like an adult, it was exciting. I think people were telling me the truth, it got easier for me as the planning went on, and I felt I am not only a client!

Pat thrived on gaining the locus of control at her meetings. As each planning meeting commenced she became more confident and less embarrassed. Pat became more and more active and told her story. The plan took on a life of its own – individualised, empowering and visually impacting on all who contributed.

Stage 2 – Development of a new scenario

Pat and the planning team were elated. Positive labels and language streamed out, and although Pat found it embarrassing at times I was very proud of the planners – all listening, interacting and thinking how and what words would be supportive to Pat. Pat embraced the genuineness.

Evaluation – What was good and bad about the experience?

Difficult. Difficult bit were my nightmares cause they scare me. My past when I was young was horrible. I don't like cruel. People can be cruel. I found it good 'cause I could take it at my own pace, slowly. J and Di explained when I got mixed up. I liked what people thought of me. It made me feel stronger. I like now to be treated as an adult. It was bad talking about me if you know what I mean, but it was good, I am an OK person. Every session got better. I looked forward to them, they were hard work.

The concept of interdependence was being introduced: 'no man is an island'. Interdependence was our starting point and has been nurtured and positively fostered throughout the planning process, together with 'can do'. The planners positively contributed well and it felt like they enthused each other. The facilitators managed the planning meeting but also provided a positive, interactive role model; everyone contributed to the process genuinely. Pat felt this too, which in turn increased her self awareness. Stages 1 and 2 of Egan's model sit comfortably within this.

Analysis – What sense can you make of the situation?

I learnt who Pat is and where she has come from. People accept me for who I am. Even my nightmares made sense in a way. The past couldn't hurt me. I realised I needed some questions answered. I also realised that maybe nobody could answer them. Who is Pat? Was the best 'cause I learnt about me and how people see me. I am an OK person after all. I feel stronger now I understand some of me. I know I have a disability and I know I can cause chaos, I am an OK person, I can deal with things more, without doing things like hurting myself. I have learnt a lot. I have learnt that it was not Pat's fault.

I enjoyed making new friends as a result of my plan. I now go on my own to my bank to see my personal banker instead of nagging J. I am working voluntarily in a shop now. I am having the right help with my nightmares. Ken Timms is my Clinical Psychologist and I am getting to know, trust him. He helps me help myself, he listens and helps me understand. He helps me deal with my past, it can't hurt me any more and it's OK for me to be angry about it. The greatest thing was to come out of my plan and for me to realise is we all need something/one to love. I now have Cinders, my rabbit. She is perfect, I love her and she loves me.

Stage 2 – Development of a new scenario – contextually within person-centred planning was a 'natural process'. The 'Who is Pat?', the dream practically supported, what Pat needed to thrive and intrinsically move forward, all identified Pat's need to belong and how she needed to fulfil this caring, loving, giving part of Pat to enable that feel-good factor (hence Cinders) on a daily basis. Longer term it also identified some unanswered questions that were not for the planning team but for Pat and Ken Timms to work together on. 'Things I need to keep me safe' (see Plate 7.3) provided the boundaries for this to be planned within and uniquely for Pat. It also highlights not only her individualism, but again the concept of interdependence.

Conclusion – What else could you have done?

Nothing. We did enough. All of us.

The plan metamorphosed into a life of its own. Total respect was upheld all of the way through. Pat was the chairperson all the way through. The action plan (Stage 3 of Egan's model) involves commitment and consideration of how to achieve the preferred scenario by those involved with Pat (see Plate 7.4) and were prioritised due to the Plan's complexities.

In conclusion, but by no means the end, Pat is now in her early thirties and lives alone in her one-bedroom flat. Pat receives four hours support worker time per week, which enables her more psychologically than practically. Pat has two voluntary jobs – Snax on Trax (local project in conjunction with the SEC providing a snack kiosk at the train station) and a charity shop – Salvation Army. Pat enjoys these work opportunities, meeting lots of people but also having a valued role within a team of people.

Pat's circle of friends has increased. As well as her longstanding friends, who she meets up with regularly, she also regularly visits her personal banker.

Pat remains quite reliant on services, seeking reassurance and, at times, approval, especially where she finds decisions are difficult to make.

Pat views her life as having collected many labels over the years and will laugh at them generally, although at other times she withdraws, feeling low and isolated. Pat's a very warm and wonderful person – she is truly a survivor. Person-centred planning – its techniques, its concepts – building on her 'positive subjectivity', has endorsed the interdependence and 'can do's in Pat's everyday life.

Egan, I feel, underpins person-centred planning throughout, illuminating people's responses and empowering and therefore enabling Pat to take that step forward. Cinders is so therapeutic – the sharing and caring is truly incredible. Cinders is the most spoilt rabbit in Worcestershire.

The last word however must go to Pat:

> I will have another plan one day, but not now, my plan has done a lot for me. I love Cinders, she is so good, we understand each other. Ken Timms is helping me to understand me. 'I am an OK person'.

Appendix 1: Key principles of person-centred planning

We are spending time thinking about how we can plan for the present and the future in a more person-centred way with people, where they are seen as having rights and control over the services they receive and the lives they lead. We are also looking at different ways of providing support for individuals we know in a person-centred way.

All person-centred planning processes share a number of key characteristics:

- The locus for the plan is the real world, not service land – person-centred planning is about getting someone a life, not getting them a service.
- The focus is on the person and their whole life – the planning meeting is not to discuss the difficulties the service or the professionals may be experiencing or the constraints they are working within.
- The control is with the focus person and their advocates, and the person and the people who love and care for the person are the primary authority.
- The professionals are there to provide specialist advice, knowledge and support – but it is not their meeting.
- Universal needs are as important as medical needs.
- The focus is on individual gifts and aspirations, not individual needs and deficiencies.
- There is a future orientation.
- There is a commitment to address conflict openly and honestly.
- There is a commitment to reach a consensus for action.
- There is a willingness to come up with non-traditional, sustainable solutions.

- When person-centred planning works it builds a desirable future for the person and engages the energy, commitment and ingenuity of others to make that future happen.
(New Possibilities, 2002)

Appendix 2: The values of inclusion

- *Everyone is born in*
We are all born as equal citizens and part of a community; we are only excluded later.
- *All means all*
Everyone capable of breathing, even if breathing requires support, is entitled to be included – no-one is too difficult, too old, too poor or too disabled to qualify.
- *Everyone needs to be in*
If people are physically excluded, they have to be physically included. Judith Snow talks about presence being the first criterion for inclusion – if you're not there, no-one will know you're missing.
- *Everyone needs to be with*
Being there is necessary – but being with takes time and effort. A community is not just a locality – it is a network of connections and relationships. We have to help people be part of and belong to communities, not just be lonely residents within them or day visitors to them.
- *Everyone is ready*
No-one has to pass a test of meet a set of criteria to be eligible – everyone is ready to be part of community now and it is community's task to find ways of including them.
- *Everyone needs support – and some need more support than others*
No-one is fully independent and independence isn't our goal. We are working towards inter-dependence and differing degrees and kinds of support at different times.
- *Everyone can communicate*
Just because someone can't or won't use words to communicate doesn't mean that they don't have anything to say – everyone can communicate and we have to work harder at hearing, seeing, under-standing and feeling wheat people are communicating to use and communicating back.
- *Everyone can contribute*
Each person has their own gifts and strengths – and each person has a unique contribution to make. Our task is to recognise, encourage and value each person's contribution – including their own!
- *Together we are better*
We do not believe the world would be a better place if everyone were the same. We are not dreaming of a world when all differences are eradicated and all disabilities are cured – we believe that diversity does bring strength and that we can all learn and grow by knowing one another.
(New Possibilities, 2002)

References

Bowlby, J. (1951) Maternal *Care and Mental Health*. World Health Organization, Geneva.

Clarke, A. M. and Clarke A. D. B. (eds.) (1976) *Early Experience: Myth and Evidence*. Open Books, London.

Department of Health (2001) *Valuing People. A New Strategy for Learning Disability for the 21st Century*. HMSO, London.

Egan, G. (1994) *The Skilled Helper*, 4th edn. Brooks/Cole, California.

Gibbs, G. (1988) *Learning by Doing: A Guide to Teaching and Learning Methods*. Further Education Unit, Oxford Polytechnic.

Hjelle, L. A. and Ziegler, D. J. (1981) *Personality Theories. Basic Assumptions, Research and Applications*, 2nd edn. McGraw-Hill, Singapore.

Maslow, A. (1970) *Motivation and Personality*, 2nd edn. Harper & Row, New York.

New Possibilities (2002) Training and Consultancy, 86 Drayton Road, Kings Heath, Birmingham B14 7LR.

Rogers, C. R. (1961) *On Becoming a Person: A Therapist's View of Psychotherapy*. Houghton Mifflin, Boston.

Rutter, M. and The English and Romanian Adoptees (ERA) Study Team (1998) Developmental catch-up and deficit, following adoption after severe global early privation. *Journal of Child Psychology and Psychiatry*, **39**, 465–76.

Skeels, H. (1966) Adult status of children with contrasting early life experiences. *Monographs of the Society for Research on Child Development*, **31**(105).

World Health Organization (1946) *Preamble of the Constitution of the World Health Organization*. World Health Organization, Geneva.

CHAPTER 8

Uncovering identities: the role of life story work in person-centred planning

Helen Hewitt

In order to engage in any meaningful care planning activity or other intervention it is essential to understand as much as possible about who the person is. In other words, we need information about the person's identity before we can help them construct an appropriate schedule of care. A sense of our identities helps us to achieve self acceptance and form relationships. So often in the past this kind of information has been absent in the care setting, especially for those people who cannot verbalise about their life experiences. It is the aim of this chapter to highlight the importance of understanding identities as a starting point for meaningful interventions regarding person-centred planning. Life story books will be introduced as a resource for enhancing, maintaining and celebrating the person's identity, from which point good-quality person-centred planning can proceed.

Identities and people with learning disabilities

Previously, within the field of learning disabilities, identities have been studied from an orthodox psychological perspective. For example, in the 1950s and 1960s theories on personality were taken directly from traditional trait theory approaches (Eysenck, 1953; Cattell, 1959). These, in their original radical form, assume that we have a fixed personality from birth, and that outside influences and environment have no influence on who we are. Personality tests and scales were used to categorise people into different personality types. Of course, these approaches were very limited, not only in their view of human beings not being able to change and develop their personality, but also in the types of tests used, which required a certain degree of verbal competence. This meant that many people would only have partially completed scales, which were of limited use.

In the 1960s two key texts were published which took a very different perspective of and approach to examining identity amongst people with learning disabilities. Both used ethnography (the study of a people) to gain insight into what life was like for people who were labelled as having a learning disability. The first was Goffman's (1963) essay on stigma, which was sub-titled 'a study of spoilt identities'. The second was Edgerton's (1967) 'Cloak of Competence'. Both of these books provide detailed descriptions of life in long-stay institutions, away from the rest of society, and the effect of this on the person's sense of self.

Following the introduction and implementation of normalisation as a new philosophy of care (Wolfensberger, 1972, 1983; O'Brien and Tyne, 1981) the advocacy movement began to flourish in the 1980s. During this time consciousness-raising was used as a way to help people with a learning disability to accept and be proud of their identity, and to locate the 'handicap' in society rather than within their heads (Szivos and Griffiths, 1990a,b). These self-help groups were very positive but, again required a certain level of verbal competence for the person to benefit from the group interaction.

More contemporary approaches to studying identity within the learning disability field have embraced the social constructionist perspective, where constructs such as identity are seen as social phenomena and are constructed through interaction with others (Clegg, 1993; Hewitt, 1997; Walmsley, 2001). This approach has encouraged the examination of biographical accounts of peoples' lives as a way of increasing our understanding of their identity (Atkinson *et al.*, 2000). There has been a proliferation of published testimonies of people with a learning disability telling their story. These help us to understand more about the individual, but also act as part of our oral history. However, as with previous approaches, it tends to be the more verbally competent people who are able to tell their stories and have them published.

Identities in the care setting

If we accept that an understanding of identity is essential for any meaningful interaction and intervention within the care setting, this has to be the starting point for any schedule of care. Not only do we need to know who the person is, we need to help them to understand who they are too. We tend to gain a sense of self through all the interactions and experiences we engage in throughout our lives, and are able to use social comparisons to gauge where we stand in the social order of things. However, this is a skill or ability that many people with a learning disability will be lacking. Helping them to tell their stories and document their experiences is one way of helping them to achieve this sense of self.

So let's consider how identities are addressed in the care setting. In order to do this we must start with the main forms of information and documentation about the clients in the places they live. This is normally a care plan. For this reflective exercise we need to think about traditional care plans prior to the introduction of more person-centred approaches. These are likely to be based on a Roper and Tierney model of care plan, where 12 activities of daily living are used to provide a 'holistic' profile of the person's care needs. During the 1990s these schedules of care were extremely popular and comprehensive. However, one of the ironies of this 'holistic' approach is that by dividing a person's life up into discrete sections, you achieve fragmentation rather then integration of the different elements of their life. In terms of identity it is extremely hard to get a picture of who the person is from reading one of these care plans.

One of the reasons that traditional care plans fail to address some of the main elements of the person's identity is related to their function. They are schedules of care and as such are future-orientated, set in the here-and-now with old action plans and information filtered out to keep them up to date. This means that information about a person's history, which is vital to their identity and how they came to be the person they are today, is absent. Life story books can be used to redress this imbalance.

Life story books

A life story book is a biographical account of a person's life including 'stories' of their experiences, relationships and significant events that have happened throughout their lives. It is important to state that there is no one 'right' way to produce a life story book. Each life story is unique and this should be reflected in the style of the life story presentation chosen. Wherever possible the person themselves should make the decisions regarding style and content. They are never complete and should be treated as an evolving tool, which should be added to at any time.

Different formats

Posters

These are probably the easiest to compile. You can help the person to select and stick photographs and other artefacts onto a piece of card and you have an instant life story, which does not have to be exhaustive, and can be added to or changed at any time. In fact, a poster is an ideal way to start a life story book, as it can act as a story board that can be fleshed out on the pages of a book.

Video diaries

Most of us have some video footage in our homes of family events and the changing development of our children as they grew. These videos can be edited and copied onto DVDs and form a video diary of the person's life. This is particularly appropriate for people who can operate a video recorder, as they can record all the people, places and events that are important to them. It is always advisable to have a backup of these recordings, as this medium can be very fallible.

Computerised versions

Again, if the person has an interest in computers and uses them as part of their daily lives then a computerised life story will be appropriate for them. There are many different ways in which a computer can be used, from typing up stories and adding graphics to creating a fully interactive program. Some people have even produced their own web sites to present their life stories. As with video recordings, computer-generated material is very fallible so backup copies are essential.

Memory boxes

Memory boxes are a sensory-enhanced format for presenting a person's life story. Objects of value and significance to the person can be kept in the box and provide a record of places visited, important relationships and events in their lives. Memory boxes are very tactile, which makes them particularly appropriate for people with sensory impairments, who rely on other senses rather than sight.

Bag books

Bag books are sensory enhanced 'books' developed for people with profound multiple and sensory impairments (Fuller, 2000; Lambe and Watson, 2002). They are built up on large pieces of card with objects of reference pertaining to the story that are recognisable to the person. Each piece of card may only have one item on it, but collectively the cards will relay a story that will be told and retold to the person several times at regular intervals. Over time it is possible to observe anticipation as the person comes to recognise the order of the story.

Bag books can convey any story, from simple daily events, such as going to the shops, to more personal stories. A life story could be developed by putting something personal on each piece of card. For example, if the person likes going swimming then a piece of their towel with the smell of chlorine could be used to symbolise this activity. An enlarged photograph of a family member could be stuck on a piece of card and objects from the family home. Likewise, objects from holidays could be used to symbolise places visited. For example, sand and shells can be very evocative of memories of beaches. This would be enhanced further if the smell of the sea could be captured in the shells.

The value of life story books

It has already been established that life story books are important for understanding a person's identity. There are, however, many more benefits and uses of life story books that make them a valuable resource in the care setting.

Hewitt (1997) explored the use of life story books for a group of people with profound learning disabilities moving from a long-stay hospital to a community home. During transitions such as these there is a risk that the stories and experiences a person has had, particularly regarding their relationships, could get lost. This is especially true if staff who have known the person for a number of years do not move with them. Life story books were found to be a useful tool for getting to know the person, defining the person in wider terms than 'client' in the here-and-now, and displaying personality. They also provide continuity across transitions in care to maintain this identity information. The books encouraged people to see the person as an individual with a unique life history (Hewitt, 1998, 2000). This moves beyond the parameters of a nursing care plan, where the information about the person is purely of a clinical nature. Life story books can act as a communication aid to assist in the initiation of therapeutic relationships.

In addition to being a tool for communication within therapeutic relationships, life story books are an aid to more general communication. This element particularly benefits people with limited verbal communication, such as people with more severe or profound learning disabilities, and older people as a tool for reminiscence. The books provide the person with a resource they can use to describe their lives. This encourages meaningful interaction by sharing personal experiences and gives other people topics of conversation and avenues to explore in order to deepen their understanding of the person. This is a two-way process, as the books also encourage shared understanding. For example, if a member of staff reads a story in a person's book about a family holiday it may be that they also have been to that place. This can then be shared and to highlight the aspects of the person that make them 'like me' rather than 'not like me'. This is a significant departure from other documentation in the care setting that highlights the differences between the 'client' and other people. Finding some common ground is fundamental to the formation of meaningful relationships, and life story books can assist in this process.

Life story books also encourage people to make sense of events that have happened in the context of their life history (Bogdan and Taylor, 1994). This is particularly useful for people with complex needs, who may have many issues they need to come to terms with. This includes traumatic events in their lives, such as abusive relationships. However, due to the sensitivity of such information care needs to be taken to ensure the person has adequate support to address any issues that are brought to light.

Regardless of the type of disability, life story books give all people a sense of self and identity that may otherwise be lacking in their day-to-day lives.

Life story books and person-centred plans

The most important feature of life story books is that the person remains at the centre of the process. This is very pertinent in the light of the White Paper *Valuing People* (Department of Health, 2001), as person-centred plans are the way forward in terms of care planning for each individual. The books can act as a tool for breaking down barriers between service provider and user by creating a better understanding of who the person is, and what they want, which is the foundation of good person-centred planning.

If a person has a life story book it provides a starting point for person-centred planning because they have already compiled a book about the things that are important to them. The life story process encourages the person to view themselves as the most important person to inform others about their life. It may be the first time that they have been treated as an expert on anything, and the acknowledgement of this expertise is what drives the person-centred planning process.

There is a danger that practitioners may incorporate life story books in person-centred plans in a prescriptive fashion. This would totally defeat the object, as life story books are unique and ideally should be compiled separately, at a time that suits the individual, rather than produced *en masse* when everyone else in the setting has their person-centred plan compiled. Of course, the information contained in the books can be duplicated in the PCP, but life story books should inform the process, rather than being completely integrated into it. This would alter their primary function from being a unique and independent identity-rich resource to merely being part of the person's care plan. Life story books and person-centred plans work perfectly together because they complement each other.

Case studies

Below are examples of how life story books were introduced and compiled for two very different people. These are fictitious cases, but they are based on real people. Following this section is advice for getting started on a life story project and how it can fit into the PCP process.

Bob

Bob is 51 and has lived in his own flat for the past seven years. Prior to this he lived in a large long-stay hospital for most of his life, as well as a couple of small group homes. He has an older brother who is married with grown-up children. They have limited contact two or three times a year, as they live over a hundred miles apart.

Bob loves drawing and painting and has always had jobs involving this skill. Even at the hospital he used to help with maintenance, mainly painting and decorating. He has also worked in craft-based workshops, producing goods for retail. Currently he works part-time in a cooperative scheme that makes furniture and gifts.

Bob has a good circle of friends who he sees most Friday nights in the local pub. He also knows a couple of his neighbours quite well. There are many friends from his past that he has lost contact with.

Bob's life story book

On the days that Bob does not work he attends a local college. It was one of the tutors here who suggested the idea that Bob compile a life story book. It was inspired by the fact that Bob is always talking about his past. Staff felt it would be an interesting project for him.

Bob discussed his ideas with one of the college staff. He wanted to contact some of the friends he had lived with in the hospital. There were also two members of staff, in particular, that he was very close to there. He was due to see his brother, so he compiled a set of questions to ask him.

He sorted through a box of old photographs he wanted to include in his book and gathered some artefacts that were very special to him.

Initially Bob was helped to write his own memories and map the events and relationships throughout his life. He used all the photos and memorabilia he had collected. Once he had done this he started to contact the other people for their stories and recollections. The whole process, to get the book up and running, took Bob two months. He spent more time decorating and adding to the book once he had collected information and written the main body of it.

Bob enjoyed reading his book over and over, and showed it to all his friends. He also went through it with his brother who was really moved by it. In fact, contact between them increased following the compilation of the book.

Jane

Jane is 37 and has severe physical and intellectual disabilities with sensory impairment. She is registered blind but has some peripheral vision, as she picks objects up and holds them close to the side of her eyes. She also relies heavily on her sense of touch and smell. She has lived in a staffed group home with four other people for the past five years. Prior to this she lived at home with her parents until they became too infirm to meet all her care needs. This was an extremely unsettling time for all the family, but there is regular contact between Jane and her family, with visits home and her parents coming to see her every week.

Jane attends a day centre two days a week but spends most of her time in the house doing activities. She enjoys aromatherapy sessions, massage and having long soaks in the bath. She also likes going on holiday, particularly where there are beaches.

Jane's life story box

The staff in the house had heard about life story books and had been on a training course. They learnt that life stories do not have to be recorded in a book, and realised there are many options for presenting this kind of information. They decided that a life story box would be appropriate for Jane, with her reliance on touch and smell.

The box was chosen by Jane by presenting different types for her to handle. She selected a very tactile box with wooden carvings, which also had an aroma of pine. Once the box had been selected the staff gathered many artefacts that they felt were important to Jane and presented them to her. Jane's parents were involved from the start and brought things from their home that had significance to Jane's relationships and to the time she lived at home.

Jane was noticeably excited and animated when handling the objects, and all the time her parents were talking about each item and recalling their own memories. Staff members learnt a lot about Jane from these sessions and continued to help her collect more mementos, and made sure the box was near to Jane for her to be able to access it whenever she wanted.

Items gathered included shells from beach holidays, enlarged photos of family members, a string of beads she has had since she was a child, some jewellery, and a pillowcase from her bedroom at home. She also kept scented candles in the box, and staff would light these for her when she was handling all the objects. This meant that Jane had a cue to her life story activity which also had the effect of enhancing the experience.

Some advice for getting started

As previously mentioned, and as the examples have highlighted, there is no one way to produce a life story book. In fact, each person's life story book should be approached with a fresh view, to emphasise the uniqueness of that person. This section provides some very general advice on how to compile a scrapbook type of life story book. It is not intended to be a recipe that is reproduced exactly. Rather, appropriate elements should be extracted and used according to individual circumstances and preferences.

There are three distinct phases of the life story process: information gathering, interpreting the information and presenting it in a book. Each phase will be considered in turn, followed by some useful tips for encouraging participation.

Gathering information

- In this phase it is essential that any interviews are recorded, so that no details are missed and full attention can be given to each respondent.
- It is a good idea to ask the person to bring any photographs or significant artefacts with them. This will help to organise their stories.
- Include as many people as possible to give a fuller account. A diverse range of people can provide added interest. For example, cleaners and neighbours who have known the person for a long time can contribute.
- Don't try to gauge the accuracy of the stories. Avoid altering the content of people's accounts.
- Devise a brief schedule to help organise the interviews, but be prepared for digression. A schedule could include the following items:
- Birth story
- The person as a baby and young child
- Early memories and experiences
- Favourite things
- Relationships with family and friends
- Places the person has lived
- Happy memories
- Significant life events
- Family members' memories and feelings

Interpreting the information

The level of interpretation required will depend on the individual. If they are able to write their own book, then they can decide what to include and how to organise it. However, most people with learning disabilities will require some assistance, especially with this phase. In some cases the learning disability practitioner may have to interpret all the information. This is an important role, as the practitioner will be responsible for how the person is represented in their life story book.

Below are some general points for interpreting the information gathered from the life story interviews.

- Try to organise the interview data into themes.
- Organise the stories in a rough chronological order.
- Report any interpretations back to the original source for verification. This may be the person themselves or their relatives and carers.

Presenting the information

As outlined earlier, there is no one right way to present a life story book. They can be as simple as a collage poster on someone's wall, a series of video diaries or audio cassettes, or a fully computerised version that allows the person to be interactive. However, the most common way to present life story information is in a scrapbook type of format. Below are a few tips for helping a person to present the information in their life story book.

- A loose leafed folder is preferable, as additions can be made at any stage.
- Mount photographs on coloured card and always write a caption and date by any photos. It is easy to forget who people are and when events took place.
- Hand write the books are far as possible, as they are more likely to be added to. Typed or computer-generated books can appear too complete, and be off putting to add to.
- Encourage people to add to their books.

Encouraging participation

There are two types of participant: the people themselves and other informants (third parties such as relatives or carers). In either case it is essential to:

- Foster a trusting relationship.
- Let the person stay in control as much as possible.
- Be clear and open about what you are doing.
- Gather artefacts that are important to the person.
- Conduct any discussions in a place where the person feels safe.

- Respect the person's decision to stop the process at any stage.
- Where the person cannot give their own account, always read the stories of others to them and gauge their reaction. You can take photos while reading the book and add the photos at the relevant points.

The three key words here are trust, respect and clarity.

Using life story information in person-centred plans

It has already been suggested that life story books provide information that highlights a person's identity, and that an understanding of this is essential for good person-centred planning. We need to uncover the person's identity before we can engage in any meaningful therapeutic intervention. Life story books should not merely be reproduced in the PCP, but the information should be used to inform the process. The books should always stand alone in addition to having a presence within the plans. The most important element of the life story book is that the person remains at the centre of the process, and their uniqueness is highlighted. This is the fundamental goal and basis of person-centred planning, which is why life story information is an essential part of the process.

References

Atkinson, D. (1997) *An Autobiographical Approach to Learning Disability Research*. Open University Press, Milton Keynes.

Atkinson, D., McCarthy, M., Walmsley, J., Cooper, M., Rolph, S., Aspis, S., Barette, P., Coventry, M. and Ferris, G. (eds.) (2000) *Good Times, Bad Times: Women with Learning Difficulties Telling their Stories*. BILD, Kidderminster.

Bogdan, R. and Taylor, S. (1987) Toward a sociology of acceptance: The other side of the study of deviance. *Social Policy*, **18**, 34–9.

Bogdan, R. and Taylor, S. J. (1982) *Inside Out: Two First-Person Accounts of What it Means to be Labelled 'Mentally Retarded'*. University of Toronto Press, Toronto.

Bogdan, R. and Taylor, S. J. (1989) Relationships with severely disabled people: the social construction of humanness. *Social Problems*, **36**, 135–48.

Bogdan, R. and Taylor, S. J. (1994) *The Social Meaning of Mental Retardation – Two Life Stories*. Teachers College Press, New York.

Cattell, R. B. (1966) *The Scientific Analysis of Personality*. Chicago: Aldine.

Clegg, J. A. (1993) Putting people first: a social constructionist approach to learning disability. *British Journal of Clinical Psychology*, **32**, 389–406.

Department of Health (2001) *Valuing People: A New Strategy for Learning Disability for the 21st Century*. HMSO, London.

Edgerton, R. B. (1967) *The Cloak of Competence*. University of California Press, Berkeley.

Eysenck, H. J. (1953) *The Structure of Human Personality*. Wiley, New York.

Goffman, E. (1963) *Stigma*. Prentice Hall, Englewood Cliffs, NJ.

Hewitt, H. (1997) *Identities in Transition: Formulating Care for People with Profound Learning Disabilities*. Unpublished Ph.D. Thesis, Loughborough University.

Hewitt, H. (1998) Life story books for people with learning disabilities. *Nursing Times*, **94**(33), 61–3.

Hewitt, H. (2000) A life story approach for people with profound learning disabilities. *British Journal of Nursing*, **9**(2), 90–5.

Linde, C. (1993) *Life Stories: The Creation of Coherence*. Oxford University Press, Oxford.

O'Brien, J. and Tyne, A. (1981) *The Principle of Normalisation: A Foundation for Effective Services*. The Campaign for Mentally Handicapped People, London.

Pietrukowicz, M. E. and Johnson, M. M. S. (1991) Using life histories to individualize nursing home staff attitudes toward residents. *The Gerontologist*, **31**, 102–6.

Ryan, T. and Walker, R. (1985) *Making Life Story Books*. B. A. A. F., London.

Ryan, T. and Walker, R. (eds.) (1993) *Life Story Work*. B. A. A. F., London.

Szivos, S. E. and Griffiths, E. (1990a) Group processes involved in coming to terms with a mentally retarded identity. *Mental Retardation*, **28**, 333–41.

Szivos, S. E. and Griffiths, E. (1990b) Consciousness raising and social identity theory: a challenge to normalisation. *Clinical Psychology Forum*, **28**, 11–15.

Walmsley, J. (2001) Normalisation, emancipatory research and inclusive research in learning disability. *Disability and Society*, **16**(2), 187–205.

Wolfensberger, W. (1972) *The Principles of Normalization in Human Services*. National Institute of Mental Retardation, Toronto.

Wolfensberger, W. (1983) Social role valorisation: a proposed new name for normalization. *Mental Retardation*, **21**, 234–9.

CHAPTER 9

Solution-focused practice

Pam Morley

Solution-focused therapy (SFT) emerged as a therapeutic approach in the 1980s and since then has gained advocates in many countries across the world. More recently it has become usual to refer to solution-focused practice (SFP), to acknowledge the way in which it has moved from the therapeutic arena into many other areas of interpersonal interaction. These include education, management, life coaching and conflict resolution. Solution-focused therapy is also part of the Brief Therapy movement alongside Possibility Therapy, Narrative Therapy and Solution Orientated Therapy. Most of these approaches share some characteristics and overlap to a certain extent – especially as regards techniques and skills.

SFP comes from a social contructionism standpoint, which is a postmodern movement that challenges the positivist and empiricist stance of the traditional 'hard' sciences; i.e. the notion that one can be a neutral, objective observer of the world around one, and that what the person observes is what actually exists. Instead, social constructionism offers the view that there is no one actual 'reality', which exists 'out there', but rather that reality is a concept developed by each individual as a result of his or her social interactions and life experiences. Thus each person constructs their own mental map of the world as they understand it, and each person's view of reality is unique – just as each individual is unique. Reality is not seen as a single static entity, but rather a dynamic phenomenon that changes from moment to moment, and each of us is in a constant state of change. In fact, Selekman (1993) highlights a belief originally rooted in Buddhist philosophy that change is inevitable and stability is merely an illusion. In a similar vein, SFP uses the idea that we live in a multiverse, rather than a universe, where there are many 'realities' that are created by the inhabitants of the multiverse.

Anderson (1997) highlights the idea that social constructionism emphasises the important role that language has in not only the construction of ideas, notions and concepts, but also in the way that problems and solutions are developed and understood. People make sense of the world around them, and the events that occur in their reality, by the use of language. An example of this occurs frequently in student nurse education when students are asked:

If you qualify, what area would you like to work in?

Now consider a similar question:

When you qualify, what area would you like to work in?

Changing the 'If' to 'When' alters the tone of the question in a powerful way, sending clear signals about the questioner's expectations of the student. This emphasis on language has been a powerful factor in the development of many of the brief therapy approaches, and certainly in SFP the practitioner is urged to be mindful of the power of the language that is used.

There is insufficient space here to venture further into the realm of social constructionism, so readers are strongly urged to consult Burr (1995) for an excellent explanation of the philosophy, and McNamee and Gergen (1992) for an enlightening discussion on the influence of social constructionism in the therapeutic field.

SFP was founded by the Brief Family Therapy Team in Milwaukee, Wisconsin, when the team noticed that some clients made progress more quickly than was expected (de Shazer, 1988). Further analysis revealed that these clients had engaged in discussion that centred on their preferred future, and how they could initiate change in their lives, rather than exploring their past and their problems. Clients were then able to collaborate with the therapist to construct solutions that were strongly linked to their preferred futures, and as the focus on the solution grew, so their attention to the problem lessened. Often clients came to see the problem in an entirely different way. This is what O'Hanlon and Beadle (1994) call 'changing the viewing'.

The team then refined the approach and developed a number of standardised interventions that could be useful for most clients. These are what de Shazer (1985) called 'skeleton keys'. This refers to the belief in SFP that it is not necessary to understand how a lock works to open it, and one does not have to have the exact key – a skeleton key is sufficient to turn the tumblers. These interventions include exception-seeking, the miracle question, scaling, helping the client to construct clear goals, giving compliments and searching for the client's strengths and resources. The team also generated a number of principles to serve as a framework to guide practitioners who wished to adopt their ideas. These principles have been listed by O'Connell (2001) as:

- Keep therapy simple as possible
- Do something different
- If it doesn't work , stop doing it
- If it works, keep doing it
- If it isn't broken, don't fix it

These principles can be successfully integrated into the framework of person-centred planning as proposed in the *Valuing People* strategy (Department of Health, 2001) as they focus on the wishes of the client. SFP is very much a model for change and so can enhance the drive to provide choice for the service user, and can empower them to make choices in a supportive atmosphere. Indeed, SFP is highly compatible with the drives to place service users at the heart of service development in both the mental health and learning disability fields, as it hinges very much on the client's agenda rather than serving the agenda of the practitioner or organisation. Also, basing one's practice on an approach that has such a clear foundation of principles, together with recognised techniques that have been subject to rigorous research, is in concordance with professional requirements to use evidence-based practice and to be able to give a full rationale for one's actions.

Keep therapy as simple as possible is a maxim that encourages practitioners to work in an efficient and uncomplicated manner. Some of the more traditional therapies offer complex theories regarding the development and maintenance of problems. However, SFP practitioners are pragmatic in their approach. This means that SFP is especially relevant to people with learning disabilities if it is modified. Fletcher (1993) recommends keeping vocabulary uncomplicated, using concrete examples and using pictures to aid understanding.

A common experience for people is that of the loss of someone or something of importance. Whilst there are many different theories of loss that explain the effects for an individual, it is crucial that the worker focuses on how the client is feeling, and how he or she is making sense of what has happened. This will guard against the possibility of the individual being viewed only in terms of the theory, and possibly being 'shoe-horned' into a category that then directs how the practitioner then responds to that person.

This principle also encourages practitioners to take a non-expert position, so no instant answers are offered. Likewise the client will not be 'told' what is wrong with them according to the practitioner's theory, or prescribed some sort of task or activity. Steve de Shazer has often said, 'we have a theory about having no theory', which suggests that anyone who lacks skill or any sort of training could claim to be solution-focused. Perhaps it is more useful to claim that we have a theory about how we can be helpful to clients as they travel from where they are now to where they want to be. Along with these ideas goes the concept that clients are not damaged, weak or disabled, but rather that they have strengths, resources and abilities that can be brought forward and built upon. Maybe all of us are disabled in some way – physically, psychologically, socially or spiritually – but we all have strengths, talents and capabilities to draw on.

The *Do something different* principle guides practitioners to be alert to identifying unhelpful patterns that the client engages in. This often includes repeated attempts at previously failed solutions. The key word here is 'Do', as simply discussing a change may not always be productive, but altering one's behaviour – even in a small way – can be like dropping a stone into a pool. The ripples may start off being small, but then expand and grow. This principle is also useful for practitioners to monitor their performance, and if the therapy does not seem to be helping the client... *do something different*! For example, Stoddart *et al*. (2001) recommend shorter sessions and the involvement of people who are close to the client in therapy. Fiddell (2000) gives an example of doing something different when she suggests that therapists should ask the service user to tell the therapist when they have had enough and want to finish the session. This not only empowers the service user, but is a much more collaborative way of working that may be very different from the previous approaches that the person has encountered.

If it doesn't work, stop doing it again looks at change – changing unhelpful behaviour in particular. For example, one mother said that she despaired of ever getting her son to school on time. He was always slow to get ready, even though his mother tried to hurry him by screaming and shouting. The question 'What could you do instead of shouting at him?' was asked. This had the effect of creating some space for the mother to consider alternative behaviour that was possibly more useful – and wouldn't give her a sore throat and a thumping headache!

Often clients see themselves in a very negative way. They can readily list their faults, shortcomings and weaknesses, but find it very hard to identify their strengths and resources. Here the principle of *If it works, keep doing it* advocates that the practitioner should listen very carefully for clues about ways in which the client is being successful. When a client recognises an area of achievement in their life they can feel much more empowered, and this may engender in them a renewed sense of hope and energy. This is a definite strength of the model, considering how people with mental illness and/or learning disabilities are marginalised in society (Stoddart *et al*., 2001). It may also be possible to use some idea or behaviour from a successful area of their life in another area that is presenting more difficulties for the client. In this way the client is not being asked to adopt new behaviour, but is merely being encouraged to expand established skills into another area. This will probably be easier for them to achieve. An example of this occurred in practice when a 12 year old boy – Tim (pseudonym) – was getting into trouble at school for being unable to control his behaviour when he got angry or frustrated. Whilst talking to Tim's parents it became obvious that Tim dealt with frustration very well at home by removing himself from the situation and sitting quietly in his bedroom by himself for a few minutes. Tim's mother was encouraged by the therapy team to adopt the role of 'expert parent' and advise Tim's teacher of Tim's ability. Together, Tim, his mother and teacher devised a 'green pass' system. Tim was given a green card and encouraged to use it by showing it to the teacher when he felt he was getting out of control. Tim would then be allowed to go to the school's quiet room for a few minutes, returning when he felt calmer. The green pass negated the need for Tim to explain how he was feeling when he needed to have time out (which was usually very difficult for Tim) and was a signal that every teacher could easily recognise. This system became so successful that it was adopted for other children and became part of school policy. This situation clearly demonstrates how a skill in one area of a client's life can be transferred to another area.

If it isn't broken don't fix it admonishes practitioners not to pathologise their client, by recognising the parts of the client's life that are positive and healthy. A basic premise of SFP is that people have problems, and that they are not problems themselves, so they are not damaged, brittle organisms in need of a complete personality overhaul. Rather, practitioners should help clients to re-experience themselves as people with talents, gifts and strengths. A useful guide is to ask whether the 'problem' is indeed a problem for the client, or actually a problem at all. An example of this was when a married couple brought their 14-year-old son for family therapy. They began by highlighting their concerns for their son and wondering what had happened to change their happy, sociable little boy into a moody adolescent, who just lay around the house, neglected his hygiene and was often confrontational and rude in the way he spoke to them. They also blamed themselves, because he had no problems at school so 'the fault must lie at home'. The team listened intently to their concerns and then engaged them in a discussion about the parenting role – helping children to achieve independence and launching them into adulthood. We then normalised some of the son's behaviour as typical of teenagers experiencing the changes of puberty. We also complimented the parents on having developed such a strong relationship with their son – so strong that he was able to practise his new-found sense of self and assertiveness with them, knowing that they would not abandon him when he made mistakes or errors of judgement due to his lack of skill and tact. The family seemed surprised and then pleased with this alternative view of their situation, and left the clinic with their sense of pride in their son reawakened.

Another concern that affects some parents of children with learning difficulties is anxiety around the need to 'let go' to allow the young person to become more independent. Again, some of this anxiety can be normalised as being similar to the experience of most parents the first time their child goes on a shopping errand alone, or walks home from school on their own, as well as countless other challenges that our children have to face. Also, the anxiety can be constructed as a helpful factor in that it drives parents to protect the child. Then the construct of 'anxiety for the child's safety' can be expanded to consider times when the anxiety is a hindrance that gets in the way of the child's development, and what needs to happen so that parents can 'throw away' some of their anxiety.

The skills of SFP are simple ideas, but ones that practitioners need to practise, evaluate and develop. Insoo Kim Berg – one of the Brief Family Therapy Team in Milwaukee – has publicly stated several times 'simple doesn't mean easy'. So, although the ideas are easy to grasp, they need effort and commitment to develop and maintain. During the practitioner's development towards a more solution-focused way of working, they will develop a style of working of their own. When viewing videos of the leading lights of SFP, or reading their accounts of therapy, it is important that would-be SF practitioners do not try to emulate the 'gurus' or become a clone of someone else. For example, Matthew Selekman is a very skilful and engaging therapist. He encourages practitioners to celebrate their client's successes, and in his own practice in America he often goes around each member of the family doing 'High-5' handclaps with them. This is a very successful strategy for Matthew, but not one that would transfer well to the author's practice in Birmingham, West Midlands. Suddenly jumping up in the middle of a session to do High-5s is likely to be viewed by clients as the therapist having 'lost the plot', and would only alienate the clients. So, whilst attention should be paid to the development of skills, the practitioner also needs to pay attention to the art of therapy and ensuring that their style of working is genuine for them and is in keeping with the principles of SFP.

Seeking exceptions is when the practitioner is looking for times when the problem is absent, or if present, is under control. These can be vital in the search for a solution, as careful enquiry regarding what was different about those times can reveal information that is very useful. Often the client has difficulty remembering an exception at first, but as they discuss it in more detail the time becomes clearer to them.

The 'Miracle Question' is perhaps the best known of the interventions listed previously. The classic miracle question is (de Shazer, 1988, p. 5):

> Imagine that tonight when you go to bed a miracle happens; and all the problems that you have today disappear. But because you are asleep you don't know that the miracle has happened. When you wake up in the morning, what is the first thing that you notice that is different?

Box 9.1 Miracle questions

What would be the first thing that you would notice that would be different?
What else?   What else?   What else?

Who would be the first person to notice the differences?
Who else?

What would they notice?

How would you recognise that they had noticed?

Take me on through the day... What else would have changed?
Who else might notice this?

Can you think of anything that suggests that some of these changes have already started happening?

It is important that the therapist concentrates on small differences, little changes that the person might notice. Otherwise the client is very likely to go off into the fantasy of 'How my life would be better if I won the lottery', which might not be very useful. The therapist should try to take the person through their 'miracle' day. See Box 9.1 for further miracle-type questions.

If the client is having difficulty conceptualising the notion of a miracle, it may be helpful to try using the idea of magic. Children in particular engage well with the question – 'If I had a magic wand here that would make all the problems you brought with you today disappear, what would be the first thing you would notice that would be different?' Alternatively, if a client talks about struggling with a problem that feels like trying to climb a mountain, the therapist could ask what life would be like at the top of the mountain. These questions help the client and therapist to establish some clear goals for the therapy, what the client wants to achieve. Well-formed goals are one of the indicators that therapy is likely to be successful according to de Jong and Miller (1995).

However, the notion of 'miracle' can be problematic in that some cultures have no word for miracle – and therefore the concept is alien to them – and some people who have strong religious beliefs object to discussing miracles as though they were everyday occurrences. An acceptable substitute for the word 'miracle' could be 'something extraordinary' or 'something marvellous'.

Scaling is another technique that is closely associated with SFP. Again, it can help to formulate clear goals and describe changes that the client would like. A typical scaling question is:

Imagine a scale from 1 to 10 where 1 is the worst that things could be and 10 is the best. Where are you right now?

It can also be useful to ask the client to imagine where the 'good enough' point might be – the point at which things are not ideal but they are reasonable. I also ask the client which point they would have to reach so that they could 'sack the therapist'! This helps to empower the client as having some control in the process, and gives me an idea of how much change the client is hoping for. When reading about the scaling technique, it is important to understand that often American authors put the scale in terms of 1 being the best and 10 the worst, whereas in the UK there is a notion that improvement comes with some effort, so the scale seems to work best going from 1 at the lowest point up to 10 as the best. It doesn't matter which way round the scale is put as long as the client understands it. If a client has difficulty conceptualising the scale it could be simplified and symbols used instead of numbers. Thus:

could represent worst to best in a way that most people would recognise. In addition Stoddart *et al.* (2001) recommend changing a horizontally aligned scale to a vertical scale.

When the client identifies where they are on the scale the therapist usually asks them what is telling them that they are at that point and not the point below? The client can often then identify some aspects of their life that are better than others – maybe even some exceptions! Then they can be asked to identify what would have changed if they were to move up one point on the scale. It is important that the client is only asked to imagine life at one point higher, as any further amount of change can leave the client feeling overwhelmed, and may lead to the 'lottery' answer – an answer so unrealistic that it could only be fulfilled if the person won the jackpot in the National Lottery. Then the client can be encouraged to consider what needs to happen so that these changes can take place. This is where the discussion moves into action planning. Scaling can be used in many ways; to address a client's motivation to change, to look for strengths, and to help them identify their current position and what small changes they could implement. Occasionally, given the options of being from 1 to 10 on the scale, a client has stated that he/she is at –3. At first the author found this difficult to deal with, but now takes this sort of response as an indication of just how tough things are for the client. This is a good point to acknowledge to the client that you have heard him loud and clear, and also to give a compliment that even though they feel so low they are still motivated to make efforts to change. It is perfectly possible to extend the range of the scale to include negative numbers, and then work with those just as with the usual scale.

It is often surprising how the changes that clients talk about are quite small. For example, one mother said that things would be one point higher on the scale if her son smiled at her when he got up in the morning. The son was asked if that was possible and he readily agreed, so the family was asked to try this as an experiment to see what happened. The son was determined that his mother should notice him smiling, and so he tried to eat his breakfast without losing his smile! Both mother and son found this so funny that they ended up laughing together. So, one simple idea led to them being able to rediscover their enjoyment of each other's company, rather than them starting the day in conflict. See Box 9.2 for a selection of scaling questions.

The final technique that will be outlined is that of giving compliments. Again, this has to be used with care – some people are so unused to receiving compliments that they have difficulty in dealing with them, or even worse start looking for the therapist's hidden agenda. Also, the compliment must be genuine and based within the client's reality. The example given above can be used as appropriate when the client describes having battled with a certain problem, or their refusal to allow the problem to 'win'. The therapist should be noticing and complimenting the client on these examples of determination and on other helpful behaviour. In this way the client can receive positive feedback even when their situation seems completely dire. It is usual to give a compliment towards the end of the therapeutic session when the therapist is summarising the conversation that has taken place.

People with learning difficulties and mental health problems often receive very negative, even damaging, feedback in their dealings with the general public. This can range from people having very low expectations of service users, or a belief that they are violent and dangerous and therefore to be avoided at all costs. Compliments can go some way towards reducing these detrimental effects. One way of sustaining the beneficial effects of compliments is the use of the therapeutic letter. This is a letter written by the practitioner that fulfils several functions. Firstly, it can summarise the main points of the discussion that has taken place with the service user so that these can be picked up and developed on the next session. Then the letter can highlight the person's strengths and abilities that the practitioner has noticed in the session, which helps to validate the person, and finally the practitioner can include their thoughts and observations. These must be of a positive nature and can give the client an alternative perspective that can empower them, and may help the client to keep trying when they experience difficulties. The beauty of a therapeutic letter is that the practitioner can include all the points they want the service user to hear without fear of overloading them with information, and the service user can read the letter over and over again to sustain their self-confidence in the face of adversity. An example of a therapeutic letter was one that the author wrote to a single parent who was living through a very difficult time in her

Box 9.2 Scaling questions

The practitioner draws a scale from 1 to 10 on paper.

This is a scale of your problem from 1 to 10, with 1 being the worst and 10 being the best that things could be. What word would you use for the worst? What word would you use to describe the best?

The practitioner or client should write those words in at the appropriate places on the scale.

It would be wonderful if we could all be at 10 all the time, but life isn't like that, so I wonder if there is a point on the scale which is 'good enough' – not perfect but good enough for you?

The 'GE' point is marked on the scale

What will tell you that you that you don't need to come for therapy any more?

Looking at this scale, where are you right now?

What is telling you that you are at 3 and not at 2? What else? What else?

If I saw you next time and you said that you had moved up one point on the scale to 4, what would be different? What else? What else?

What needs to happen so that those changes can be made?

What do you need to do to make these changes?

What sort of help do you need and from whom?

Of all the things that we have talked about with this scale, is there one thing that you think you might like to try between now and the next time we meet?

NB This last question must be asked in a very tentative tone of voice, as the object is not to tell the client what to do, but help them to identify what they might like to try for themselves.

life. This client was unable to accept compliments about herself, and showed obvious discomfort if one was offered. So, a therapeutic letter was written which focused on how well-behaved her children were, and how well they could express themselves considering their young age. The letter stated that the children had obviously received a lot of attention and encouragement from their mother, and perhaps she could take pride in a job that had been done so well. At the following appointment, three weeks later, the mother talked about her pride in her children and how the letter had revived her sense of achievement at having brought her children up well. She removed the letter from her handbag – now a very tatty bit of paper – and apologised for the state of it, explaining that she had needed to read it several times a day on the bad days. By offering a compliment that focused on her children the mother was able to accept some of the 'reflected glory' and this had obviously helped her cope on difficult days. For more information and examples of therapeutic letter writing, consult Milner (2001).

Conclusion

This chapter has attempted to give an outline of Solution-Focused Brief Therapy, and to highlight some of the more important aspects of the approach. It began by discussing the areas in which SFP is used, and its roots in social constructionism. The origins of SFP were then highlighted, and the principles of the approach were discussed, together with their congruence with current trends in learning disability and mental health services.

The chapter then went on to identify a number of skills that are commonly used in SFP, namely seeking exceptions, the miracle question, scaling, giving compliments and the use of a therapeutic letter. Hopefully, readers will now be able to see that this approach is not only a way of working collaboratively with their clients – which often improves levels of concordance or compliance – but also a way of placing the client at the heart of their clinical practice to ensure that they are working in a person-centred way. The approach can by used to discover solutions to problems, and also to help clients decide on their hopes and aspirations for their future and how these can be achieved.

Readers who would like to know more are urged to use the reading list given below, or to contact the Brief Therapy Practice for details of their SFP courses. The BTP web site address is included, together with a number of web sites that offer further information.

References

Anderson, H. (2004) *Postmodern Social Construction Therapies.* http://www.harlene.org/Pages/PostmodernTherapiesChapter.htm Accessed on 24 September 2004.

Berg, I. K. and Miller, S. D. (1992) *Working With the Problem Drinker: A Solution-Focused Approach.* W. W. Norton, New York.

Burr, V. (1995) *An Introduction to Social Constructionism.* Routledge, London.

De Jong, P. and Miller, S. D. (1995) How to interview for client's strengths. *Social Work*, **40**(6), 729–36.

Department of Health (2001) *Valuing People: A New Strategy for Learning Disability for the 21st Century.* HMSO, London.

De Shazer, S. (1985) *Keys to Solutions in Brief Therapy.* W. W. Norton, New York.

De Shazer, S. (1988) *Clues to Solution in Brief Therapy.* W. W. Norton, New York.

Fidell, B. (2000) Exploring the use of family therapy with adults with a learning disability. *The Association for Family Therapy and Systemic Practice*, **22**, 308–23.

Fletcher, R. J. (1993) Individual psychotherapy for persons with mental retardation. In: *Mental Health Aspects of Mental Retardation* (eds. R. J. Fletcher and A. Dosen). Lexington Books, New York.

McNamee, S. and Gergen, K. J. (eds) (1992) *Therapy as Social Construction.* Sage, London.

Milner, J. (2001) *Women and Social Work: Narrative Approaches.* Palgrave, Basingstoke.

O'Connell, B. (2001) *Solution Focused Stress Counselling*. Continuum, London.

O'Hanlon, B. and Beadle, S. (1996) *A Field Guide to Possibility Land: Possibility Therapy Methods*. BT Press, London.

Selekman, M. (1993) *Pathways to Change: Brief Therapy Solutions with Difficult Adolescents*. Guilford Press, New York.

Stoddart, K., McDonnell, J., Temple, V. and Mustata, A. (2001) Is Brief better? A modified Brief Solution Focused Therapy approach for adults with a developmental delay. *Journal of Systemic Therapies*, **20**(2), 24–40.

Further reading and web sites

O'Connell, B. (1998) *Solution Focused Therapy*. Sage, London.

Selekman, M. D. (1993) *Solution Focused Therapy with Children: Harnessing Family Strengths for Systemic Change*. Guilford Press, New York.

O'Hanlon, B. and Beadle, S. (1996) *A Field Guide to Possibility Land: Possibility Therapy Methods*. BT Press, London.

http://www.brieftherapy.org.uk/: The site for the Brief Therapy Practice in London, who provide therapy, organise training workshops and conferences and have an extensive booklist from which you can order texts that may not be held by general bookshops.

http://www.psychnet-uk.com/psychotherapy/psychotherapy_brief_solution_focused.htm: A collection of links to some articles and other brief therapy sites.

http://www.brief-therapy.org/ The home website for the founders of the approach – Insoo Kim Berg and Steve de Shazer. Lots of explanations of the approach and books to buy, and you can email them if you have a particular question!

Alternatively, just type 'Solution Focused Brief Therapy' into the search box on http://www.google.co.uk/

CHAPTER 10

Cognitive behavioural therapy

Mark Alison

The expectation that people with a learning disability will take a full participatory role in society is endorsed by the Commission of the European Communities (1998) who have embraced a rights-based model of disability. This includes an equal opportunities right to social inclusion. In *Valuing People* (Department of Health, 2001) the Government mapped out key objectives that would reflect these principles. These included a right to good health, and enabling people to have more control over their own lives. The emphasis of this document was on equality of access to mainstream services. However, it is recognised that people with a learning disability have an unequal struggle in asserting these rights. They are more likely to live in poverty, be unemployed and have lower educational attainment. All these are known risk factors for poor health. Health is defined by the World Health Organization as the interaction of physical health, mental health and social well-being.

This chapter deals with one side of the health triangle, i.e. mental health. It has long been recognised that people with a learning disability are more likely to experience mental health problems than the general public, though they often go undetected and untreated (Hardy and Bouras, 2002). Rates of psychopathology are high amongst the learning disabled population. The prevalence of a mental health problem has been reported at varying rates from 20–64% (Dosen, 1993), to 20–39% (Hatton and Taylor, 2005), to 10–80% (Borthwick-Duffy, 1994). This compares to a prevalence rate of 25% in the general population (Taylor, 2005).

In spite of this vulnerability, people with a learning disability have been denied access to the same sort of treatments currently available to the general public with mental health needs, especially psychotherapy. Indeed, the diagnosis of learning disability has been an exclusion criterion from psychotherapy in the past. This is in spite of the evidence which would seem to indicate that psychotherapy can be beneficial with this client group (Royal College of Psychiatrists, 2004; Health Evidence Bulletin, 2001).

Although the use of psychotherapy in the field of learning disabilities is rather small by comparison to other interventions, such as applied behavioural analysis and pharmacology, it has an important part to play in treating mental health problems in people with learning disabilities.

This chapter is about using one modality of psychotherapy with an excellent record in treating common mental health problems – cognitive behavioural therapy (CBT) – and applying it to people who have mild learning disabilities and mental health problems. This will be illustrated through a case study with reference to the adaptations required to make this possible.

There will also be further discussion on the changes in attitude and service delivery that may increase the use of CBT with this client group.

Cognitive behavioural therapy

Cognitive behavioural therapy is considered perhaps one of the most recent forms of psychotherapy, but it has steadily increased its impact on mental health service provision. This has been helped mostly by the organisation and commissioning of services on an evidence-based approach. Whilst there is a wide range of psychological treatments available on the NHS, few if any can claim the efficacy and clinical effectiveness of CBT, and across such a comprehensive span of clinical applications. Its usefulness for common mental health problems such as anxiety disorders and depression has been recognised by the National Institute for Clinical Excellence (NICE). It has published clinical guidelines for anxiety and depression which makes the recommendation that CBT is one of the psychological treatments of choice for these mental disorders (NICE, 2004a,b).

A quick trawl of the literature will produce a range of uses for CBT. These vary widely, from helping with needle phobias (Patel *et al.*, 2005) through relieving depression in someone with diabetes (Lustman *et al.*, 1998) to the management of schizophrenia (Siddle, 2000).

CBT began its life in the 1960s with essentially three different fathers. It started with Beck's (1967) experimental work on depression, Ellis's (1962) observations from working with couples, and Meichenbaum's (1969) work with schizophrenia. Each brought their own unique findings to the understanding of mental disorder and how to treat them.

Beck's contribution was that he recognised systematic distortions in the thinking patterns of his psychiatric patients. These were identified by him as following themes according to the type of mental disorder, e.g. themes of loss in the thoughts of people with depression.

At the core of Ellis's discovery was that human thinking and emotions are interrelated. He argued that a person's symptoms are a result of their beliefs, activated by experience. He suggested that those beliefs tended to take the form of absolutist or unrealistic demands on themselves or others.

Meichenbaum recognised the internalisation of self-talk as a necessary requisite in the control of one's own behaviour. He observed that patients trained in verbal self-commands could bring their behaviour under control.

The principles of CBT

CBT is a term used to describe psychotherapeutic interventions that aim to reduce psychological distress and maladaptive behaviour by altering cognitive processes (Kaplan *et al.*, 1995). CBT is formed from a simple premise, 'It is not events that affect us, but our interpretations of them' (Epictetus, AD 55–135). CBT is based on the underlying assumption that affect and behaviour are largely a product of cognitions, and as such cognitive and behavioural interventions can bring about changes in thinking, feeling and behaviour (Stallard, 2002; Kendall, 1991).

In summary, CBT is thus an active, directive, time-limited structured approach based upon an underlying rationale that individuals' affects and behaviour are largely determined by the way in which they structure their world (Beck *et al.*, 1979).

CBT is used to describe a range of interventions which share a number of core features.

It is active therapy with the client playing an important part in treatment. Clients learn skills so that they can tackle future problems on their own. It facilitates self-control as clients identify their own goals, setting targets and experimenting, and practising what they have learnt. They are expected to monitor their own performance and measure their progress. The aim is to change the mutually agreed focal problem.

An important element in the success of treatment is the therapeutic relationship. Regardless of how 'technically skilled' the therapist may be, it is important to recognise the human nature of psychotherapy. Therapists therefore have to demonstrate the basics in terms of developing a sound therapeutic relationship, which will require them to have the ability to be warm, empathic, interested and non-judgmental. The therapist's character is considered to be eight times more important than the treatment techniques they use (Theriault and Gazzola, 2005; Lambert 1989).

CBT is about self-help in the short and long term. By utilising what is learnt from sessions, clients are set homework which builds on what is discussed in therapy. Homework is about the clients understanding their problems better, possibly through the use of behavioural experiments. Behavioural experiments test the validity of the clients' existing beliefs, test new, more adaptive beliefs and assist in the progression of therapy. Therapy follows a structured approach which involves agenda setting. At the beginning of each session the client and therapist decide between them what needs to be covered. This collaborative approach is an essential feature of CBT. One of the early parts of therapy is socialising the client to the model, explaining how this relates to their problems.

The theoretical implication of the CBT model is that in order to understand people's distress we have to understand their individual way of perceiving. Therefore an individual's idiosyncratic interpretations of events are responsible for their own unique difficulties. It is important for clients to learn that beliefs and thoughts are opinions, not facts. They learn about this with reference to the CBT model, which focuses on the role of cognitions in creating mental distress. By changing their cognitions, they learn to influence their own behaviour, emotions and physical reactions.

Cognitions can be divided into three levels for the purpose of therapy:

- Core beliefs
- Schemas
- Negative automatic thoughts

These could be considered to operate at different levels. Negative automatic thoughts, being more at surface level, can be triggered by everyday situations. A student on the way to his exam might think 'I haven't learnt enough for this exam and I won't be able to answer any of the questions'. He may conclude 'I am going to get all the answers wrong'. Schemas tend to operate at a deeper level. They can take the form of assumptions and tend to be expressed as 'if–then' statements, e.g. '*If* I don't get 100% in the exam *then* I am a failure'. These act as conditional rules by which people live, and are more easily disputed and challenged than core beliefs. Core beliefs consist of the most sensitive component of the self and are absolutist by nature, e.g. 'I am a failure'. When the conditions for activation of the core belief get met, e.g. when the student doesn't get 100% in his exam, the core belief, 'I am a failure', is triggered.

From this example we can also see the style of cognitive distortion involved. At a negative automatic level this style of thinking might be described as catastrophising, i.e. looking for the worst possible case scenario and predicting that it will come true – without evidence to back up this thought. There are other common types of cognitive distortion that people have, including:

- **Filtering**: Looking for part of the evidence that fits with an existing view. This selective attention creates a tunnel vision, so that people only see what they want to see and ignore information that runs contrary to their pre-existing beliefs.
- **Polarised thinking**: This is about seeing things in black and white terms, good or bad, wonderful or horrible. In this distortion there is no middle ground, no room for ambiguity or uncertainty.
- **Overgeneralising**: This distortion is about basing an absolute belief on very little or biased evidence.
- **Mind reading**: These clients have a crystal ball for seeing into what other people think and often act on these predictions as if they were true. They rarely check out the accuracy of their predictions and imagine that people must think like them too.
- **Shoulds/musts etc.**: These are inflexible rules which are applied to others and themselves. These dictate how things ought to be. They are right and therefore not for disputing. This tends to be very judgmental and can lead to upset when the unreasonable rules are not adhered to by oneself – e.g. perfectionism or when others don't obey our version of what is right.

Clients are taught to recognise these distortions for themselves. They are shown the importance of thoughts in affecting mood, behaviour and physical reactions. A useful tool to assist in this is the Dysfunctional Thought Record (DTR). By collecting information about setting events, and the corresponding thoughts the person has, it can be used to track the connection between the thoughts and these bodily responses. A cornerstone of therapy is to re-evaluate negative thinking and come up with more useful or balanced alternatives. In this way emotional disorders are affected and changed. Typical questions asked by the therapist are framed so as to hear the evidence for that belief.

Another useful style of questioning is Socratic questioning (Padesky, 1993). This draws clients' attention to relevant information which may have been out of their focus previously. In this way it aims to bring clients to awareness through carefully guided discovery.

Therapy begins with a referral and an assessment of the problem. CBT theory has problem-specific models of the psychological processes which maintain problems. This begins with the general, abstract model as it applies to the problem, e.g. we know that panic often begins with a fear of something which acts as a trigger, which then leads to avoidance of the fear, which maintains the panic cycle.

When gathering information about the problem, the therapist is categorising information into cognitive, emotional, behavioural and physiological aspects of its presentation. They also ask about childhood, critical incidents, triggers and maintenance factors of the problem, as well as the current impact on the individual (see Figure 10.1). The therapist is interested in generating a formulation or a 'working hypothesis' which they then share with the client. If this formulation 'holds water' with the client, i.e. it makes sense of their problem, treatment is based upon this. This is reviewed regularly to see if it accurately captures the client's problems, and adjustments are made as necessary.

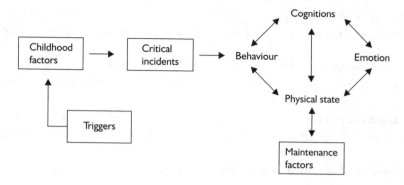

Figure 10.1

Cognitive behavioural therapy and learning disabilities

The use of psychotherapeutic interventions with people who have learning disabilities is now widespread practice. The most common form of this is behavioural interventions (Willner, 2005). However, there is evidence that psychologists are increasingly using CBT with their clients, but mainly in the use of self-instruction (Nagel and Leiper, 1999). These types of self-management strategy are aimed at cognitive deficits and not cognitive distortions. This approach therefore has limited use, since there tends to be a difficulty in generalising what is learnt to novel situations (Stenfert Kroese, 1998). Nonetheless, CBT is now widely used in the treatment of learning-disabled sex offenders (e.g. Lindsay *et al.*, 1998; Blumenthal *et al.*, 1999) and anger management (e.g. Taylor *et al.*, 2002; Howells *et al.*, 2000; Whitaker, 2001; Willner *et al.*, 2002).

There have also been those who have dealt with mental health problems, such as depression, in learning disabled clients. Reed (1997) used a CBT-focused approach with a woman who had Down's Syndrome and was depressed. Lindsay *et al.* (1993) reported on the use of CBT for depression with individuals with mild learning disabilities. They reported being able to isolate negative automatic thoughts, identifying underlying assumptions and generating alternative balanced ways of thinking. They reported improvements in the clients' mental state as a result of therapy. Others have reported on the use of CBT to address the attitudes of carers working with people with a learning disability (Kushlick *et al.*, 1997).

An important factor in CBT and people with learning disabilities is whether they will be able to use it. Willner (2005) has identified some basic requirements to assess for before commencing therapy. He suggests the person will need to be able to distinguish between antecedent events and associated cognitions and emotions, and have an ability to recognise that cognitions mediate the effects of events on emotions and a willingness to engage in collaborative empiricism.

Dagnan, Chadwick and Proudlove (2000) studied the abilities of 40 people with mild learning disabilities to see if they could accurately identify emotions and link emotions to situations. They found that over 75% of the sample could do these tasks.

One area of difficulty in gauging a person's emotional intelligence is the way they display it. This is perhaps more important than their intellectual intelligence, but may be correlated. Glick and Zigler (1995) have suggested a developmental progression with people with higher functioning internalising their distress and more severely disabled clients externalising their emotions, resulting in acting out behaviours (e.g. temper outbursts, assaults).

There have been a number of methods used to assess clients' emotional awareness. Dagnan and Proudlove (1997) have reported on the use of Makaton symbols consisting of facial expressions to test emotional awareness. Gioia and Brosgole (1988) have used line drawings to similar effect. Pictures can also be used to assess emotional awareness and even role playing, with the therapist acting out certain emotions for the client to identify. Another useful vehicle for this may be TV soap operas. Using selected video clips, it is possible to guide the client to describe why a character is reacting or feeling a particular way.

Another important feature of CBT is accessing thoughts. Children as young as three have been found to be able to provide information about their thoughts (Hughes, 1988). Therefore simple questions like 'What are you thinking?', or 'What thoughts run through your head when...? ' may identify necessary information such as clients' negative automatic thoughts. Metaphors might also be a useful way to exploring a client's understanding of abstract concepts and make them more concrete (Stallard, 2002).

Other areas of assessment include the behavioural and physiological components of mental health problems. Behavioural effects include avoidance of situations and environments or a reluctance to engage in certain activities. Again, simple questions can be asked about whether the person has stopped doing something recently or have started doing something they used not to. Third party information may assist in identifying and observing these changes.

The physiological effects of mental disorders vary according to the problem. Depression often correlates with changes in appetite and sleeping patterns. People may report lethargy as energy levels drop. In anxiety, typical physiological presentations are about heightened threat responses, so they may appear vigilant, have an increased pulse/heart rate, display rapid, shallow breathing etc.

At the end of the assessment the therapist should be able to produce a working hypothesis of the problem based on the model of Figure 10.1. This information will assist in the therapist producing a preliminary formulation. This may be done on the initial consultation or may take several sessions to compile.

When all of these components have been identified the therapy can then progress to the treatment stage. It must be noted that some information may be missing, especially the person's full life history, so a 'probabilistic' approach may have to be employed in order to progress therapy. This framework will now be applied to a case study.

Case study

Ben lives alone in a flat. He has a mild learning disability and a borderline personality disorder. He started to develop sleep problems and loss of appetite. He was seen by his psychiatrist, who diagnosed depression. He was referred for a short course of CBT.

On assessment Ben described his current situation, and identified having no friends, no job and little money as being his main problems.

Using the Beck Depression Inventory the level of depression he was currently experiencing was assessed as moderate/severe, i.e. he had a score of 30. This assessment reflected his statement about his job and friend situation. There were high scores for loss of interest, hopelessness and helplessness.

Assessment

Ben was interviewed and consent was sought to gather further information from other sources about his past. It transpired that Ben's parents split up when he was aged three. There were incidents of domestic violence which he witnessed. He describes his mother as being very protective towards him.

The session went on to identify what thoughts went along with his current mood. He identified thinking that he was 'useless' and a 'waste of space'. Ben talked about not being able to hold down a job because he didn't seem able to get on with work colleagues and he tended to make lots of mistakes in whatever job he did get. This usually led him to be dismissed. He was asked about his view of the future, which he described as pretty miserable, and his view of the world, which he said didn't care about him. He divulged a relationship break-up with a girlfriend because of his drinking and spending money on non-essential items like gambling.

Formulation

- **Core beliefs**: It is hypothesised that Ben has core beliefs such as 'I am useless' and 'I am unlovable'. He may have reached these conclusions through his experience as a child. He may have developed beliefs as a result of his early experience that include feeling vulnerable and a failure. One of his compensatory beliefs is about entitlement, leading to irresponsible behaviour.
- **Schemas**: At a schema level he is making the assumption there is nothing he can do to change his feelings and that he cannot change things for the better, so he has taken this to mean that it is not worth attempting to change his situation.
- **Critical incidents**: Ben's view of himself as being undesirable and incompetent was formed from his employment experience. His insufficient self-control has led him to being unable to tolerate any frustration or discipline, and therefore he has been unable to curb his addiction to gambling and drinking.
- **Triggers**: The most recent trigger to Ben's depression has been the break-up with his girlfriend. This has led to the current symptoms he is experiencing, which are:
  - Negative automatic thoughts, such as 'What's the point in living like this' and he is 'just a nuisance to everyone'.
  - Physical symptoms: these were identified as loss of appetite and feeling lethargic.
  - Behaviours: these were identified as poor sleep, difficulty concentrating, drinking and gambling.
  - Emotion: the primary emotion was depression, but he was also feeling frustrated and had low self-esteem.

Ben was then invited to a course of treatment sessions. These are summarised in Table 10.1.

Table 10.1 Ben's treatment sessions.

	Session tasks	**Homework tasks**
1	Introduction to the cognitive model Setting agendas Agree problem list Measuring level of depression (Beck Depression Inventory)	Listen to audiotape of session Monitor activities rate for mastery and pleasure Small incremental steps in activity levels, e.g. housework and seek debt advice
2	Review homework Agree agenda Developing therapeutic alliance Targeting thoughts to dispute	Listen to session tape Increase level of activity. Introduce more pleasurable experience – visiting friend
3	Review homework Agree agenda Review formulation and adjust if necessary Recording automatic thoughts	Listen to session tape Record automatic thoughts, including situation Feelings and thoughts
4	Review homework Agree agenda Testing validity of thought (where's the evidence)	Listen to session tape Behavioural experiment: testing out prediction 'All my friends will reject me'
5	Agree agenda Feedback from experiment Reflecting on prediction-testing assumptions	Listen to session tape Behavioural experiments – testing out assumptions
6	Agree agenda Generating alternative balanced thoughts	Listen to session tape Disputing thoughts and generating alternative balanced ones
7–20	Repeat of above with adjustments as necessary to formulation	Listen to session tape Behavioural experiments Activity scheduling

Session 1

Ben highlighted that his main problems were drinking, being in debt and the unhygienic state of his flat. Ben had difficulties reading and writing, so an assessment of his current level of depression was undertaken using the Beck Depression Inventory (BDI), with some modifications. These were that the questions were read out by the therapist. An analogue scale of circles was used so that Ben could indicate how much he was experiencing the particular symptom by pointing to the corresponding size of circle. Homework was set, which was to keep a diary of his daily activities. Due to his difficulty in reading and writing, this needed some modification too. He was encouraged to draw stick men to keep a record of what he did, with whom and when.

Session 2

Ben's activity schedule was gone through. It painted a picture of spending lots of time sleeping or watching TV with very little else going on. Some changes to this schedule included a visit to a friend, and one morning he attended a drop-in centre. These were explored to see if they helped with his mood, and he was able to see a very slight difference on these days compared with others.

Session 3

Recording of dysfunctional thoughts was introduced. Also the connection between thoughts, emotions, physical symptoms and behaviour was made. Ben was given a diagram which showed each of these factors connected to one another. Thoughts were represented by a head and a thought bubble. Behaviour was shown as a person walking. Emotions were characterised by two faces – one sad and one happy – and physical symptoms were represented by someone with a thermometer in their mouth.

Ben was asked to monitor his own thoughts by writing down a sequence of events using stick men. He was shown thought examples, to illustrate what was going on around him at the time, and was then asked to capture his thoughts by what he said in terms of how he saw himself. He was to draw what he thought he looked like, so if it was 'I'm a waster', what example could he give for this? He came up with lying in bed. In this way he was encouraged to make a connection between events and his thoughts.

Session 4

The event–thought connection was reviewed. It still needed some reinforcement, but he was sufficiently consistent to introduce the next step, which was identifying the emotions that went with these thoughts. He was asked to describe these by drawing the expression of this emotion as a representation on a face, e.g. a down-turned mouth and drooping eyes represented sadness. The activity schedule was also used to introduce previously abandoned interests. These were decided upon as visiting friends. He made a negative prediction that his friends would reject him. In the session he was encouraged to draw out the sequence of events and the homework was to test out this belief by visiting some friends to see if the prediction came true.

Session 5

There seemed to be some lift in Ben's mood, so it was re-evaluated using the BDI. His score had indeed dropped to 21, indicating a moderate depression. This information was shared with Ben, who acknowledged he was feeling somewhat better. The behavioural experiment had gone well in that he was not rejected by his friends and that he could acknowledge the discrepancy in his expectation as indicated by his previous drawing and what actually happened.

Ben made gradual progress over the next few months until he was subsequently discharged when his BDI score indicated a consistent score of 9, suggesting that he was no longer suffering from depression.

Discussion

This chapter has been about using approaches to people's mental health problems which have not found widespread use in the field of learning disabilities. We will explore some possibilities as to why this might be.

There are issues about vicious circles. By engaging in low expectancy beliefs about the individual, we may not currently consider referring them on to mainstream psychotherapy services for their mental health problem. This is in spite of current policy, which encourages an inclusion philosophy. As a result, a culture of ignorance is bred into services as we underestimate people's abilities. This reinforces pre-conceived ideas in those providing psychotherapy that people with learning disabilities are a client group that would not benefit from it. It leaves the therapist impotent, since their beliefs about learning disabled people and what they can offer is left unchallenged. The training required to practice at a higher level such as a psychotherapist has largely ignored the needs of this group, thus perpetuating the problem, as psychotherapists are largely drawn from the mental health field. The Royal College of Psychiatrists (2004) has recommended that all organisations and courses that train psychotherapists should include modules on working with people with a learning disability. Furthermore, psychotherapists working in the NHS should accept patients with a learning disability for treatment, seeking supervision from disability psychotherapists as appropriate. This could be a way of breaking the vicious circle.

This brings us on to some of the wider service and system issues that may account for the lack of CBT use in learning disabilities.

There has been a history of separate services for the Mental Health and Learning Disability Directorates within Trusts. Service configurations have emphasised separateness and difference. Budgetary arrangements, management structures and provision have all been largely divorced. Each empire has been maintained in relative isolation. This has had several negative effects on the learning disability population who have mental health problems. These concerns are reflected in the report *Meeting the Mental Health Needs of Adults with a Mild Learning Disability* (Royal College of Psychiatrists, 2003). It recommends that there should be protocols to share expertise and that learning disability professionals should work with other mental health colleagues to meet the psychological needs of this group.

This chapter has reviewed the use of CBT with people with learning disabilities. It has endorsed the use of CBT whilst recognising some of the reasons why this form of psychotherapy is not yet widely used with this client group. One reason may be the evidence base, which is still emerging. Also, the evidence base that does exist still mainly consists of single case studies. This may be the main reason why so little is known about this therapeutic approach for people with learning disabilities. Success breeds success, and the lack of research means its current use will remain with a well-meaning dedicated few until the body of research reaches critical mass. The hope for CBT is that when this happens it will be seen as the right philosophical approach to people's mental health problems, i.e. that it is empowering and self-affirming. It puts the individual in charge of their own problems, able to do something about these problems, without ultimately having to rely upon others to do this. In this way CBT could become the 'third way' in learning disabilities.

Acknowledgements

Acknowledgements are due to Lisa Lodwick and Karen Amner.

References

Beck, A. T. (1967) *Depression; Causes and Treatment.* University of Pennsylvania, Philadelphia.

Beck, A. T., Rush, A. J., Shan, B. F. and Emery, G. (1979) *Cognitive Therapy for Depression.* Guilford Press, New York.

Blumenthal, S., Gudjonsson, G. and Burns, J. (1999) Cognitive distortions and blame attribution in sex offenders against adults and children. *Child Abuse and Neglect,* **23**(2), 123–43.

Borthwick-Duffy, S. A. (1994) Epidemiology and prevalence of psychopathology in people with mental retardation. *Journal of Consulting and Clinical Psychology,* **62**(1), 17–27.

Commission of the European Communities (1998) *A New European Community Disability Strategy.* Document 98/0216 (CNS). Commission of the European Communities, Brussels.

Dagnan, D. and Proudlove, J. (1997) Using Makaton drawings to assess the ability to recognise facial expression of emotion in people with learning disabilities. *Clinical Psychology Forum,* **105**, 3–5.

Dagnan, D., Chadwick, P. and Proudlove, J. (2000) Towards an assessment of suitability of people with mental retardation for cognitive therapy. *Cognitive Therapy and Research,* **24**, 627–36.

Department of Health (2001) *Valuing People: A New Strategy for Learning Disability for the 21st Century.* HMSO, London.

Dosen, A. (1993) Diagnosis and treatment of psychiatric and behavioural disorders in mentally retarded individuals: the state of the art. *Journal of Intellectual Disability Research,* **37**(suppl. 1), 1–7.

Ellis, A. (1962) *Reason and Emotion in Psychotherapy.* Stuart, New York.

Glick, M. and Zigler, E. (1993) Developmental differences in the symptomology of psychiatric inpatients with and without mild mental retardation. *American Journal of Mental Retardation,* **99**, 407–17.

Gioia, J. V. and Brosgole, L. (1988) Visual and auditory affect recognitions in singly diagnosed mentally retarded patients, mentally retarded patients with autism and normal young children. *International Journal of Neuroscience,* **43**, 149–63.

Hardy, S. and Bouras, N. (2002) The presentation and assessment of mental health problems in people with learning disabilities. *Learning Disabilities Practice*, **5**(3), 33–8.

Hatton, C. and Taylor, J. L. (2005) 'Promoting health lifestyles' and 'Mental health and illness'. In: *Learning Disability: A Life Cycle Approach to Valuing People* (eds. G. Grant, P. Goward, M. Richardson and P. Ramcharan). Open University Press, Maidenhead.

Health Evidence Bulletin (2001) *Wales Learning Disabilities (Intellectual Disabilities)*, p. 36.

Howells, P. M., Rogers, C. and Wilcock, S. (2000) Evaluating a cognitive/behavioural approach to teaching anger management skills to adults with learning disabilities. *British Journal of Learning Disabilities*, **28**, 137–42.

Hughes, J. N. (1988) *Cognitive Behavioural Therapy with Children in Schools*. Pergamon Press, New York.

Kaplan, C. A., Thompson, A. E. and Searson, S. M. (1995) Cognitive behaviour therapy in children and adolescents. *Archives of Disease in Childhood*, **73**, 472–5.

Kendall, P. C. (1991) Guiding theory for treating children and adolescents. In: *Child and Adolescent Therapy Cognitive Behavioural Procedures* (ed. P. C. Kendall). Guilford Press, New York.

Kushlick, A., Trower, P. and Dagnan, D. (1997) Applying cognitive behavioural approaches to the carers of people with learning disabilities who display challenging behaviour. *IABA Newsletter*, **II**(4).

Lambert, M. J. (1989) The individual therapist's contribution to psychotherapy process and outcome. *Psychology Review*, **9**, 469–85.

Lindsay, W. R., Howells, L. and Pithcaithly, D. (1993) Cognitive Therapy for Depression with Individuals with Intellectual Disabilities. *British Journal of Medical Psychology*, **66**, 135–141.

Lindsay, W. R., Neilson, C. Q., Morrison, F. and Smith, A. (1998) The treatment of six men with a learning disability convicted of sex offences with children. *British Journal of Clinical Psychology*, **37**, 83–98.

Lustman, P. J., Griffith, L. S., Freeland, K. E., Kissel, S. S. and Clouse, R. E. (1998) Cognitive behaviour for depression in type 2 diabetes mellitus; a randomized control trial. *Annals of Internal Medicine*, **129**, 613–21.

Meichenbaum, D. H. (1969) The effects of instructions and reinforcement on thinking and language behaviours of schizophrenics. *Behaviour Research and Therapy*, **7**, 101–14.

Nagel, B. and Leiper, R. (1999) A national survey of psychotherapy with people with learning disabilities. *Clinical Psychology Forum*, **129**, 14–18.

NICE (2004a) *Anxiety: Management of Anxiety (Panic Disorder, With or Without Agoraphobia; and Generalised Anxiety Disorder) in Adults in Primary, Secondary and Community Care.* Guideline 22. http://www.nice.org.uk/cg022niceguideline.

NICE (2004b). *Depression: Management of Depression in Primary and Secondary Care.* Guideline 23. http://www.nice.org.uk/cg023niceguideline.

Padesky, C. (1993) *Socratic Questioning: Changing Minds or Guiding Discovery?* Keynote Address Delivered at the European Congress of Behavioural and Cognitive Therapies, London, 24 September.

Patel, M. X., Baker, D. and Nosarti, C. (2005) Injection phobia. A systematic review of psychological treatments. *Behavioural and Cognitive Psychotherapy*, **33**(3), 343–50.

Reed, J. (1997) Understanding and addressing depression in people with learning disabilities. In: *Cognitive Behavioural Therapy for People with Learning Disabilities* (eds. B. Stenfert Kroese, D. Dagnan and K. Loumidis). Routledge, London.

Royal College of Psychiatrists (2003) *Meeting the Mental Health Needs of Adults with a Mild Learning Disability*. Council Report CR115. Royal College of Psychiatrists.

Royal College of Psychiatrists (2004) *Psychotherapy and Learning Disabilities. The Present Position and Options for Future Development*. Council Report CR116. Royal College of Psychiatrists.

Siddle, R. (2000) The management of schizophrenia: cognitive behaviour therapy. *British Journal of Community Nursing*, **5**(1), 20–5.

Stallard, P. (2002) *Think Good – Feel Good. A cognitive Behaviour Therapy Workbook for Children and Young People*. John Wiley & Sons, Chichester.

Stenfert Kroese, B. (1998) Cognitive-behavioural therapy for people with learning disabilities. *Behavioural and Cognitive Psychotherapy*, **26**, 315–22.

Taylor, J. (2005) *BABCP Magazine*, **33**(3), 14.

Taylor, J. L., Novalo, R. W., Gillmer, B. and Thorne, I. (2002) Cognitive behavioural treatment of anger intensity among offenders with intellectual disabilities. *Journal of Applied Research in Intellectual Disabilities*, **15**, 151–65.

Theriault, A. and Gazzola, N. (2005) Feelings of inadequacy, insecurity and incompetence among experienced therapists. *Counselling and Psychotherapy Research*, **5**(1), 11–18.

Whitaker, S. (2001) Anger control for people with learning disabilities: a critical review. *Behavioural and Cognitive Psychotherapy*, **29**, 277–93.

Willner, P. (2005) The effectiveness of psychotherapeutic interventions for people with learning disabilities: a critical review. *Journal of Intellectual Disability Research*, **49**, 73–85.

Willner, P., Jones, J., Tams, R. and Green, G. (2002) A randomized control trial of the efficacy of a cognitive-behaviour anger management group for clients with learning disabilities. *Journal of Applied Research in Intellectual Disabilities*, **15**, 224–35.

CHAPTER 11

Transactional analysis and people with learning disabilities

Isabel Robinson

Introduction

Transactional analysis is a contractual and goal-oriented psychotherapy, sharing complementary principles with current learning disability practice and the philosophy of *Valuing People* (Department of Health, 2001) and person-centered planning (PCP). This chapter will demonstrate the contribution of transactional analysis as an approach in helping people with learning disabilities make significant changes and developments in their lives. Such people have often been categorised as a homogeneous group, rather than being seen as individuals with different competencies, understanding and personalities. Three case illustrations are included which show the diversity of each person, and provide examples of transactional analysis in practice. In order to protect confidentiality pseudonyms are used.

What is transactional analysis?

Transactional analysis, or TA as it is commonly known, was founded by the late Eric Berne (1910–1970) He was a psychiatrist, who went on to study psychoanalysis. However, owing to theoretical disagreements he decided not to complete his training. Instead he continued to develop his own theories of transactional analysis, which evolved into a new school of psychotherapy. Today the International Transactional Analysis Association defines it as a '...theory of personality and a systematic psychotherapy for personal growth and change'. It provides a theoretical framework including evidence-based models of personality (ego states), communication skills (transactions), recognition (strokes), human development (life-scripts), emotions (rackets) and repetitive relationship patterns (games). These provide an explanation for developing psychological stability and disturbance. Philosophically rooted within the humanistic tradition, TA values the whole person, body, mind and spirit. Human beings are considered to be fundamentally positive and worthwhile, even though their behaviour and relationships may have become dysfunctional. The basic assumption is that 'people are OK (Ernst, 1971), and with sufficient motivation are capable of intrapsychic (inside the mind), interpersonal and behavioural change.

It is impossible to give a full explanation regarding the complete theoretical framework of transactional analysis within such a short chapter. Instead, we will focus on the major elements of ego states and script, and provide examples of how these may be integrated into clinical practice. For readers who are interested in developing a wider knowledge it will be useful to read the following books: Stewart and Joines (1987), Stewart (1996) and Joines and Stewart (2002).

Background regarding TA and learning disabilities

There is a deficiency of published research within the area of transactional analysis and learning disabilities, exceptions being Beazley-Richards (1992, pp. 99–116), Sichem (1995, pp. 259–64) and Haimowitz (2000, pp. 84–90).

Historically, this client group has been excluded from traditional psychotherapy treatment, with assumptions being made that people require high levels of intelligence, insight and verbal articulation to benefit from it (Sinason, 1992; Royal College of Psychiatrists, 2004, p. 170).

In TA clinical practice there appears to be little involvement with people who have learning disabilities. Possible reasons may be that transactional analysts do not consider that they have the necessary skills or specialist knowledge to work with this client group. Others may presume that such people lack a sufficiently developed adult ego state (see below), and are unsuitable for therapy. However, Berne made specific reference to the contrary, stating 'That every individual (including children, the mentally retarded and schizophrenics) is capable of objective data processing if the appropriate ego state can be activated. . . . Everyone has an Adult' (Berne, 1964, p. 24). This suggests that a person, whatever their range of disability, is capable of using therapy to make changes and developments in their lives. Differences exist regarding intellectual ability, communication, and particular issues relating to disability which may affect the process and outcome of therapy. Therapists need to have the confidence, competence, flexibility and creativity to modify their approach and interventions appropriately to meet the needs of each individual client.

Theoretical framework

The ego state model of personality

> Parent, Adult and Child represent real people who now exist or who once existed, who have legal names and civil identities. (Berne, 1961)

The structural model explains how personality develops through the content and interaction of three different ego states, and examines the impact of these on emotional health and mental stability. Structural analysis of the personality is used to help people make sense of who they really are. Eric Berne (1964) defined an ego state as 'a consistent pattern of feeling and experience directly related to a corresponding pattern of behaviour'.

The structural model of ego states

Berne used everyday titles of Parent, Adult and Child (capital letters denote ego states) to identify separate components within the ego state model (Figure 11.1). This choice of language was intended to make TA accessible to non-medical people who had not trained in psychiatry or psychoanalysis. However, generalisations and over-simplifications are sometimes made. For instance, talking about someone as being in a Child ego state might be construed as a derogatory statement. This does not mean that they are behaving in a childish or immature manner. In TA terms it means that the person is re-experiencing aspects of their own childhood (which will include positive and negative elements) as if they were happening within the present moment. Perceptions of situations are imprinted throughout the various stages of child development (Mahler, 1975; Stern, 1985). Different stimuli will reactivate these in the present, causing people to move into Child ego states. Sometimes these will be joyful experiences, where the person is free to be spontaneous, creative and intuitive. Alternatively an overly compliant or rebellious state may manifest irrational fears, phobias and delusions.

Berne (1964, p. 24) stated: 'That every individual was once younger than he is now, and that he carries within him fixated relics from earlier years which will be activated under certain circumstances.... Everyone carries a little boy or girl around inside of him.

Working with the Child ego state

Gordon is a 26-year-old with mild learning disabilities, whose history includes sustained periods of child abuse, neglect and multiple care placements. During assessment, he reports uncomfort-

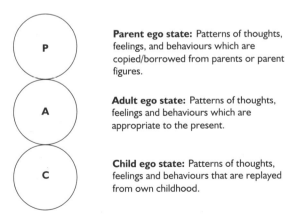

Parent ego state: Patterns of thoughts, feelings, and behaviours which are copied/borrowed from parents or parent figures.

Adult ego state: Patterns of thoughts, feelings and behaviours which are appropriate to the present.

Child ego state: Patterns of thoughts, feelings and behaviours that are replayed from own childhood.

Figure 11.1 The structural model of ego states.

able feelings of anger towards men, and feels distressed whenever he is in the proximity of any. The therapist invites him to tell her about a specific situation when this happened. She notices that his behaviour changes as he relates his experience. He leans forward, holds his head in his hands and closes his eyes. She asks him what he is feeling, to which he replies, 'I'm all right'. Rather than accepting this retort, she picks up on his body language and her own intuition that he might be re-living painful memories. She invites him to focus on his physical sensations. He reports that he is experiencing a 'burning feeling' inside his head; 'sharp chest pain', 'cold shoulders' and 'shakiness' all over his body. In processing these with the therapist, he remembers similar sensations when he was a young boy enduring abuse. Gordon's anger towards *all* men appears to be a result of his previous abuse by *specific* men. Underneath this anger he is scared and frightened of being harmed. Being in the vicinity of any man is now enough to reactivate his traumatised Child ego state. The therapist aims to help him reassemble his story in the present and develop a boundary between his overwhelming Child experiences of the past. She encourages him to utilise his current grown-up context and resources. Her invitation to work with his bodily sensations offers a more direct route to his experiences than straight talking or listening might. This offers Gordon a model that provides an opportunity for him to re-experience significant memories and beliefs from the past affecting his present life. It is the beginning of a process that will help him to re-contextualise his trauma.

The Parent ego state

A person does not have to be a grown-up or a biological parent to have a Parent ego state. This part of the personality structure evolves as children become influenced by patterns of thoughts, feelings and behaviours borrowed from their own parents. Other authority figures, such as grand-parents, foster carers, teachers and elder siblings are also assimilated. Parent-type behaviours can be observed in young children playing and interacting with each other, e.g. mimicking words, phrases and actions used by their own parents.

Internally, the child records a selection of 'Parent tapes'. These contain attitudes, values, rules, beliefs, advice and information from various sources. Some will be positive and growth enhancing, yet others will be confusing, stunting or harmful.

The contents of Parent ego states differ from person to person. This depends upon which parent figures were perceived as the most important and subsequently internalised by the individual child. People of any age can shift into a Parent ego state, copying or repeating things modelled by their own parents, such as nurturing or disciplining children. On a subconscious level they may be adapting their thoughts, feelings and actions to comply with their Parent messages.

As a defence against making contact with the therapist a client may communicate rigid beliefs, which are exclusive Parent responses. This is because such contact psychologically challenges the client's habitual values and attitudes.

Berne (Berne, 1964, p. 24) emphasised 'That every individual has had parents (or parent substitutes) and that he carries within him a set of ego states that reproduce the ego states of those parents (as he perceived them), and that these parental ego states can be activated under certain circumstances.... Everyone carries his parents around inside of him'.

Gordon arrives for his therapy session in an agitated state. He delivers an account of something that has happened during the week. The therapist observes him enter a lengthy monologue and his speech becomes faster. His eyes and facial expression show anger, intensity and a lack of contact with his environment. The therapist experiences being talked *at*, rather than *to*, lectured even. She recognises that this is stimulating her own Child ego state, and to 'ground' herself she shifts her attention towards her own internal response. Recalling previous information from Gordon concerning his experiences of punitive parenting, she feels as though such a character is in the room with her now. She recognises that he has shifted into a Parent ego state that restricts his capacity to respond more flexibly.

The Adult ego state

In TA terms a developed Adult ego state does not mean physical maturity. This occurs when a person is not reacting from their Parent or Child ego states, but fully experiencing here-and-now reality. The person is not in script (see below) and is therefore able to act objectively, by considering options and developing strategies relevant to their current level of development. Authentic patterns of thoughts, feelings and behaviours are experienced.

The therapist observes that Gordon's speech is even and coherent. He is aware of his physical surroundings, and she experiences him as motivated, logical and interesting. As the therapy progresses his Adult becomes stronger, and he starts to learn some behavioural and cognitive techniques to help manage his symptoms of anger and panic.

Structural pathology

Damage occurs within the structure of the personality when the Adult becomes contaminated by Parent prejudices and/or Child fears. The Adult loses the ability to differentiate current reality from past experiences and feelings. Unconsciously, 'the individual will mistake Parent beliefs and Child delusions for Adult facts' (Joines and Stewart, 2002).

Throughout his childhood Gordon was ridiculed and assaulted by people, including his parents, foster parents and siblings for 'being disabled'. He received prejudicial verbal and non-verbal messages that people with disabilities are 'freaks to be laughed at' which he ingested as a Parent belief. His Child ego state agreed, 'I am a freak; I hate myself', causing a 'Double Contamination' of his Adult (see Stewart and Joines, 1987, pp. 50–2). Without realising, he now seeks out situations which will reinforce this position, e.g. entering a public place and perceiving that he is being scorned by people as 'an idiot' and experiencing symptoms of panic, including accelerated breathing and heart rate, sweating and tension. He discounts the effects of his negative beliefs and the possibility that he is projecting these onto other people.

Severe levels of contamination may cause a person to block out and exclude one or more of their ego states. As Berne (1964) observed 'Exclusion is manifested by a stereotyped predictable attitude which is steadfastly maintained as long as possible in the face of any threatening situation'.

Gordon expresses a rigid belief that 'All men are evil'. In stating this view his Parent ego state not only contaminates his Adult, but also excludes his Child (Stewart and Joines, 1989, pp. 53–5). This is a defence mechanism to guard against experiencing his Child vulnerabilities; instead he becomes angry and derisive of others who disagree with his opinions.

Clinical practice

Case illustration 1

Scott, a 41-year-old man with mild learning disabilities, had asked his GP for a referral, so he could talk about his depression and self-harm. At a pre-therapy meeting he describes feelings of anxiety, depression and frustration. He wants to understand these concerns and if they are related to his past experiences of being 'put away in a mental handicap hospital when I was four years old', and states 'I want to find out the truth about my past'.

In order to support her explanation of what the service offers, the therapist uses an information sheet and pre-therapy agreement form, designed with colleagues from Speech and Language Therapy Services. These provide information which is client-friendly and accessible. Picture communication symbols (Curriculum Online, 2006) are used to show reasons why someone might seek psychotherapy treatment (Figure 11.2). The agreement form illustrates ground rules such as confidentiality, and methods that might be used in working together (Figure 11.3). Scott demonstrates understanding of this explanation, and is able to make an informed choice regarding acceptance of further appointments. An initial contract is made to meet for four individual assessment sessions.

Case illustration 2

Carol is a 30-year-old woman with severe learning disabilities and restricted language (one or two words and phrases; vocalisations; repetitive sentences). At the pre-therapy meeting she is unable to explain her reasons for seeking therapy. Her key worker informs the therapist that Carol has been referred for several issues, including periods of withdrawn behaviour, aggressive outbursts and eating problems. The care staff hope that therapy will provide Carol with the means of expressing herself in more constructive ways and alleviate some of her problems.

The therapist reflects on Carol's background information, which consists of early childhood separation, suspected abuse, and long-term hospital care. She formulates that the client's presenting problems are symptoms of emotional distress caused by these traumatic experiences.

Carol is unable to make an informed choice regarding the offer of further assessment sessions. Ethical dilemmas are common in relation to issues around the consent and capacity of people with learning disabilities. However, as Matthews (2003) states: 'Practitioners have a duty to make a decision about what is in the client's best interests, and act accordingly'. In this case, if Carol's problems were symptoms of emotional trauma, psychotherapy would be an appropriate approach for her to sample. Ten appointments are arranged in order to assess her suitability.

PRE- THERAPY INTERVIEW

Name: _____   Date:

Why are you here today?

Is this the right kind of help for you?

How I work.

You talk to me in confidence.

We will not hurt   each
other.

Do you want to come again?

Su M T W
Th F Sa

Actions:
You come here to see me for _____ weeks.

Other:

SIGNED:
Isabel Robinson: _____   Name: _____

Figure 11.2 Information sheet.

Assessment procedure

The initial purpose of assessment is to estimate a person's level of motivation and to evaluate the capacity of their Adult ego state to engage safely and effectively in psychotherapy treatment.

In mainstream services people are expected to make their own way to appointments. However, many people with learning disabilities do not have the capacity to do so, and are dependent on someone else to escort them. The consequence of this might be attendance out of compliance with others, or non-attendance due to circumstances outside of the client's control.

Scott had the necessary independence skills and was punctual and regular in his attendance, making it easier for the therapist to assess his initial level of motivation. However, Carol required escorting and had communication difficulties; therefore a longer assessment period was required. To avoid the pos-

PSYCHOTHERAPY AND COUNSELLING

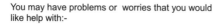

WHAT IS IT?

When people want to make changes in their lives, it can help to work with a therapist.

You may have problems or worries that you would like help with:-

* Someone may have hurt you

* You may feel like hurting yourself

* You may be upset that someone has died

* Or just feeling scared, angry or fed up

* There may be other things that you want to talk about in confidence

WHO IS IT FOR?

Adults and young people with learning disabilities

WHO WILL I SEE?

Sessions will be with Isabel Robinson, who is a qualified and experienced therapist

WHAT DO I DO NEXT?

 If you would like to know more please ring Isabel Robinson at Bridge House on 01254 695698 (or get someone else to ring e.g. carer, friend, community nurse etc). Isabel will help you decide if this is the right help for you.

Figure 11.3 Pre-therapy agreement form.

sibility of over-compliance, the therapist requests Carol's key worker to provide information regarding her capacity to make choices. She also asks her to monitor, and give feedback concerning Carol's behaviour and mood before setting off, during the journey to, and following her appointments.

In mainstream psychotherapy practice involvement from a third party is considered highly inappropriate, and presents boundary issues. However, significant differences arise in working psychotherapeutically with people who have severe learning disabilities. Owing to the level of support Carol requires for all aspects of her daily living and social care, it would be impossible and counterproductive to work in total isolation. The psychotherapist therefore clearly defined her role and specific boundaries with the key worker and other professionals involved. She explained the type of therapy being offered, and how she intended to work with Carol. A commitment was negotiated regarding the provision of transport and escort staff that would remain in the building while Carol was having her session. For therapy to be effective, regular attendance is of paramount importance. Escorts need to be reliable; initially Carol only stayed for a few minutes and someone familiar needed to be in reception to meet her. Confidentiality was explained, i.e. the actual details and content of what happens within individual sessions will not be shared, but relevant insight into the work and recommendations will. Regular review meetings are held by the therapist for this purpose. These help to monitor and gain feedback, including examples of what effect the therapy is having on the person's everyday life. General information and concerns can also be discussed.

Theoretical considerations

An important function of TA assessment is the collection of data and information concerning ego states and script. The therapist will use these to plan treatment interventions, and consider any potential risks.

For the therapist, the importance of assessing both Carol and Scott was to find reasons for their presenting problems, and whether these resulted from early childhood decisions. In order to do this she needed to gather information concerning their ego states and life script. Berne (1972) wrote '[the script is] a lifeplan made in childhood, reinforced by the parents, justified by subsequent events, and culminating in a chosen alternative'.

Process of assessment: Carol

For people who have a severe level of learning disability, such as Carol, there is a more complex need to focus attention on creating a safe therapeutic space. It is important to take into account the possible effects of everyday stimuli: perceptional differences, and increased sensory arousal (e.g. lighting, temperature, sound, smell, décor). Mutual routes of communication, trust and interaction need to be developed. This was facilitated by the therapist noticing her own sensory responses as she 'listened' to Carol's non-verbal communication and body language. She provided a range of resources which she hoped would help Carol to express herself at her current level of development. Rather than talking or asking questions during the assessment sessions, the therapist remained as unobtrusive as possible. She sat on the floor with Carol, who was looking into a box of toys, and was careful not to invade her personal space. Through paying attention to any signs of contact that Carol made towards her, she was able to respond accordingly, allowing Carol to take the lead regarding engagement. Over a period of time she started to mirror some of Carol's behaviours (e.g. pointing, pausing, touching a toy dog on top of its head, making chirruping sounds), and a level of rapport and communication developed between them.

Analysis of information

The therapist noted Carol's repetitive use of the phrases 'Don't cry... dry your eyes' when distressed, and the standard response from her care staff of 'No, don't cry', stated in kindly voice tones. She observed how Carol held tension and rigidity throughout her torso, and often exhibited a frozen facial expression. She interpreted this as Carol listening to Parent voices inside her own head telling her not to cry. This was being reinforced unintentionally by her carers' responses: 'No, don't cry'. These and other *body script* signals communicated how Carol used muscular tension to stop herself releasing authentic emotions. Her limited intellectual abilities and language problems added to the difficulties of being able to get significant people to understand or respond effectively to her emotional needs. The therapist was offering a relationship-oriented therapy, based on Erskine's (2002) concepts of *contact* and *attunement* to relational needs. He defines this as:

> ...a two-part process that begins with empathy – being sensitive to and identifying with the other person's sensations, rhythms, and developmental level of functioning, as well as also responding with reciprocal affect to the other's feelings. Attunement to the client's affect of sadness, fear, anger and joy provides an interpersonal contact so necessary for human relationship.

A review meeting towards the end of the assessment period provided feedback that Carol was enjoying her appointments; appeared less depressed; and was eating well and communicating more. She was still having occasional aggressive outbursts. As the therapist started to engage with Carol on a significant level, therapeutic change was already occurring.

Methods of assessment: Scott

Initial data was collected via the interview format and the use of a script questionnaire (Stewart, 1996). The therapist also incorporated methods of ego state diagnosis (see above). This material was collated on a *script matrix*: a model developed by Claude Steiner (1966) which illustrates how individual parents and care givers unconsciously transmit messages, known as *injunctions*; *permissions*; *counter injunctions* and *programs* to babies and young children. The earliest injunctions (negative) and permissions (positive) are conveyed non-verbally, via the parents' body language, and the quality of their response to emotional, physical and relational needs On the basis of such stimuli, and not out of any rational level of awareness, the infant makes very 'early decisions', about self, others and the world, which if left unrevised, become the foundations of a life script (Stewart and Joines, 1987, pp. 134–47).

Script analysis evidenced that Scott received *Don't Exist, Don't Belong* and *Don't Be Close* familial and cultural injunctions in relation to being born with a 'mental handicap'. He defended against the full potential of the *Don't Exist* injunction (killing himself; by 'accident' or on purpose), by adapting to the later verbally transmitted counter injunctions of *Be Perfect* and *Be Strong*. In complying with these parental commands he decided that he could exist if he shut down his feelings and didn't make a fuss.

Extract from Scott's psychotherapy: Session 20

Scott began telling the therapist about a recent funeral he had attended. Although he had felt sad, he had been unable to cry, and wanted to know why. He stated, 'I never cry, I don't even know if I cried when I was a baby'. The therapist asked him to make a contract with her about what he wanted to focus on during his session. Scott identified that he wanted to explore his emotions, and the reason he finds it difficult to express them. Rather than distancing himself from his emotions through talking 'about' them, the therapist invited him to show her what he was feeling through using the art materials. This would increase his Adult awareness and enable him to *feel* his feelings, rather than *just* talk about them. As Rogers (2000) wrote, 'The expressive arts – including movement, art, writing, sound, music, meditation and imagery – lead us into the unconscious. This often allows us to express previously unknown facets of ourselves, thus bringing to light new information and awareness'.

The therapist sat as a silent observer, whilst Scott expressed himself using black and blue crayons to create an image with captions (Plate 11.1).

To avoid stunting his creativity by inviting an overadaptation from his Child ego state, the therapist did not make judgments or offer any evaluation of his picture. Instead she invited him to tell her about his drawing. As he spoke, she made empathic responses, and paid attention to his body process. She was looking for evidence of body script signals. Throughout his childhood, Scott experienced environments where survival meant the suppression of spontaneous emotions. He blamed himself for having been 'hyperactive' and 'too difficult for mum to handle'. A natural need for parental love and approval (*strokes*) had caused him to suppress his feelings. As the therapist helped him to process his drawing and pay attention to his physical feelings, Scott started to release repressed childhood memories. He recalled his mother telling him to 'Stop crying!' after being bullied at school because, 'They'll think you're a little kid'. Another memory surfaced concerning 'older lads' on the ward of the 'mental handicap' hospital where he had spent a significant part of his early childhood. According to Scott these boys had 'been brave and never cried', and had provided him with significant role models. They transmitted messages of how to survive in adverse conditions, e.g. 'Here's how to hide your scare and avoid getting bullied', which he interjected into his script *program*. As Scott related these incidents to the therapist, he reported a sensation of 'feeling tears at the back of my eyes'. He was starting to move out of script, and re-experience authentic emotions.

Ending therapy

Three years into therapy Scott and the therapist agreed he had fulfilled his overall treatment contract, which was:

> To develop self understanding and confidence i.e.: to know who I really am, to be able to talk clearly with people, explain my thoughts, know what I am feeling and express emotions.

Several behavioural markers had been used during the therapy to demonstrate that he was achieving the changes identified in his contract. These included him:

- Drawing a life path (during sessions)
- Writing to a residential school that he had attended, requesting any photographs they had kept of him (home task)
- Using psychodrama techniques to practice talking clearly to his boss (during sessions)
- Using 'two cushion' work to re-enact early Child scenes, and express thoughts, feelings and behaviours relating to these (during sessions)

Post-therapy evaluation

Ten months after completing therapy Scott provided a colleague with the following feedback:

> Less stressed and moody; not needing to see psychiatrists; not needing tablets or injections to cope with problems; not thinking the worst-thinking better; not getting as upset as before; have more friends; not hearing voices; not seeing strange things; better at talking to people; listening and understanding them more; less frustrated; less depressed; no longer self harming.

Conclusion

This chapter provides evidence that throughout the range of learning disabilities, psychotherapy treatment can benefit those presenting with emotional distress. Clients with moderate to mild levels of disability are able to comprehend the key concepts of TA when presented to them in a creative and simple manner. Many express relief at finding an explanation which helps them to make sense of their own lives. The therapist has found these clients to be as enthusiastic as those without disabilities in using TA and achieving therapy goals and treatment contracts.

People with severe and profound levels of disability are not cognitively able to understand such concepts; however, they are still able to benefit from psychotherapy. As Pat Frankish (2001) said, 'All people with learning disabilities have a lot to say if we are able to listen'. The theoretical framework of TA provides the therapist with psychodynamic reasons for apparently incomprehensible signals of behaviour and communication. This helps her to listen, understand and plan appropriate interventions to facilitate therapeutic change.

Current evidence suggests that few transactional analysts work with clients who have learning disabilities. This reflects the position of psychotherapy treatment in general, and '...demonstrates that there is neither inclusion nor equity for this needy client group in accessing psychotherapy services from which evidence shows they can benefit' (Royal College of Psychiatrists, 2004).

TA theory illustrates that major script decisions are made at a pre-verbal stage of development, where therapists study human development and understand intrapsychic, relational and behavioural levels of communication. This knowledge is equally important regarding the needs of individuals with learning disabilities. However, if clinical application is delivered by therapists who rely predominantly on verbal articulation and cognition, many people with learning disabilities will be discriminated against. As stated in the Royal College of Psychiatrists (2004) report regarding psychotherapy and learning disability:

> For psychotherapies to be effectively delivered to this group, established, models of therapy can be modified to accommodate differences in intellectual ability and the particular issues of the disabled individual that affect not only the content but also the process of therapy.

Recommendations

- Psychotherapists need to develop ways of working independently within a multidisciplinary framework, and have access to clinical supervision from psychotherapists who specialise in the field of learning disabilities.
- Include psychotherapy and learning disability core modules in TA training courses.
- Develop TA training courses for residential care staff which helps them to recognise their own ego states and the effect this has on their communication with service users.

References

Beazley-Richards, J. (1992) Transactional analysis as a theory of interpersonal behaviour and as a psychotherapeutic model. Cited by Conboy-Hill, S. (1992) *Psychotherapy and Mental Handicap*. Sage, London

Berne, E. (1961) *Transactional Analysis in Psychotherapy*. Grove Press, New York.

Berne, E. (1964) *Games People Play*. Penguin, London.

Berne, E. (1972) *What Do You Say After You Say "Hello"?* Corgi, London.

Curriculum Online (2006) Boardmaker™ V5 Picture Communication Symbols. http://www.curriculumonline.gov.uk/

Ernst, F. H. (1971) The OK Corral: the grid for get-on-with. *Transactional Analysis Journal*, **1**(4), 231–40.

Erskine, R. G. (1998) Attunement and involvement: therapeutic responses to relational needs. *International Journal of Psychotherapy*, **3.5**(3).

Erskine, R. G. (2002) Relational needs. *EATA Newsletter*, No. 73, February.

Frankish, P. (2001) Everyone has the right to be seen and heard. *Institute of Psychotherapy and Disability Conference*, London, 13 December.

Department of Health (2001) *Valuing People: A New Strategy for Learning Disability for the 21st Century*. HMSO, London.

Haimowitz, C. (2000) Maybe it's not 'Kick me' after all: Transactional Analysis and Schizoid Personality Disorder. *Transactional Analysis Journal*, **30**(1), 84–90.

Joines, V. and Stewart, I. (2002) *Personality Adaptations*. Lifespace Publishing, Kegworth.

Mahler. M. (1975*) The Psychological Birth of the Human Infant*. Basic Books, New York.

Matthews, D. (2003) Learning disability consent and capacity. *Learning Disability Practice*, **6**(2).

Rogers, N. (2000) *The Creative Connection: Expressive Arts as Healing*. PCCS Books, Ross-on-Wye.

Royal College of Psychiatrists (2004) *Psychotherapy and Learning Disability*. Council Report CR116. Royal College of Psychiatrists, London.

Steiner, C. (1966) Cited by Stewart, I. and Joines, V. (1987) *TA Today*. Lifespace Publishing, Kegworth.

Stern, D. (1985) *The Interpersonal World of the Infant*. Basic Books, New York.

Stewart, I. and Joines, V. (1987) *TA Today*. Lifespace Publishing, Kegworth.

Stewart, I. (1996) *Transactional Analysis Counselling in Action*, 2nd edn. Sage, London.

Sichem, V. (1996) Learning disabilities and script. The brain suggests, the environment predisposes, and the individual decides. *Transactional Analysis Journal*, **25**(3), 259–64.

Sinason, V. (1992) *Mental Handicap and the Human Condition*. Free Association Books, London.

Tilney, T. (1998) *Dictionary of Transactional Analysis*. Whurr, London.

Waitman, A. and Conboy Hill, S. (eds.) (1992) *Psychotherapy and Mental Handicap*. Sage, London.

Further reading

American Psychiatric Association (1995) *Diagnostic and Statistical Manual of Mental Disorders*, 4th edn. American Psychiatric Association, Washington DC.

Department of Health (2004) *Organising and Delivering Psychological Therapies*. HMSO, London.

Niedecken, D. (2003) *Nameless, Understanding Learning Disability.* Brunner-Routledge, London.

Stewart, I. (1994) *Eric Berne.* Sage, London.

Staunton, T. (ed.) (2002) *Body Psychotherapy.* Brunner-Routledge, London.

West, J. (1992) *Child-Centred Play Therapy.* Edward Arnold, London.

Woollams, S. and Brown, H. (1978) *Transactional Analysis.* Huran Valley Institute Press, USA.

CHAPTER 12

Therapy in bereavement

David Elliott

I no longer feel part of a team
(Quote by a bereaved person with learning disabilities)

Introduction

The government white paper *Valuing People* (Department of Health, 2001), is based on the following four principles: inclusion, rights, choice and independence. Only recently have these principles been considered and acted upon in relation to bereavement and loss issues for people with learning disabilities (Blackman, 2003; Read, 1996) (see Box 12.1).

Box 12.1 *Valuing People*'s **four principles.**

Inclusion ⎫ In relation to decision-making in regard to the death of a loved one (e.g.
Rights ⎬ attending chapel of rest, funeral arrangements, accessing appropriate
Choice ⎭ bereavement support)

Independence – as a result of bereavement support/interventions
(Department of Health, 2001)

Bereavement and the four principles

Historically, people with learning disabilities have had little or no say in events surrounding the death of a loved one (Department of Health, 1999; Bicknell, 1983; Raji *et al.*, 2003). One reason postulated by Hollins and Grimer (1988) is that parental mortality and their own mortality can be thought of as one of the 'secrets' of learning disability, and is therefore considered a taboo subject. This resulted in avoidance of discussion of bereavement and loss issues in their lives, and denying them access to appropriate support (Oswin, 1991). Thankfully this situation has started to change and these issues are now being increasingly recognised and addressed. For some bereaved people with learning disabilities their grief is associated with major negative health changes and distress (Dowling *et al.*, 2003; Hollins and Esterhuyzen, 1997). Hollins (2003) has suggested that for these people counselling or psychotherapy would be of benefit to them. The aim of these interventions would be to support the grieving person in a dynamic way by providing appropriate support and information, and helping them come to terms with their loss, in a positive and healthy sense (Hollins, 2003; Conboy-Hill, 1992; Read, 1996; Stroebe and Schut, 1999; Stroebe and Stroebe, 1993).

Health implications of bereavement

Parkes (1998a,b) and Jacobs (1993) have indicated that after a major loss 'such as the death of a spouse or child, up to a third of the people most directly affected will suffer detrimental effects on their physical or mental health, or both'. One would also expect the proportion of people with learning disabilities who experience equivalent losses to be similarly affected, although as yet very little research has been undertaken in this area.

Negative physical health changes have been noted following a bereavement. These changes include an excess of heart disease (Kaprio *et al.*, 1987), cancer deaths (Mellström *et al.*, 1982), liver cirrhosis (Stroebe and Stroebe, 1993) and mortality from infectious diseases resulting from joint unfavourable environments (Helsing *et al.*, 1982). One would expect similar patterns to emerge with people with learning disabilities.

Emotional and mental health consequences of bereavement include anxiety (Zisook *et al.*, 1990), elevated levels of distress and depressed mood (Gallagher *et al.*, 1983), and a particularly high risk of suicide in those recently bereaved (Kaprio *et al.*, 1987).

In the case of people with learning disabilities, their grief needs are not always openly acknowledged (Oswin, 1991). This results in them experiencing 'disenfranchised grief' (Doka, 1999). Doka (1989, 1999) has defined it as 'the grief experienced by those who incur a loss that is not, or cannot be, openly acknowledged, publicly mourned or socially supported'. As Dowling *et al.* (2003) have said, 'risks to health are increased when loss experiences are not acknowledged or are hidden'.

In research which has focused specifically on people with learning disabilities, Hollins and Esterhuyzen (1997) found a greater frequency of aberrant behaviour and psychopathology in parentally bereaved people with learning disabilities compared with a control group. In addition, day centre keyworkers noted a negative change in client health following a parental bereavement. In a follow-up study, Bonell-Pascual *et al.* (1999) concluded that having a learning disability is a 'significant predictor of mental health problems following bereavement'.

Incremental grief

People with learning disabilities often experience multiple losses following the death of a parent (Read, 2003). Possible losses incurred following parental death include:

- loss of main carer/confidant
- loss of parental home
- loss of acquaintances/neighbours
- loss of typical routines
- loss of daytime activity/work placement
- loss of control over life

A model which can be adapted to explain their sense of loss at this time is the incremental model of grief (Cook and Oltjenbruns, 1998). Incremental grief, according to Cook and Oltjenbruns (1998) is the additive factor of grief due to multiple related losses.

When a person with learning disabilities experiences the death of a parent (primary loss), they experience primary grief. If this results in the person having to enter residential care, they then experience secondary losses (loss of family home, neighbours, friends and daytime placement). A secondary loss in this context has been defined as 'any loss, either physical or symbolic, that develops as a consequence of the death of a loved one' (Rando, 1984). Secondary losses give rise to secondary grief. This results in an increase in felt grief, and has been termed 'incremental grief' (Cook and Oltjenbruns, 1998).

Incremental grief might have the potential to have a profound and devastating impact on a person with learning disabilities, who is particularly at risk. Risk factors can be categorised as either traumatic or linked to a person's vulnerability (Parkes, 1998a). Traumatic factors include parental death (especially in early childhood/adolescence), problematical deaths (for example suicide, murder or manslaughter) and multiple loss situations, whereas vulnerability factors include poor self-esteem, lack of trust in others, history of poor mental health and dependant and/or ambivalent attachment to the deceased (Parkes, 1998a). Those people with learning disabilities identified as being particularly at risk and who experience incremental grief might require a therapeutic bereavement intervention.

A taxonomy of helping

Before supporting a bereaved person with learning disabilities, it is necessary to undertake an assessment of their bereavement needs. Blackman (2003) offers a useful framework for making a detailed assessment. In addition Elliott (2003) has devised a comprehensive bereavement assessment tool for people with learning disabilities. Areas which might be usefully and sensitively explored with the bereaved person with learning disabilities and their carers include:

- Current professional support on offer.
- Current health status of the bereaved person. Have any changes been noted following the death? Has the person additional complex care needs (e.g. mental health needs, autism) which need to be taken into account?
- Social relationships/support on offer.
- Cultural/religious factors which need to be taken into account.
- Participation by the bereaved person in rituals associated with the death (e.g. visiting the chapel of rest, attendance at the funeral).
- Other losses experienced by the bereaved person following the death.
- How well is the bereaved person coping with their loss? What stage are they at in the grieving cycle?

On the basis of this assessment, a decision can be made in conjunction with the person with learning disabilities about what, if any, bereavement intervention might be helpful. O'Driscoll offers the following taxonomy of helping (O'Driscoll, 1999; Young and Black, 1999).

- **Humanitarian**: Supporting and comforting the bereaved person with learning disabilities
- **Preventive**: Facilitating the grieving process
- **Therapeutic**: Working with pathological grief reactions

This taxonomy fits in with Cawley's (1977) levels of psychotherapy, as outlined by Hollins (2003). The aim of helping is to reduce the person's level of distress, and help them come to terms with their bereavement, thus enabling them to move on with life.

Developing a therapeutic alliance

When establishing a therapeutic alliance with a bereaved person with learning disabilities it is important to develop an 'emic' perspective rather than an 'etic' perspective (McNally, 2003; Goode, 1984). According to McNally (2003) an 'etic' perspective is 'how professionals believe the person with learning disabilities experiences the world'. In this case, how the professional bereavement counsellor believes the person is making sense of and coping with their bereavement. Whereas McNally (2003) recommends the development of an 'emic' perspective, which is 'understanding the person's own actual experience of reality' (Goode, 1984), in this case their bereavement. According to McNally (1999), this can only be achieved by knowing the person, through 'establishing a meaningful and mutual basis for their relationship' (Klotz, 2004). This takes time, commitment and great sensitivity on the part of the bereavement counsellor who is developing a therapeutic alliance.

An integrated model of helping

Elliott (1995, 2003) has outlined how Worden's (1991) task model of grief can be constructively used to support a bereaved person with learning disabilities. This model focuses primarily on loss-

Table 12.1 An integrated model of helping (Stroebe and Schut, 1999; Worden, 1991).

Loss-orientated aspects of grief	Restoration-orientated aspects of grief
Accepting the reality of the loss	Encourage person with learning disability to talk about the life changes following their loss
Experiencing the pain of grief	Identify new skills/hobbies developed by bereaved person with learning disabilities. Discuss daytime activities that the person is now engaged in.
Adjusting to an environment in which the deceased is missing	Explore with bereaved person with learning disabilities how their social world has changed
Emotionally relocating the deceased and moving on with life	Discuss with the person with learning disabilities new roles/relationships/identities developed following their loss

orientated aspects of grief, whereas Stroebe and Schut (1999) advocate that a healthy resolution of grieving involves oscillating between both loss-orientated and restoration-orientated aspects of grief in a dynamic and flexible manner. This process has been outlined in their dual process model of coping with bereavement (Stroebe and Schut, 1999). Loss orientation in this context involves helping the bereaved person with learning disabilities concentrate on their loss experience. Helping the person work through their grief is an important part of this process, whereas restoration orientation involves helping the person with learning disabilities adjust to their changed life situation following their loss. They are helped to solve new problems and fulfil new roles, and are supported when coping with changing routines and daily challenges. The person with learning disabilities is also encouraged to 'take time off' from their grief.

An integrated model of helping based on the dual process model of coping with bereavement (Stroebe and Schut, 1999) and Worden's (1991) task model of grief can be effectively used with bereaved people with learning disabilities (see Table 12.1).

The bereavement counsellor would help the bereaved person with learning disabilities to focus on both aspects of their grief. This would be facilitated in a dynamic manner, and would involve oscillation between both aspects. By doing so, this would help to ensure a healthy bereavement outcome for the person with learning disabilities.

Therapeutic narration

The bereaved person with learning disabilities is encouraged to narrate their loss story, during the therapeutic process. McCleod (2003) has described narration as 'a general process of creating an account of what has happened. A narrative may include several discrete stories, but may also include commentaries on these stories, linking passage and explanations'. Neimeyer and Anderson (2002) have identified three types of narration. They are:

- **External narratives**: Here the bereaved person with learning disabilities gives a clear and unambiguous account of what happened, for example events surrounding the death and funeral of the loved one. The bereavement counsellor might explore in greater detail certain aspects of the account which appear to have additional significance.
- **Internal narratives**: Here the focus is on the emotional response to the events being narrated. These responses might range from sadness and despair to anger. The bereavement counsellor might identify such responses either in language used (for example 'I felt sad...') or observe emotional reactions in the person (for example crying). These can be explored in greater depth by the bereavement counsellor.
- **Reflexive narratives**: These involve the bereaved person with learning disabilities attempting to make sense of their loss. Questions the bereaved person might ask include 'Am I partly to blame for the death of...?' and 'What does it all mean?'. The bereaved person might require a great deal of support as they work through these issues.

Neimeyer and Anderson (2002) suggest that 'people tack back and forth among these narrative forms, although different individuals often show a characteristic orientation toward one narrative process over others'. The bereaved person with learning disabilities will require sensitive support as they narrate their story.

Transference and countertransference

The bereavement counsellor needs to have an awareness and understanding of transference and countertransference issues. These are powerful feelings, rooted in psychoanalytic and psychodynamic approaches. Transference occurs when a person with learning disabilities 'displaces feelings onto the therapist, which derive from earlier relationships' (Blackman, 2003), whereas countertransference describes 'the conscious and unconscious reactions and feelings of the therapist to the patient and to the transferred feelings from the patient' (Blackman, 2003).

Ongoing clinical supervision is essential for the bereavement counsellor. It helps them reflect on very distressing life events and provides them with the opportunity to deal with feelings 'stirred' up by the counselling sessions (Lendrum and Syme, 1992), including those associated with transference and countertransference.

Case study

The following is a case study of a person I supported following a traumatic bereavement that he experienced. Certain biographical details have been changed in order to preserve the person's anonymity.

Biographical details

Mark and his partner Janet had mild learning disabilities, and had received support from the statutory agencies over many years. They lived in separate flats, which were located near to each other. Janet had found coping with life increasingly difficult and decided to take her own life one evening. Mark tragically found her body in her flat in the morning. He alerted the emergency services and assisted them in relation to the death of Janet. This involved assisting the paramedics and giving a statement to the police. I received a referral, requesting support for Mark, one month after Janet's death.

Assessing Mark's needs

I assessed Mark's bereavement needs using a variety of assessment tools, including one I had devised (Elliott, 2003). The assessment highlighted a number of health concerns. Mark informed me that he was seeing his general practitioner on a regular basis in relation to these. In addition the assessment highlighted that Mark was finding it very difficult coping with his loss and the emotions related to it.

Helping Mark

Mark gave me permission to offer him bereavement counselling and to inform his general practitioner of my intention. I undertook counselling with him over approximately 16 sessions, each of one hour duration. I utilised the integrated model of helping (Stroebe and Schut, 1999; Worden, 1991) in a very flexible and non-prescriptive way when supporting Mark. Whilst supporting him I acknowledged and respected his cultural, spiritual and religious beliefs.

After getting to know Mark, I focused on both loss-orientated and restoration-orientated aspects of his grief. I helped him move backwards and forwards between these components (i.e. oscillate) as delineated by the model.

The loss-orientated aspects of Mark's grief were:

- Helping him to focus on events surrounding Janet's death and her funeral. His telling of the story (narration) was essentially external in nature (Neimeyer and Anderson, 2002). He gave a graphic account of finding Janet's body and the ensuing events. He also gave a clear account of the funeral. Towards the end of his account it became reflexive in nature. He said he felt partly to blame for her death. I helped him reality-test his thoughts concerning this.
- Emotions associated with his loss. Mark felt a range of emotions following the death of Janet. These included profound sadness at her loss, anger towards the statutory services, guilt as a result of feeling partly to blame for her death, and fear for the future without his partner. I helped Mark ventilate his emotions and explore them in greater depth.
- I explored with Mark how he was coping following his bereavement: what tasks he was able to achieve, and what aspects of his life he had difficulty coping with.

- I helped Mark reminisce about Janet, using photographs and items which had special significance to him. This helped him relocate Janet in his emotional world (Worden, 2001).

The restoration-orientated aspects of Mark's grief were:

- Life changes that occurred to Mark following the death of Janet. These included shopping and cooking for himself. Also only having to think about himself, whereas before he had to think about Janet and her wishes.
- The development of new skills. Mark now had to deal with his daily finances, budgeting, paying bills and correspondence. Previously Janet had dealt with these tasks. We discussed ways in which Mark might be able to cope with these new challenges.
- Changes to his social world. I explored with Mark how he spent his time, and the people he visited following Janet's death.
- New roles and relationships. This involved highlighting new roles and relationships he had developed since his bereavement. New roles for Mark included cook, budgeter and shopper. In addition, Mark had started to visit his sister on a regular basis following Janet's death.

Additional support

Mark required additional support at times throughout the bereavement process. This was particularly the case when he was asked to attend the coroner's court, and also when the death of his partner was reported in the local newspaper.

Endings

Towards the end of the planned sessions, I informed Mark that the bereavement counselling would be coming to an end. I helped him identify his support networks, and who could provide him with ongoing support once the sessions had finished. Mark informed me that he had found the bereavement counselling very helpful, and felt he could move on with his life.

Reflection on the case study

Supporting Mark following the tragic death of his partner Janet was at times challenging and painful, yet very rewarding. At times Mark's grief appeared to overwhelm him, whilst at others he felt better able to cope, and be in control of his life. Two important events for Mark were the inquest at the coroner's court, and the positioning of the headstone at his partner's grave. For Mark these symbolised 'Janet lying at peace', and gave him partial closure to the tragic events he had experienced. As the counselling sessions progressed Mark appeared visibly to 'look better', although he will probably require practical support and help in the years ahead.

Conclusion

Oswin (2000) has stated that it is 'as if all our lives we are trying to cope with loss – either the fear of it, or the memory of it, or its raw immediate presence', and that includes the death of a loved one. Bereavement in the lives of people with learning disabilities poses and highlights many questions and challenges. In order to effectively address these bereavement needs professionals offering support need:

- An awareness of the life–death transition (Todd, 2004), and the ongoing support needs of the person with learning disabilities, their family, friends and carers.
- To offer both proactive and reactive bereavement support, by utilizing person centred plans and health action plans (Department of Health, 2001). These approaches can be used to map out anticipatory losses, and identify appropriate support.
- To be able to offer a 'continuum of bereavement support' (Read, 2005). This involves providing educational, participation, facilitation and therapeutic opportunities and interventions as and when required (Read, 2005).
- To provide a 'secure base' (Bowlby, 1988; Parkes, 1998a,b) for people with learning disabilities who are grieving. This involves identifying a professional who has the time, commitment and expertise to offer bereavement support in a respectful and valuing way.

By having these support systems in place, the bereaved person with learning disabilities will receive the appropriate help they require. The outcome of this support will hopefully be a healthy resolution of their grief, so they can carry on living in a meaningful way.

Acknowledgements

I would like to express my thanks to South Staffordshire Healthcare Trust for the support given to me in writing this chapter. In particular I would like to thank Mrs Judy Morris (Clinical Director – Learning Disabilities), Mrs Penny Pritchard (Clinical Co-ordinator – Learning Disabilities) and Mrs Sandra Brickley (Community Nurse Manager – Learning Disabilities) whose support I found invaluable.

Resources and contacts

The following resources and contacts might be of use to a professional supporting a bereaved person with learning disabilities.

Resources

Books Beyond Words series, in particular:

Hollins, S. and Sireling, L. (1991) *When Dad Died*. Books Beyond Words, St George's Hospital Medical School and Gaskell Press, London.
Hollins, S. and Sireling, L. (1991) *When Mum Died*. Books Beyond Words, St George's Hospital Medical School and Gaskell Press, London.
Both very useful books, to be used with parentally bereaved people with learning disabilities.

Blackman, N. (2003) *Loss and Learning Disability*. Worth Publishing, London.
This gives a very comprehensive overview of loss and learning disabilities. It also gives practical advice on how to support people at this time.

Oswin, M. (2000) *Am I Allowed to Cry?*, 2nd edn. Souvenir, London.
A ground breaking book in this historically neglected area.

Useful addresses

The National Network for the palliative care of people with learning disabilities – Co-ordinator Linda McEnhill. Telephone 01284 715578. Address: Head of Family Support, St Nicholas Hospice, MacMillan Way, Hardwick Lane, Bury St Edmunds, Suffolk.

In relation to death by suicide the following organisation can provide useful help and support:

Survivors of Bereavment by Suicide (S.O.B.S): National Office – 01482 610728; National Helpline – 0870 2413 337

Useful Web addresses include:

Bereavement And Learning Disabilities: http://www.bereavementanddisability.org.uk/
Learning about Intellectual Disabilities and Health: http://www.intellectualdisability.info/
The Arc: http://www.thearc.org/

References

Bicknell, D. J. (1983) Inaugural lecturel: the psychopathology of handicap. *British Journal of Medical Psychology*, **56**, 167–78.
Blackman, N. (2003) *Loss and Learning Disability*. Worth Publishing, London.

Bonell-Pascual, E., Huline-Dickens, S., Hollins, S., Esterhuyzen, A., Sedwick, P., Abdelnoor, A. and Hubert, J. (1999). Bereavement and grief in adults with learning disabilities: a follow-up study. *British Journal of Psychiatry*, **175**, 348–50.

Bowlby, J. (1988) *A Secure Base: Clinical Applications of Attachment Theory*. Routledge, London.

Cawley, R. H. (1977) The teaching of psychotherapy. *Association of University Teachers of Psychiatry Newsletter*, January, 19–36.

Conboy-Hill, S. (1992) Grief, loss and people with learning disabilities. In: Psychotherapy and Mental Handicap (eds. A. Waitman and S. Conboy-Hill). Sage, London.

Cook, A. S. and Oltjenbruns, K. A. (1998) *Dying and Grieving. Life Span and Family Perspectives*, 2nd edn. Harcourt Brace College Publisher, Fort Worth.

Department of Health (1999) *Once a Day One or More People with Learning Disabilities Are Likely to Be in Contact with Your Primary Healthcare Team. How Can You Help Them?* Department of Health, London.

Department of Health (2001) *Valuing People: a New Strategy for Learning Disability for the 21st Century*. Department of Health, London.

Doka, K. (1989) *Disenfranchised Grief: Recognising Hidden Sorrow*. Lexington Books, Toronto.

Doka, K. (1999) Disenfranchised grief. *Bereavement Care*, **18**(3), 37–9.

Dowling, S., Hubert, J. and Hollins, S. (2003) Bereavement interventions for people with learning disabilities. 'My mother's name was Marjorie'. *Bereavement Care*, **22**(2), 19–21.

Elliott, D. (1995) Helping people with learning disabilities to handle grief. *Nursing Times*, 25 October, pp. 26–9.

Elliott, D. (2003) Loss and bereavement. In: Contemporary Learning Disabilities Practice (eds. M. Jukes and M. Bollard). Quay Books, Wiltshire.

Gallagher, D., Breckenridge, J., Thompson, L. W. and Peterson, J. A. (1983). Effects of bereavement on indicators of mental health in elderly widows and widowers. *Journal of Gerontology*, **38**, 565–71.

Goode, D. A. (1984) Socially produced identities, intimacy and the problem of competence among the retarded. In: Special Education and Social Interests (eds. L. Barton and S. Tomlinson). Croom Helm, London.

Helsing, K., Comstock, G. and Szklo, M. (1982) Causes of death in a widowed population. *American Journal of Epidemiology*, **116**, 524–32.

Hollins, S. (2003) Counselling and psychotherapy. In: *Seminars in the Psychiatry of Learning Disabilities* (eds. W. Fraser and M. Kerr). Gaskell, London.

Hollins, S. and Esterhuyzen, A. (1997) Bereavement and grief in adults with learning disabilities. *British Journal of Psychiatry*, **170**, 497–501.

Hollins, S. and Grimer, M. (1988) *Going Somewhere: People with Mental Handicaps and their Pastoral Care*. SPCK, London.

Jacobs, S. (1993) *Pathologic Grief: Maladaptation to Loss*. American Psychiatric Press, Washington DC.

Kaprio, J., Koskenvuo, M. and Rita, H. (1987) Mortality after bereavement: A prospective study of 95,647 widowed persons. *American Journal of Public Health*, **77**, 283–7.

Klotz, J. (2004) Sociocultural study of intellectual disability: moving beyond labelling and social constructionist perspectives. *British Journal of Learning Disabilities*, **32**(2), 93–104.

Lendrum, S. and Syme, G. (1992) *Gift of Tears*. Routledge, London.

McCleod, J. (2003) *An Introduction to Counselling*. Open University Press, Berkshire.

McNally, S. (1999) Professionals and user self-advocacy. In: *Professionalism, Boundaries and the Workplace* (ed. N. Malin), pp. 47–64. Routledge, London.

McNally, S. (2003) Helping to empower people. In: *Learning Disabilities Toward Inclusion* (ed. B. Gates). Churchill Livingstone, Edinburgh.

Mellström, D., Nilsson, A., Oden, A., Rundaren, A. and Svanborg, A. (1982) Mortality among the widowed in Sweden. *Scandinavian Journal of Social Medicine*, **10**, 33–41.

Neimeyer, R. A. and Anderson, A. (2002) Meaning reconstruction theory. In: *Loss and Grief: A Quick Guide for Human Service Practitioners* (ed. N. Thompson). Palgrave, Basingstoke.

O'Driscoll, D. (1999) The six-week therapeutic assessment. In: *Living with Loss: Helping People with Learning Disabilities Cope with Bereavement and Loss* (ed. N. Blackman). Pavilion, Brighton.

Oswin, M. (1991) *Am I Allowed to Cry? A Study of Bereavement Amongst People Who Have Learning Difficulties*. Souvenir, London.

Oswin, M. (2000) *Am I Allowed to Cry?*, 2nd edn. Souvenir, London.

Parkes, C. M. (1998a) Coping with loss: bereavement in adult life. *British Medical Journal*, **316**, 856–9.

Parkes, C. M. (1998b) Coping with loss: facing loss. *British Medical Journal*, **316**, 1521–4.

Raji, O., Hollins, S. and Drinnan, A. (2003) How far are people with learning disabilities involved in funeral rites? *British Journal of Learning Disabilities*, **31**(1), 42–5.

Rando, T. A. (1984) *Grief, Dying and Death: Clinical Interventions for Caregivers*. Research Press, Champaign, IL.

Read, S. (1996) Helping people with learning disabilities to grieve. *British Journal of Nursing*, **5**, 91–5.

Read, S. (2003) Bereavement and loss. In: *Learning Disabilities: Themes and Perspectives* (eds. A. Markwick and A. Parrish). Butterworth Heinemann, Edinburgh.

Read, S. (2005) Loss, bereavement and learning disabilities: Providing a continuum of support. *Learning Disability Practice*, **8**(1), 31–7.

Stroebe, M. and Schut, H. (1999) The dual process model of coping with bereavement. Rationale and description. *Death Studies*, **23**(3), 197–225.

Stroebe, M. and Stroebe, W. (1993) The mortality of bereavement: a review. In: *Handbook of Bereavement: Theory, Research and Intervention* (eds. M. Stroebe, W. Stroebe and R. Hansson). Cambridge University Press, Cambridge.

Todd, S. (2004) Death counts: the challenge of death and dying in learning disability services. *Learning Disability Practice*, **7**(10), 12–15.

Worden, J. W. (1991) *Grief Counselling and Grief Therapy: A Handbook for the Mental Health Practitioner*, 2nd edn. Tavistock Routledge, London.

Worden, J. W. (2001) *Grief Counselling and Grief Therapy: A Handbook for the Mental Health Practitioner*, 3rd edn. Brunner-Routledge, East Sussex.

Young, B. and Black, D. (1997) Bereavement counselling. In: *Psychological Trauma. A Development Approach* (eds. D. Black, M. Newman, J. Harris-Hendriks and G. Mezey). Gaskell, London.

Zisook, S., Mulvihill, M. and Shuchter S. R. (1990) Widowhood and anxiety. *Psychiatric Medicine*, **8**(4).

CHAPTER 13

Neuro-Linguistic Programming: therapeutic magic or a model for successful human communication?

John Anstey

Introduction

Neuro-Linguistic Programming (NLP) concerns itself with the structure of human subjective experience and how we organise what we see, hear and feel, as well as how we edit and filter the outside world through our senses. NLP explores how we describe our experience, the language we use and our resulting behaviour, both intentional and unintentional (O'Connor & Seymour, 2002). It should be noted that NLP has not been without its critics. Hostility has been levelled towards claims of therapeutic magic and assertions that NLP can achieve accelerated and more effective change (or cures), which will be covered later in this chapter.

Recognising that NLP expressions can be less than reader-friendly, O'Connor and Seymour (2002) assist with demystifying the somewhat cumbersome terminology:

'**Neuro**' acknowledges the idea that our behaviour stems from our five neurological processes of sight, sound, smell, taste and touch. We experience 'our' world through these processes and literally make 'sense' of information received through our central nervous system from the outside world and act upon it. Our neurology, it is argued, covers more than just our invisible thought processes. Our visible physiological reactions to ideas and events are also encompassed and one simply reflects the other at a physical level. Body and mind forming an inseparable unity, freeing us to explore our spirit.

'**Linguistic**' refers to our language and system of communication. It indicates that we use language to order our thoughts and behaviour and as a means of communicating with others. In a sense, the way we perceive the outside world is coded and transmitted through language.

The '**Programming**' element refers to the choices we make in organising our ideas and actions in order to produce results. We therefore interact in systems and our experiences are made up of sequences (or programmes).

Historical perspectives and key features

It is some 30 years since Richard Bandler and John Grinder introduced the intriguing notion of NLP, during which they have enjoyed something amounting to guru status from followers of the NLP approach to enhancing quality of life.

The two NLP originators studied three highly regarded therapists. Fritz Perls, an innovative *Gestalt* therapist; Virginia Satir, an extraordinarily successful family therapist; and Milton Erickson, a world-renowned hypnotherapist, were observed to have an extraordinary ability to communicate and 'tune in' with their clients. Bandler and Grinder, it is suggested, had no intention of starting a new school of theory or therapy, but rather sought to identify successful patterns used by outstanding therapists that could be modelled and taught.

O'Connor and Seymour (2002) highlight the 'profound' contribution of British anthropologist and writer Gregory Bateson. Bateson also happened to introduce Bandler and Grinder to 'this strange old guy' (Milton Erickson), who he said was, 'a brilliant therapist, but nobody knows what he's doing or how he does it'! Other significant influences and 'co-developers' include Alfred Korzybski, Noam Chomsky, Leslie Cameron, Judith Delozier, Robert Dilts, David Gordon and Tad James.

It has also been suggested that NLP was designed to fill the gap in psychological thinking due to the shortcomings within the classical, theoretical schools of thought (O'Connor and McDermott 2001). The latter assert that the value-based psychological systems were conspicuously missing out in respect of the 'how to' – the capability level – and that NLP stepped into this gap by providing step-by-step procedures, making excellence or simply improvement easily learnable.

As NLP techniques have developed, two concepts have remained constant: firstly, the question of how people do what they do, and secondly, the continued search for excellence in order to model it, use it and increase elements of choice. NLP involves practical skills aimed at achieving favourable results while creating value for individuals in the process. Successful techniques have been developed for education, counselling, business, sales and therapy. Andreas and Andreas (1990) also reference the use of NLP in nursing, sports and medicine, where it is claimed to achieve more effective communication, personal development and accelerated learning. Many NLP techniques make useful 'tool kit' additions for practitioners working in mental health and learning disability services, helping to pursue a deeper understanding in order to bring about tangible improvements in those we provide care for.

Presuppositions

In NLP terms, presuppositions could be described as 'basic operating instructions' (O'Connor and McDermott, 2001). When we presuppose things we act as if they are true and then take note of our findings. This is a kind of working hypothesis where 'Is this useful?' is deemed more relevant than 'Is this true?'. Some commonly used presuppositions include:

- Every behaviour serves a positive intent
- People may have all the resources they need

- The meaning of a communication is the response you get
- Nothing has any meaning except the meaning we give it
- It is not possible to not communicate
- The map is not the territory
- There is feedback rather than failure
- Choices are made with the best available resources at the time
- The mind and body form a unified system
- When you know how to listen words have more meaning.

It should perhaps be noted that some of the aforementioned have a well-worn flavour and can be a source of irritation when offered as a casual linear explanation of human experience.

Representational systems

This is described as the processing system used to engage a particular sensory modality during our moment-to-moment experiences, and over time to code, store and retrieve personal information (Bailey, 1997). The sensory modalities through which we take in and make sense of information are said to be predominantly visual, auditory or kinaesthetic (the latter applies to touch). These are described as the 'primary' representational systems. The missing senses of taste (gustatory) and smell (olfactory) are included in the kinaesthetic sense where they serve as powerful and immediate links to sounds and pictures associated with them (O'Connor and Seymour, 2002).

An individual's preferred words or predicates (e.g. verbs, adverbs and adjectives) are thought to be primarily visual, auditory or kinaesthetic (VAK), and by listening carefully to these predicates we should learn much about the sensory components of their experience and be able to tell in which modality the individual is representing their world. The following examples illustrate how we might respond to an individual in the three modalities:

Auditory – 'I can *HEAR* what you're *SAYING* and it *SOUNDS* as if you would like to *TELL* me more about not being *LISTENED* to.'

Visual – 'I can *SEE* it from your *PERSPECTIVE* and it *LOOKS* as though you'd like to *REVEAL* more about your own *POINT* of *VIEW*.'

Kinesthetic – 'I can *GRASP* that it *TOUCHES* on a *RAW NERVE* when you sense you're being *HANDED* little opportunity to express more of your *FEELINGS*.'

The most effective communicators are highly proficient in all three modalities and can move from one to another at will and with ease. It should be noted, however, that no individual is totally auditory, visual or kinesthetic, but each of us has a favoured system (Dailey-Knowles, 1983) and it is perhaps no coincidence that we each have favoured learning styles. As predicate-matching skills are developed it is possible to make powerful moves towards greater communication and rapport as we begin to literally speak our client's language.

Here are some other examples of sensory-based predicates:

V	A	K
picture	vocal	stuck
observe	talk	hold
show	speak	do
sight	discuss	firm
appear	ask	grip
watch	told	sore
focus	echo	catch
image	call	heavy
visualise	voiced	contact
glimpse	audible	hurt
scene	enquire	stress
insight	overtone	sensitive
frame	eavesdrop	abreast
reflect	earful	numbed
review	unheard	pressure
notice	outspoken	heated
outlook	rings	cool
illusion	harmonise	tackle
transparent	resonate	arouse
snapshot	tune	relaxed

Predicates therefore are not metaphorical when they are sensory related, and if someone says, 'It *appears* quite wrong to me', they are likely to be making meaning by accessing internal pictures. Likewise, if someone says, 'It *sounds* good to me' they are representing information to themselves auditorily, or if they say 'It *feels* the right thing to do' they are acting kinaesthetically.

Submodalities

Submodalities are subclassifications within each sensory system associated with qualities of internal representations such as colour, brightness, distance, position, volume, pitch, pressure, temperature, intensity and duration (Bailey, 1997). As we will discover, these universal elements (Bandler, 1985) can be changed to great advantage.

Character types

Grinder and Bandler (1976) proposed a kind of character profile of the favoured representational systems. These might already be predictable to the reader. The Visual person often stands or sits with their head and body erect, with eyes upwards and breathing from the top of their lungs. They often sit forward in chairs and have a tendency to be neat, organised, well-groomed and orderly. They memorise by seeing pictures and are less distracted by noise. They experience difficulty in remembering verbal instructions, as their minds tend to wander. Visual people will be interested in how your programme looks, because appearances are important to them.

The auditory person will tend to move their eyes sideways and breath from the middle of their chest. They typically chat to themselves, even moving their lips to do so, and are easily distracted by noise. Things can be repeated back with relative ease and they learn by listening. Music and telephone conversations are enjoyed and there is a tendency to memorise by means of steps, procedures and sequences. They like to be told how they are progressing and respond to certain tones of voice or sets of words. The auditory person will be interested in what you have to say about your programme.

The kinaesthetic person typically breaths from the bottom of their lungs; therefore the stomach tends to move in and out as they breath. They are likely to move and talk slowly, are tactile and may have a tendency to look down. They respond to physical rewards and it is suggested that they are likely to stand closer to people than, say, a visual person might. The kinaesthetic person will be interested in your programme if it feels right.

Bandler and Grinder also proposed the 'auditory digital' profile. They suggest that people who fit this spend considerable time talking to themselves. The auditory digital person can exhibit characteristics of the other representational systems and will want to know if your programme makes sense. OK, hands up...?!

Matching a person's style of verbalising thoughts and emotions therefore has little to do with magic and everything to do with demonstrating a level of empathy. What is different is the deliberate analysis of the client's speech in order to discover their primary representational system.

Eye accessing cues

As indicated above, In addition to listening out for predicates Bandler and Grinder (1990) provided us with another means of determining whether a person is thinking in terms of pictures, sounds or feelings. They invite us to take part in an exercise aimed at demonstrating that we move our eyes in different directions when we are thinking in certain representational systems and we are able to determine unequivocally which internal system is being utilised at any given point in time by observing these directions.

As we face a normally organised right-handed person (Figure 13.1) the visual accessing cues are likely to be looking upwards, or possibly the eyes may be defocused (usually straight ahead and will not move). In the case of the latter it has been suggested that by observing which side of the body moves, we are also able to determine whether the dominant or non-dominant hemisphere of the brain is being activated. If the person looks up and to *their* left (visual remembered) this indicates that they are visualising something that they have seen before. Looking up to the right (visual constructed) indicates they are visualising something that has not been seen before, or perhaps picturing something differently, e.g. what a camel with three humps might look like or their house painted a different colour.

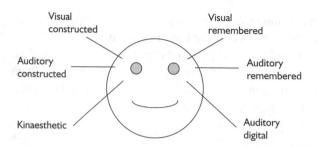

Figure 13.1 Eye cues.

If the eyes move from side to side the person is likely to be listening to or remembering words or sounds. If they move towards the left ear (auditory remembered) the person is hearing sounds that have been heard before; movement towards the right ear (auditory constructed) indicates imagining either a sound that has not been heard before or perhaps one that has, but in a different way.

Another auditory cue involves the person looking down towards their non-dominant hand, and on this cue (auditory digital) it is suggested that internal dialogue is taking place where the person is discussing sounds, words etc. A person looking down towards their dominant hand indicates a kinaesthetic accessing cue whereby they are likely to be experiencing feelings, emotions and sensations relating to touch. As previously mentioned, this could also involve smell and taste.

There are certain pitfalls that are likely to be encountered, such as using words that are unspecified in NLP language. Otherwise they assert that such observations constitute a powerful source of information about a person's unconscious processes, and even with inconsistencies (say, looking upwards for feelings and down for pictures) eye movements will be systematic for *them* at that time. I recall an example of this when asking a client what the colour of their front door was. The information, 'A kind of mushroom' was accessed following an auditory remembered cue, to which I enquired, 'That sounds an interesting colour?'. The client responded with 'The painter advised me on what colour to have'. She was remembering his description before actually picturing the door, which we might not have expected. A word of caution here: do guard against being a smart-alec – it's not a stage show.

Meta model

O'Connor and Seymour (2002) describe this as a model that identifies language patterns which obscure meaning in a communication through a process of generalisation, deletion and distortion (GDD). It provides a systematic way of gathering information in order to determine more precisely what someone means and promotes the use of precise words that will have meaning in the other person's 'map'. NLP asserts that language exists at a deep, unconscious level (deep structure) and we shorten our explanations to be clearer and succinct (surface structure).

A person's model of the world evolves as a result of these three universal modelling processes, and because individuals generalise, distort and delete they may not realise the several meanings that could be associated with a set of 'facts' (Pesut, 1991). The meta model therefore seeks to unravel language, fill in missing information, reshape the structure and elicit information in order to make sense of what is communicated (O'Connor and Seymour, 2002).

Generalisation is a process by which our model becomes detached from the original experience and comes to represent the entire category of which the experience is an example. *Deletion* is a process by which we selectively pay attention to certain dimensions of our experience and exclude others. *Distortion* is a process by which we are able to make shifts in our experience of sensory data.

Generalisation, deletion and distortion can be further broken down into subsets or patterns. In my introduction I referenced the fact that NLP expressions can be cumbersome. I will endeavour to keep the terminology simple, as some descriptions add little in terms of the reader's understanding. I can recall the effect these had on me! Generalisation, deletion and distortion have also been described as the three gatekeepers at the doors of perception (O'Connor and McDermott, 2001). It is also suggested that these gatekeepers are both an asset and a liability. If we did not delete sensory information we would be overwhelmed, but we might delete something of great significance, such as important feedback from others. Likewise, if we did not distort we would be stifling our creativity, but if, through distortion, we decide that a communication received is unfriendly we run the risk of our response being equally unfriendly. Generalisations are a fundamental part of learning, but what if we decided that, based on a difficult relationship, all men or all women are the same and shouldn't be trusted?

Have you ever been astonished by someone's response when you thought you were being really sensitive? Perhaps your own understanding of some comment turned out to be other than what was intended (Figure 13.2). O'Connor and McDermott (2001) point out that when we com-

Figure 13.2 The pitfalls of mismatch.

Figure 13.3 The meaning in a communication is the response that you get.

municate something we cannot decide what the signal will actually mean to the recipient, only what we intended it to mean. The message that we put across may not be what was intended, but if we pay close attention to the other person's response and be guided by it (i.e. 'How am I triggering this behaviour?') we can avoid the need to mind-read (a distortion) and prevent misunderstandings. Hence the meaning of the communication is the response you get (Figure 13.3).

The meta model is considered a powerful way of gathering information and creating more choices by clarifying meanings and identifying limits in an individual's thinking. Indeed, questions are interventions and can take a person's mind in new, life-changing directions (O'Connor and Seymour, 2002). The latter add a caution in that questions need to be in keeping with mutually agreed outcomes and within a context of rapport, as we will discover. They also point out that repeated questions could be experienced as aggressive and too direct. Therefore instead of asking, 'How specifically do you know that?' a preferable question might be, 'I'm curious to know exactly how you knew that?'. Rapport-enhancing skills will also assist this process, as will guarding against being a meta model bore – some have been known to experience difficulty in this regard!

Rapport

If NLP was used only for enhancing rapport it would still be justified as an adjunct to therapy – indeed, rapport first, last and always (Bailey, 1997). During the early development of NLP it was noted that people who are in deep rapport with each other match one another non-verbally. Two people sitting, deeply involved in a café, for example are often seen to be matching body posture, voice tone and tempo. The smooth communication cycle is interrupted if one or the other suddenly alters the tempo or volume (Andreas and Andreas, 1990) or indeed if they opt to answer their mobile phone. The effect can be quite startling! There is a similar effect if someone is, say, tapping their foot or tapping on a table too quickly (faster than the speech rhythm). In many respects the notion of rapport should feature first in an NLP text, but the 'tuning-in' process seems to makes more sense after interrelated elements have been described. A colleague once said that it grates if you're not in rapport (Gasson, 1995). It certainly can – as the reader will know if you've ever felt rushed into making a comment because the other person is saying, 'Mmm, mmm, yeah, yeah, yeah...' etc.!

In NLP terms rapport is used to describe a relationship of trust and responsiveness and an ability to meet individuals in their model of the world. We are all unique individuals with different beliefs, capabilities and identities (O'Connor and McDermott, 2001). In order to understand an individual, NLP emphasises the importance of joining them in their world because people operate as if their model is the real world itself and understanding is the crucial bridge between our model of the world and theirs. This does not mean that we agree with their model, but the rapport we have aims to create an ideal climate for growth and change (Lewis and Pucelick, 1982). Bateson (1972) illustrated the distinction between 'reality' and our models with his menu card analogy. If a menu card in a restaurant merely represents the food, we might consider the menu to be a model or map of reality. However, if we decided to treat the menu like we often treat our own models of the world (as actual reality) we would begin to eat the menu. We mistake map for territory; hence 'the map is not the territory'. Our models of the world are not constructed in a haphazard or disorganised way. Indeed, we are highly efficient in the way we make sense of information from our experiences, how we form building blocks and how we operate our filtering processes (Lewis and Pucelick, 1982). As Richard Bandler noted 'people work perfectly'. They or we might not like what is happening, but they can repeat things systematically. They're not broken; they're doing things differently and may need to change.

We build rapport on many different levels. As previously mentioned, three master communicators, Satir, Perls and Erickson, demonstrated a quite natural ability in being able to behave in ways that their clients interpreted as familiar and friendly. This was achieved by matching the client's own position, not in an obvious imitative fashion but in a gradual respectful and natural way (Dailey-Knowles, 1983). Virginia Satir sat like her clients, breathed with them, matched their blink rate, tone of voice and movements. The distinction between mirroring and matching is that *matching* focuses on adopting another's behaviour with the intention of enhancing rapport, whilst *mirroring* is a more precise (mirror image) matching of certain portions of behaviour such as tapping the index finger of the right hand if the client was tapping their left (Bailey, 1997). *Crossover mirroring* refers to the matching of another's body language with a different type of movement, such as tapping your foot in time with a client's speech rhythm. *Pacing* is the term given to the gaining and maintaining of rapport with another person over a period of time by joining them in their model of the world. Erickson's two favourite maxims were 'join the patient' and 'speak in the patient's language' (Rosen, 1991). You can pace beliefs and ideas as well as behaviour (O'Connor and Seymour, 2002). Body language, voice tonality, matching predicates whilst respecting beliefs, values, moods and interest are all a feature. *Leading* refers to the therapist changing their behaviour with sufficient rapport for the client to follow, leading to new possibilities. Leading cannot work without the rapport of pacing. Ultimately, we achieve mutual orientation by using the client's sensory representational language, their eye movements, body language, and tonality (Bailey, 1997). Erickson was able to lead his patients deeper into their own internal reality and was therefore able to access unconscious resources by distracting the conscious mind. He also used open, permissive, vague language and metaphors. Erickson's body language, voice tonality and ability to mark sections of his speech (through change of pitch or hesitation) aided his ability to lead. Essentially, his approach enabled therapists to learn about clients' background, culture and areas of 'stuckness' as well as desires, goals, strengths and talents, ultimately understanding the person as a total psychosocial–spiritual–sociocultural being with values and behaviours in concert with that wholeness (Zahourek, 2002).

Erickson used metaphors and story telling *per se* to great effect, and if we decide to build, say, an outcome-orientated therapeutic metaphor we do need to ensure that it suits the clients cognitive map. Bailey (1997) asserts that metaphors pervade our conscious awareness and are woven into our lives at every level. They are designed to bypass our conscious understanding as their meaning enters our unconscious mind.

Rapport comes from showing others by our behaviour that we accept the validity of *their* experience. By doing so we create a basis for cooperative communication, which is not the same as agreeing with their world view. We can disagree and still remain in rapport (McDermott and Jago, 2001) and should find that competing perspectives will be more readily accepted. Rapport is a powerful tool, which earns you the rights to influence others. Otherwise we are simply being authoritative rather than working with our client's map of reality. It should be emphasised that in terms of achieving favourable outcomes there are huge benefits in being able to establish good relationships with our clients, as opposed to hiding behind the trappings of power roles and assumed professional expertise.

Reframing

Reframing is a way of changing the reference orientation of the client in order that they experience a different meaning for the same referent (Bailey, 1997). Bailey points out that provided the rapport is good, sensory-based reframing (working with the client's representation of reality) perceptions can be nudged in very different directions. As we will see with the case of Tim, changing the frame in which events are perceived changes the meaning and the person's responses.

Anchoring

Our 'state' will be associated with or changed by certain stimuli as we react to our environments. O'Connor and McDermott (2001) point out that the sight of a newborn baby, the sound of an advertising jingle, the feel of a handshake, the smell of flowers or a certain taste can evoke specific feelings and memories. This may trigger a rapidly received response (Bailey, 1997) where an internal state is accessed (sensory experience – thought processing – physiology). We seldom choose the anchors that access associations and memories because this is outside of our conscious awareness. We can, however, set or 'fire' sensory (VAK) anchors in order to produce resource states in a different context, which is a relatively simple but powerful process. O'Connor and McDermott (2001) provide us with a simple exercise aimed at anchoring a resourceful state:

- Decide what state you want (i.e. facing a new challenge with humour or patience).
- Remember a time when you had this very state (see what you saw, hear what you heard and get the feeling back as strongly as possible).
- Change state by coming back to the present (this is best achieved by moving position).
- Decide what associations (anchors) you want to trigger the state (a visual anchor – something that can be visualised in your mind's eye; an auditory anchor – a sound that can be repeated to yourself; an inconspicuous kinesthetic anchor – digital pressure, say, on one of your knuckles.
- Go back and fully experience that resource state and just before it peaks, see the picture, hear the sound and apply the digital pressure.
- Break state again and change physiology by thinking of something else.
- Now test the anchors. See the picture, hear the sound and apply the digital pressure and notice the return of the resource state. This can be repeated until total satisfaction with the anchors is achieved.

It may not be necessary to use all three anchors. One might be fine. Favoured representational systems will determine what will work best. We can teach our clients how to use this process, and changing states can produce life-changing, control-gaining behaviours.

NLP practitioners working in mental health and learning disability fields may decide to assist this process by applying the kinaesthetic anchor to the client themselves. This would occur after observing the client's physiology and when we link observable states in this way it is referred to as *calibration*. The anchor would be set after noticing the strong positive experience. This process sometimes involves setting negative anchors beforehand, and anchors can also be '*chained*', and '*stacked*'. NLP texts tend not to reference the fact that we should never touch our clients without their express permission, and practitioners should carefully consider whether this is necessary or whether we can assist the client in setting their own anchors. These are issues that need to be considered in a broader context of reflective enquiry within clinical supervision, which is an integral part of our clinical practice and our decision-making duties towards safe and effective care.

Ecology – a caution

In our assessment of clients it is crucial to understand precisely why change needs to be affected, i.e. what purpose it would serve, what will happen if you change, what will happen if you don't change etc. Again, when someone suggests that part of them is uncomfortable, this may not be metaphorical. An ecology check is essential, as change can affect a person's sense of reality. If we agree that someone needs to be more assertive it would not be deemed a positive outcome if they began alienating all of their friends. When deeply in rapport we can ask if any 'part' of the client might object to the intended change/new choices. Our calibrating skills need to be sensitive to any signal of disapproval because when we tap into someone's web of meanings we may be challenging all their cherished beliefs and values. Bandler and Grinder's (1990) suggestion that a 'part' might not want the conscious mind to be aware of something (in case it couldn't handle it) was emphasised with the example of a lady who successfully lost weight but couldn't maintain her progress. No part of this lady objected to losing weight, but one part did fear that she might become physically attractive and might not trust herself to remain faithful to her husband. Therefore part of her used being overweight to protect her marriage. Hence being overweight was 'working'! Remember, all behaviour serves a positive intent, where secondary considerations can become a feature when a new resource is acquired. Rebalancing can occur quite naturally, but secondary outcomes or 'gain' can become an obstacle to change. If change fits the ecology it is likely to be smooth and permanent.

Case illustration – the case of Tim

Principles and key features are often best brought to life by way of an illustration covering all concepts. Figure 13.4 considers the broader elements of a responsive psychosocial NLP assessment, and the following case example integrates the NLP system. Verbatim narrative has been edited to capture only the elemental dialogue.

Assessment – some considerations

Colleagues working within mental health and learning disability fields would undoubtedly emphasise the importance (a generalisation I know!) of the assessment process. Yet closer inspection of some practice might often reveal this to be a separate entity that precedes something that may or may not be offered. With some assessments the therapy or change process might not be deemed to have started. Less still, that the assessment process might be deemed an intervention in its own right. When someone walks through the door I believe a therapy of sorts has already begun, rather than this idea that we are engaging in some kind of pre-meeting. It might not work for everyone, but it can be pleasantly surprising to see a favourable 'shift' in someone's thinking during an initial meeting and feel that this is sufficient in order for them to depart and build on the change that is already occurring – a point not lost on some healthcare professionals in Birmingham.

A piece of work around person-centred psychological therapies (Anstey and Mattis, 1999) highlighted the need for a skills development programme for the benefit of primary care. GPs and practice nurses were particularly attracted by techniques that had a favourable impact despite time constraints as they could be utilised during brief consultations. In terms of effecting change within the cognitive-behavioural domain, a reframe, metaphor or some respectful challenging whilst in rapport can certainly be very useful. We also discovered that successful outcomes did not necessarily depend on deploying carefully crafted methods of intervention. Listening, reflecting, reframing, and discovering strategic, pragmatic solutions (informed by expectation and client world view) could form the base from which all interventions are delivered and may of themselves

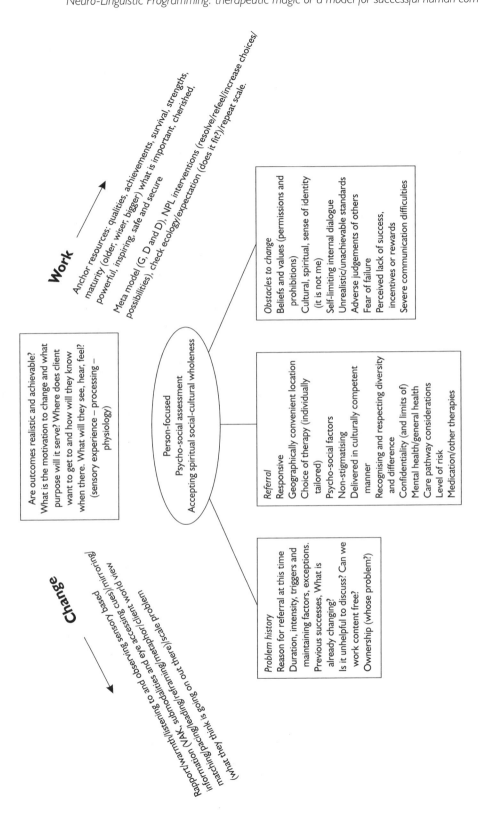

Figure 13.4 Elements of a responsive psychosocial NLP assessment.

prove sufficient for life event-related psychological distress.

Again, remember questions are also interventions. The meta model is a powerful way of gathering information, meaning and insights into the limits of someone's thinking. Obtaining the desired state of someone who is dissatisfied may be crucial to a successful outcome (What would they rather have? Where would they rather be? How would they rather be feeling?).

The case of Tim

Tim (anonymity protected) had been referred by his GP, who had diagnosed Tim as suffering from post-traumatic stress disorder (PTSD) characterised by a phobia of gas appliances, severe anxiety and flashbacks. The GP described Tim as a pleasant but troubled figure with a learning disability. His mental health problems were seemingly impacting on family relationships.

On the day of our initial contact I approached Tim in the waiting room and introduced myself (I warmly greet clients, thank them for attending and ask if they found our location OK – was the map helpful? It is pure folly not to take some time in putting service users at their ease in order to get them over the initial threshold. On this occasion I also had to ask if a colleague who had recently joined the team and was undergoing an induction programme could sit in on the session. Many readers will identify with this situation, especially having increased numbers of students 'in tow'. It goes with the territory in health and social care, and the pros, cons and dilemmas have been well debated. I think it is unfair to ask the client in front of the person who would like to join the session – this is additional pressure they can possibly manage without. Therefore I always provide an option ahead of introductions.

As it turned out, Tim had no difficulty with my colleague joining us ('two for the price of one' he suggested. 'We could probably throw in a third', I replied!). It has been suggested that humour should not always be utilised as it can either enhance or destroy relationships (Mackay, 1989). This is a risk I intuitively balance, and as Andreas and Andreas (1990) point out, humour can be of strategic use if we need to dissociate from a problem.

JA: 'Have a seat Tim. Anywhere is fine... make yourself comfortable. Well, as comfortable as you can in our every-expense-spared chairs' (there I go again!). 'Tim, there are different types of therapy available and we can discuss the choices that you have, but I just wondered if it might be helpful to remind ourselves why your GP asked us to see you and then perhaps you can let me know in your own words what's been happening.'

TIM: 'That's OK.' (*After* concurring with the content of the referral from his GP – clients certainly don't always – Tim explains what's been happening. He explains that he can't see an end to his suffering. He is anxious all the time and can't concentrate on anything. He has been arguing with his wife and Tim thinks that she may even leave him.)

TIM: 'I never get things right. My Mrs shouts at me all the time. She doesn't have time for me anymore. If she knew what I was going through she wouldn't do it. I hope you can help me. Things just seem to get worse. It started last year after I had my accident at work when a furnace exploded. My face, neck and hands were burnt...'

I am aware that Tim has been uncomfortable since he arrived. He has remained on the edge of his seat, firmly gripping the arms of the chair. In an attempt to begin mirroring and matching portions of Tim's behaviour, I had also remained on the edge of my chair and in a subtle fashion had begun gripping my legs. When he frowned so did I. He began to loosen the collar of his shirt at which point, I held my chin (again, in subtle not imitative fashion). I matched his speech rhythm and began to notice that my responses, verbal and non-verbal, were making him more relaxed, and we were both gradually sitting further back in the chair. I was aware that Tim's favoured representational system was visual. The directional movements of my eyes were also reflecting those of Tim's. I took an opportunity to ask Tim where he saw himself on a scale of 1–10 (10 being good) and he estimated around 3. With this kind of scaling, solution-focused therapists would enquire what would be happening in order to get to 4, but I simply require his own subjective measure.

As we can see, open 'grand-tour' questions like 'what's happening?' are useful in terms of gathering information but there are pitfalls. Tim kind of blurted it all out and I noticed that Tim was able to repeat his thoughts and feelings verbatim, which I found both resourceful and helpful. He repeated his plight about four times in all and each time more slowly, which provided an opportunity to consider some meta model 'violations'. Now, if we consider Tim's language there is a considerable volume to pick up on during the 60 or so words that he used.

TIM: 'Things just seem to get worse for me.' (This deletion includes not being specific and omitting the standard of comparison).

JA: 'How exactly is this happening, Tim, and worse than what?'

TIM: 'I keep going through this horrible experience where I keep seeing the accident.'

JA: 'Hmmm, Tim, it *appears* that you're very *focused* on *pictures* that you'd rather not *see*, but *clearly* these same *pictures* brought you here to resolve some issues.' (I try to use a reframe whenever the opportunity arises. They can be so useful, and I can see from Tim's response that this one has evaluated well with him. See Bailey (1997) for further examples of this).

TIM: 'Yes but I never get things right' (This kind of generalization is referred to as a universal quantifier and does not consider exceptions).

JA: 'Never Tim? How do you know that you never get things right?'

TIM: (Looking thoughtful) 'Well, she just shouts all the time and I think she really doesn't have time for me any more.' (This kind of distortion is referred to as a complex equivalence and involves connecting two separate statements to make up one meaning).

JA: 'Hmmm, I guess you're not *seeing eye to eye* with your wife at the moment and you're *seeing* the clock go back to a time when you did. Hmmm... Tim, how does shouting at you mean that she doesn't have time for you any more... I mean, have you ever shouted at someone that you did have time for?

TIM: (Remaining thoughtful as he processes this information, but also looking increasingly more relaxed. His frown is disappearing.) 'I just think that if she knew what I had to go through she wouldn't do it.' (I sensed a slight lack of conviction in this statement as Tim awaited my response. From this assumption – another complex equivalence – we might presuppose from what he has said that: (a) Tim goes through an unpleasant experience;

(b) Tim's wife behaves in a certain way; (c) his wife does not know that he goes through an unpleasant experience.)

JA: 'Tim, it *appears* to me that we need to be *clear* about three things here and we'll *focus* on them one at a time: what specifically are you going through, how is your wife behaving and how do you know that she doesn't know what you're going through?'

Tim explained that his experiences seemed worse because his wife thinks he should have got over his industrial accident by now. He believes that is wife is 'more clever' than he is and she tells him to 'move on'. His wife was worried that he would not be able to work again – Tim feared this also – and that the family will face financial hardship. Tim's solicitor had been instructed to negotiate an out of court settlement on his behalf.

JA: 'Could you *see* yourself working for the same company when you are able to Tim?'

TIM: 'I can't if I go for compensation – they wouldn't have me back.' (I could see this generalization – a modal operator of possibility – was another source of pressure for Tim, but I was also aware that he hadn't mentioned being unable to work.)

JA: (Looking up – again I could see Tim had pictured this scenario) 'How do you know that Tim?'

TIM: 'I know them and they wouldn't have me back.'

JA: (Smiling and nodding) 'Hmmm'

TIM: (A kind of puzzled smile) 'What do you think then John?'

JA: 'I was just reminded of this story about a farmer...'

'Believing we know the future' and 'mind reading' are generalisations and distortions respectively. I had stage-managed an opportunity to share one of my favourite metaphors with Tim. Briefly, it concerned two neighbouring farmers, Farmer Jones and Farmer Giles. Farmer Jones' combine harvester had broken down at the crucial time of the harvest and try as he might he was unable to buy or hire another one. Believing that he faced ruin, Farmer Jones jumped into his Land Rover and headed for neighbouring Farmer Giles's farm with a view to sharing Farmer Giles's combine harvester. *En route* Farmer Jones sees himself in his mind's eye knocking on Farmer Giles's door and imagines how the conversation will develop. He tells farmer Giles his tale of woe and Farmer Giles sympathises but asks the inevitable question, 'But what can I do about it?' When Farmer Jones proposes that they share the one machine, Farmer Giles explains that this is out of the question – he will need his own machine around the clock. Farmer Jones's repeated pleas that he faced ruin and if the situation were reversed he would share with Farmer Giles were to no avail. Farmer Giles simply suggested that was easy to for him to say because he was the one with the broken machine. While all this is going on in his mind Farmer Jones actually arrives at Farmer Giles's. He knocks on the door and when Farmer Giles opens the door and says, 'Oh hello', Farmer Jones responds with, 'Well, you can stick your combine harvester...!' Tim smiles and I'm relieved that I don't have to try to explain what I mean. Explaining a metaphor is like having to explain a joke – rather pointless.

My rapport with Tim is very good at this stage as I continue to match the speed and frequency of Tim's hand and body movements, noticing the words he emphasised through tone and body language. Moreover, he is nicely relaxed and I'm hoping he will now be receptive to establishing some well-formed goals – goals are what we seek, outcomes are what we create (O'Connor and McDermott, 2001). If Tim's outcomes (where he wants to get to) are realistic, there is a good chance that they are also achievable. However, while Tim is relaxed I also want to take an opportunity to determine some of his resources. It is important to establish what is going well in Tim's life, as these resources can be introduced and anchored. Tim reveals that his DIY efforts at home include many treasured achievements. He is very fond of his football and we enjoyed some rivalry banter! Tim was also able to visualise his lovely garden, which might be very useful later on. An individual will usually be able to identify achievements and successes on some scale (what might have worked/be working well in their lives – generally and in connection with the problem, i.e. are there times when this isn't a problem?). If so can we find ways to do more of the same?

Tim is clear in that he doesn't want to keep re-experiencing his accident (once was plenty!). He doesn't want to fear gas appliances and he wants to be able to work. I mention to Tim that I was just wondering if he thought it might be helpful to tell me more about his accident at work. It might seem strange to ask such a question given that he has declared a desire to rid himself of this burden, but we have to recognise that some individuals may find this unhelpful. If this is the case it is possible to work content free using certain techniques within NLP. Sexual abuse cases are a noteworthy example of where this might be more helpful. Tim, however, was prepared to take me through his experience, and he reiterated that things were OK prior to his accident.

Tim explained that when the gas hob on the cooker or the gas fire needs to be lit his wife would now always do it. On one level Tim knew that this did not make sense, but he was utilising avoidance strategies in order to reduce his anxiety (all behaviour serves a positive intent). This was not entirely successful, as his wife's irritation was also anxiety-provoking. Tim also mentioned that he relived the experience when he went to bed and I asked Tim if he wanted to close his eyes as if he was attempting to go to sleep. Tim's eyes defocused as he looked out straight ahead. He blinked for a few moments and closed his eyes. I noticed that without any further prompting he was beginning to re-live the experience. It is unlikely that this could have been achieved without the level of rapport that we had. There is a large intake of breath from Tim followed by a gulping swallow.

JA: 'What's happening Tim?'

TIM: 'I don't know but I'm in the factory. It's very noisy. There's a lot of banging and I can hear shouting.'

JA: 'Who is shouting?'

TIM: 'The workers.... You have to shout because of the noise.' (I am aware that Tim is becoming increasingly more uncomfortable as I calibrate his physiology).

JA: 'What's happening now Tim?'

TIM: 'I'm going over to the furnace.' (Tim's breathing rate has become rapid, more shallow and higher in his chest. There is rapid eye movement visible despite his eyes being closed. His face and lips became pale – the lower lip appears to be thinning. His skin appears clammy and Tim has again grasped the arms of the chair. His facial muscles are contorting and he is frowning intensely).

JA: 'I'd like you to open your eyes Tim and return to this room where you are safe with me. Now you'll be relieved to know that we're not going to do that again... I promise! Can I get you a drink Tim... oh, and are you OK for time...? (smiling) You haven't got a more pressing engagement to dash off to have you?' (Tim smiles and gradually begins to relax again.)

The latter small talk was contrived and designed to break state in a friendly manner. This kind of pre-test is helpful, as it becomes possible to recognise Tim's phobic response in order to know if it is occurring again or, ultimately, if it changes (Andreas and Andreas, 1990). It seemed that the action of Tim closing his eyes (influenced by our dialogue) produced an automatic, internal visual and auditory remembered, associated image of the accident. His physiology reflected the resulting kinesthetic responses.

Now Tim has returned to his relaxed state we are able to try a phobia cure intervention if Tim is happy to do so. I reassure Tim that this technique is very simple to follow and doesn't usually involve any discomfort.

JA: 'Tim, I would like you to imagine that you are in a cinema, somewhere in the middle of the auditorium, and up on the screen is a still picture of you as you are now... at this moment in time. Perhaps this might be easier with your eyes closed. (I might have begun by asking Tim to close his eyes in order to remove any distractions. However, as he spontaneously imagined being at the factory before, I needed to avoid this same cue. His physiology tells me that he is not doing that this time.) Are you able to see a picture of yourself on the screen Tim? (Tim nods and I sensed that this would be easy for him). Now, I want you to gain a sense of floating out of your body that's in the seat in the cinema... backwards towards the projection room at the back of the cinema so that you can watch yourself down in the seat, watching yourself on the screen. Can you do that Tim? (I repeat this.)

TIM: 'Yes I can see that?'

JA: 'Seem a bit strange to you? (Tim smiles and nods.) OK Tim, I want you to stay in the projection room, seeing yourself down in the seat, watching the black and white still picture of yourself back then on the screen. Now, I want you to turn the picture on the screen into a moving black and white film of your bad experience. (Tim can watch the accident itself or one of his reruns of the accident. He/his unconscious mind can choose.) You can do that now Tim, and run it from the beginning when things are OK until just beyond the end of the experience when you felt safe again, while you stay in the projection room. Then stop the film.'

The accompanying words I use are very deliberate when speaking to Tim in the here and now whilst describing an event affecting 'Tim over there on the screen back then'. Dissociating in this way enables an event to be experienced in a neutral state. Tim can observe his own physiology, i.e. watch himself in a highly anxious (flooded) state over there. Depending on the severity of the experience, where, say, his physiology begins to collapse into the phobic state, additional distancing can feature. If this occurred I would ask him to blank the screen in preparation to restart the film. He could also now be sitting in the back row of the cinema in a triple dissociated state; hence, watching himself, watching himself, watching himself on the screen. Andreas and Andreas (1990) suggested sitting behind a glass screen in the projection booth (with holes in order to hear the movie. Submodalities can also help here by making the screen smaller, darker, further away etc.).

We could also put a picture of his lovely garden on the screen and turn 'up' the beautiful colour of the flowers if required.

JA: 'Can you let me know when you've reached just beyond the end of the film and felt safe Tim? Well done Tim, you're doing very well. Now, in a few moments I'm going to ask you to leave the projection room and the seat in the cinema and step into the picture on the screen just after the end of the film where you feel safe and comfortable. Can you do that Tim (Tim nods)? Good Tim. Then I want you to turn the still picture to colour and add the sound. Then we are going to run the film backwards to the start at high speed. The whole thing will take only a couple of seconds. Can you imagine what that will be like Tim – watching a film with sound running backwards at that kind of speed? (Tim nods again.) Good Tim. I want you to do that now Tim. Do it Tim!' (Tim jolts.)

Tim: 'Phew!'

JA: 'Did you get to the other end Tim?'

Tim: (Shaking his head and looking perplexed) 'I did!'

JA: 'Seem a bit strange Tim?'

Tim: (Smiling and still looking a bit bewildered) 'Very!' (Tim opens his eyes and chuckles. I'm mind reading of course, but he also looks less than convinced.)

JA: 'Well done Tim. You did very well with that. How long do you think we've been talking now (a question to break state)? Hmmm, now imagine the next time you expect to experience that....' (Future pace)

Tim: 'Accident – it was a terrible thing.'

JA: 'It was, Tim, and suffering once with it was enough, right? Can you close your eyes Tim and picture that scene for me?' (Associated. Tim had shown a keen willingness to cooperate through the entire process and duly obliged.)

Tim: (Holding the chair as he had previously and frowning, saying nothing for about 20 seconds before opening his eyes again) 'That's amazing. It isn't there.'

JA: 'What isn't there Tim?'

Tim: (Shaking his head) 'All that stuff... that fooom noise with the heat and the pain and the burning smell (With major trauma incredible amounts of sensory information can be taken in. Tim turns to my colleague and repeats) 'That's amazing.'

After Tim departed my colleague referenced the speed with which the technique worked. One of my own criticisms of NLP surrounds claims of quick fixes. This diminishes the carefully crafted rapport building and information gathering process, without which the technique would not be possible.

An alternative version advocated by O'Connor and Seymour (2002) involves (when stepping into the screen) giving the younger self support, encouragement and reassurance: 'I'm from the future and you survived – you will not have to go through it again'. The present-day person has the strength and resources to cope with the incident (it is very reasonable to retain a healthy respect and anxiety for heating appliances where a genuine danger can exist).

Metaphorical representations arranged in this way are powerful and emphatic, whilst being gentle and respectful. The most profound example of achieving this that I have witnessed would be the inner child work developed some 25 years ago by Sue Washington (Mnemodynamic Therapy™). The resourceful person in the safety of the here and now takes the feeling of the younger person on the screen and is then able to give the younger person on the screen adult insights into the difficulty. This particular arrangement of psychotherapeutic 're-feel' techniques has a psychodynamic influence, and even the most harrowing traumatic events can be resolved or cognitively reappraised.

Whilst it might be nice to reference a successful outcome during the writing of a chapter, we had not quite achieved this yet. I had arranged to see Tim the following week to evaluate our work. On departure from our initial session Tim had scaled himself at 10, which is not untypical for someone who believes that they have rid themselves of an unwanted burden with powerful neurological connections. In a sense responses like Tim's are a remarkable achievement, and as Walker (2004) suggests 'an exquisite example of one-trial learning'. Now when Tim returned to see me he reported some residual anxiety due to experiencing occasional images of the accident. These images were nowhere near as intense and he still felt 'much better' (scaled at 7), but was anxious that the images might get worse again. This was remedied with some submodality work. After establishing rapport with Tim I asked him to access the images and enabled him to turn down the colours, sound, heat, size and intensity of the 'image'. Tim practised this technique twice successfully before leaving and departed happy in the knowledge that he had gained control over his situation. I spoke with Tim over the telephone a month or so later and he was free of all symptoms, much to his and his wife's delight.

What counts is what works – evidence and policy drivers

During the 1990s it was hard to imagine that anything surpassed mental health in terms of the number of policy initiatives that were produced, culminating in the National Service Framework for Mental Health (NSFMH) (Department of Health, 1999). In fairness some client groups had waited a long time to have their needs taken into account, but nowhere was this more evident than for people with learning disabilities. *Valuing People* (Department of Health, 2001a) was the first meaningful strategy for some 30 years! Knowledge, skills, access, responsiveness and person-centeredness would be the new 'currency' and the NSFMH and LD Strategies would promote extending elements of choice around locally tailored, evidence-based interventions, available in geographically convenient locations. There would be a common entry point for all referrals, care pathway protocols to cater for more specialised referrals, and high-quality, equitable access to the best available therapies, delivered in a culturally competent manner to working age adults irrespective of ability, gender, culture, religion, class or sexual orientation. Otherwise, apart from meaningful service user and carer involvement and developing service priorities through clinical governance, there is not much else to consider! Counselling and psychotherapy provision within primary care will also need to consider the advent of the new GP Contract (GMS 2), the threats, opportunities and challenges in which are ably highlighted by Lilley (2003). Providing solutions to common mental health problems, occupying an estimated 25% of routine GP consultations (Goldberg and Huxley, 1992) is also a well documented 'must do'.

What works best then? I sense many readers will recognise that this would require a whole book rather than a paragraph or two. One of the customary contentions one has to consider is the 'time-limited' versus 'open-ended' therapy debate. Some argue that this is irrelevant compared to the plurality of therapeutic provision based upon empiricism and client choice/need (Coren, 2002; Balick, 2004). In terms of evidence-based interventions, this currently predominates the management and provision of therapies with the familiar debate between notions of objective reality and client world view (Loewental, 2001).

My planning and lead roles within primary care enabled me to attend the launch of various Government healthcare initiatives. During the NSFMH launch, Peck (1999) highlighted some fundamental flaws in the evidence underpinning the strategy. The evidence, graded i–v, and predominantly from psychiatric literature only, included findings such as: 'No strong relationship between the strength of evidence base and rate of adoption, therefore linear models of implementation were deemed to be seriously misleading and likely to lead to implementation deficits'; and 'So-called scientific evidence being, in part, a social construction as well as "objective" data'. The implication here is that there is no such entity as the 'body of evidence', only competing bodies of available evidence, and that different forms of evidence are differentially accepted by different individuals and occupational groups, highlighting the need for some explicit joined-up thinking.

I was also a participant at the 'Psychological Therapies in the NHS: Realising the NSF' conference some 14 months later, which included consideration of the 'extensive scientific review' aimed at producing best practice guidelines on 'appropriate' psychological therapies. This research was a huge undertaking by Glenys Parry and colleagues (Department of Health, 2001b), which reminded us (just in case we needed reminding) that nowhere else is the gap between research and practice wider than in this field. Indeed, paradoxically, the most prevalent interventions were the least researched. In essence, the recommendations were based on best available evidence, utilising processes aimed at reducing bias. They emphasised a degree of uncertainty in the guidelines due to gaps in scientific evidence, methodological limitations of trials and the pitfalls of generalising research findings to clinical populations and patient heterogeneity. Economic appraisal was also identified as being extremely sparse and has only recently been considered by researchers and health economists.

The study also recognised that many NHS therapists formulate difficulties using more than one theoretical framework and choose a mix of techniques from more than one therapy approach. The therapy is therefore pragmatic and tailored to the individual. Such interventions would be described as 'eclectic' therapies rather than a formal, theoretical and methodological integration as with integrative therapy. By their very nature, the former would present difficulties for the purposes of research (like the others don't!). Significantly, learning disabilities along with psychosis, child and adolescence disorders, drug and alcohol addictions, sexual dysfunctions, organic brain syndromes and brain injury, were not addressed by the development group as 'an already difficult task would become impossible unless the scope of the guidelines were limited'.

The two-day conference itself, however, did include learning disability perspectives. A noteworthy example would include a poignant presentation on how the emotional development and emotional difficulties of people with learning disability has been ignored over the years (Nadirshaw, 2001). Such limitations have been compounded by the existence of a predominantly untrained and unqualified workforce (Department of Health, 2001b). It was asserted that there has been a recent, but very gradual, recognition that psychotherapeutic methods from mainstream adult mental health services are being translated towards the psychological needs of people with learning disabilities. It was noted that the Royal College of Psychiatrists joint working party would be examining 'psychiatry of learning disability' and making proposals for future developments.

The conference concluded with an entertaining debate and subsequent vote on whether CBT was best placed to realise Standard 2 of the NSFMH. The proposal was eventually defeated following competing assertions that 'science belonged in laboratories' and 'art belonged in museums'. The latter 'artists' (of a psychodynamic persuasion) won the day, seemingly due to their greater numbers. Subsequently, however, there has been better news for CBT in that its outcome and efficacy studies have left the analytical therapies well behind (Walker, 2004).

Such contentions have undoubtedly provided good entertainment value over the years, particularly between the three classical theoretical schools of thought. A significant example would include the kind of 'discontents' edited by Dryden and Feltham (1992). With its many useful perspectives, it is difficult to single out a favourite, but the suggestion that 'most, if not all, psychotherapy is conducted by enthusiasts with vested interests', does seem to capture a historical 'truth'. Another might be 'beneficial results in the absence of any mechanism that we fully understand should be a cause for celebration'.

We are periodically reminded that theories on which practitioners base their approach tend to reflect the configuration of positions taken on the basic assumptions about human nature and by studying these theories we learn more about the theorists themselves than about their viewpoints or what they actually do (Hjelle and Zeigler, 1981; McDermott and Jago, 2001). O'Hanlon and Hudson (1996) argue that what psychologists really don't want us to know is that nobody knows why we do the things we do! They highlight the widespread disagreement, suggesting that protagonists are probably all correct to some degree and that our behaviour is not caused by any one factor but influenced by many.

Corey (1991, Chapter 13) illustrates how a single case study can highlight contrasts, parallels and certain attributes between different approaches. From a United Kingdom Council for Psychotherapy (UKCP) perspective NLP tends to 'belong' in the Experiential Constructivist Section, and although NLP professes to have no affiliations with any theory, there is an inevitable flavour of other paradigms. Walker (2004) suggests that NLP is an unashamed plagiariser of other fields, elucidating and distilling effective interventions. He also highlights the cross-fertilisation of ideas and techniques between NLP and CBT over the same time frame. The latter of course, is the most researched therapy of modern times, whilst NLP has offered little meaningful research to support the efficacy of its interventions. Bailey (1997) agrees that 'NLP counselling' is cognitive-behavioural in its assumptions and is most useful when adopted as a person-focused approach (with a Rogerian 'validity-of-the-person' kind of importance). The subjective nature of NLP would sit comfortably alongside humanistic perspectives in that there is a focus on subjective awareness and how individuals experience themselves and their worlds and perhaps also in terms of increasing available choices.

There is a 'flavour' of Aaron Beck within the meta model and evidence of behaviourism, notably anchoring, which is similar to classical conditioning. I find Brief Solution Focused Therapy integrates well with NLP, particularly 'scaling', 'exception finding', 'miracle question' and 'problem-free talk' (all worthy of borrowing!). In order to achieve change an Ericksonian (de Shazer, 1988, 1994) shifts the focus away from 'what's wrong' and once client and therapist are focused on solutions, the therapy process is accelerated.

Overall conclusions – why NLP?

It could be argued that NLP commentators advance an optimistic view in terms of what we are able to achieve. Despite the scant evidence and gaps in the literature – almost entirely due to the notion that no two solutions could be deemed the same – there is a validity and an integrity about its approaches. It is wholly person-centred.

Some of the hostility levelled at the marketing, the selling and the scant research data surrounding NLP, particularly within psychology circles, is understandable (Sharpley, 1986; Heap, 1991). The latter notably took a dim view of claims that 'magic' and 'miracles' were being carried out by NLP 'wizards' and 'magicians'. O'Connor and Seymour (2002) have long since held the view that 'there is no magic, only magicians and people's perceptions'. Indeed, things only seem magical when we don't know what's happening. Richard Bandler's almost inexorable criticism of psychologists' inertia and incompetence will not have endeared him to the profession. Bandler (1985) highlighted the fact that professionals were paid more for taking longer with clients (incompetence being rewarded), and therefore innovations took longer to become part of the mainstream and other schools of thought often responded to such innovations by defending their own paradigms. In terms of 'learning disability', NLP commentators have argued that such conclusions are often an indication that the teaching isn't working and that the term 'learning disability' is unclear as regards who actually has it!

NLP certainly doesn't seem to be the preserve of experts, sharing truths and offering guidance from behind the trappings of power roles and assumed expertise, which is to its credit. It also works rather well too. Put simply, the aim is to increase our clients' responsiveness, and to that end their unique insights teach us all we need to know, reducing the need for speculative theorising. The clear and necessary prerequisite for change is in recognising that the client needs to feel understood – a principle that the Government now acknowledges is paramount (Department of Health, 2001c). I would have to declare a bias here, but discovering things that work well sits fairly comfortably within my own neurological model of the world! That said, I'm fairly eclectic and have tried to offer a balanced view, as I don't believe any paradigm, purist or otherwise, has cornered the market with the wisdom and knowledge to assist all individuals in all situations.

In the face of inadequate time, space and resourcing, those who aim to improve the lives of people with a learning disability, mental health problem or both are expected to deliver time-limited, outcome-orientated, cost-effective, evidence-based (add your own double-barrelled term!) interventions. NLP lends itself as a useful addition to the toolkit of the hard-pressed clinician and offers a valuable range of methods that often sit comfortably alongside or integrated with other schools of thought. In terms of extending informed choice of therapy we can see from Tim's experience that this might at times be an unrealistic expectation. Apart from the fact that all information on therapeutic choice contains an inevitable element of therapist bias, was I ever likely to change tack as regards offering Tim an NLP intervention? Unlikely, I suspect, but in the spirit of person-centredness the principles and applications within the NLP paradigm would seem to be in keeping with the wisdom of the day. 'No magic – only magicians and people's perceptions' has been suggested. It's possibly not even as profound as that. At the end of the day, what counts is what works. Finding something that works (and doing more of it) might just be all that's required.

References

Andreas, C. and Andreas, S. (1990) *Heart of the Mind*. Real People Press, Moab, Utah.

Anstey, J. and Mattis, H. (1999) *Primary Care: The Next Step*. Selly Oak Primary Care Group Strategy Document – Unpublished.

Bailey, R. (1997) *NLP Counselling*. Winslow Press, Bicester.

Balick, A. (ed.) (2004) Plurality in psychotherapy. *The Psychotherapist*, **22**, 4–11.

Bandler, R. (1985) *Using Your Brain For A Change*. Real People Press, Moab, Utah.

Bandler, R. and Grinder, J. (1990) *Frogs into Princes*. Eden Grove, Enfield.

Bateson, G. (1972) *Steps to an Ecology of Mind*. Ballentine, New York.

Coren, A. (2002) Short-term work is well suited to clinical work in primary care. *Healthcare Counselling and Psychotherapy Journal*, **2**(1), 3–5.

Corey, G. (1991) *Theory and Practice of Counselling and Psychotherapy*. Brooks and Cole, Monterey.

Dailey-Knowles, R. (1983) Through Neuro-Linguistic Programming. *American Journal of Nursing*, July, 1011–14.

De Shazer, S. (1988) *Clues: Investigating Solutions in Brief Therapy*. Norton, New York.

De Shazer, S. (1994) *Words Were Originally Magic*. Norton, New York.

Department of Health (1999) *National Service Framework for Mental Health*. HMSO, London.

Department of Health (2001a) *Valuing People: A New Strategy for Learning Disability Services for the 21st Century*. HMSO, London.

Department of Health (2001b) *Treatment Choice in Psychological Therapies and Counselling: Evidence-Based Clinical Practice Guideline*. HMSO, London.

Department of Health (2001c) *Choosing Talking Therapies*. HMSO, London.

Dryden, W. and Feltham, C. (eds.) (1992) *Psychotherapy And Its Discontents*. Open University Press, Milton Keynes.

Gasson, B. (1995) South Birmingham Mental Health NHS Trust – Personal communication.

Goldberg, D. and Huxley, P. (1992) *Common Mental Disorders: A Biosocial Model*. Routledge, London.

Grinder, J. and Bandler, R. (1976) *Structure of Magic II: A Book About Communication and Change*. Science and Behavior Books, Palo Alto.

Heap, M. (1991) Neuro-Linguistic Programming: a personal view. *Counselling News*, December, 8–10.

Hjelle, L. A. and Zeigler, D. J. (1981) *Personality Theories, Basic Assumptions, Research and Applications* (2nd edn). McGraw-Hill, London.

Lewis, B. A. and Pucelik, F. (1982) *Magic Demystified: A Pragmatic Guide to Communication and Change*. Metamorphous, Oregon.

Lilley, R. (2003) *The New GP Contract: How to Make the Most of It*. Radcliffe, Oxford.

Loewental, D. (2001) Questioning psychotherapeutic 'evidence' (and research). *The Psychotherapist*, **17**, 44–5.

Mackay, D. (1989) Behavioural psychotherapy. In: *Individual Therapy in Britain* (ed. W. Dryden). Open University Press, Milton Keynes.

McDermott, I. and Jago, W. (2001) *The NLP Coach: A Comprehensive Guide to Personal Well-Being and Professional Success*. Piatkus, London.

Nadirshaw, Z. (2001) Overview of diversity and difference, with reference to people with learning disabilities. *Psychological Therapies in the NHS: Realising the National Service Framework*, 20–21 February, Brighton.

O'Connor, J. and McDermott, I. (2001) *NLP*. HarperCollins, London.

O'Connor, J. and Seymour, J. (2002) *Introducing NLP: Psychological Skills for Understanding and Influencing People*. HarperCollins, London.

O'Hanlon, B. and Hudson, P. (1996) *Stop Blaming, Start Loving: A Solution-Orientated Approach to Improving Your Relationship*. Norton, New York.

Peck, E. (1999) Is policy evidence based? *National Service Framework For Mental Health Conference*, 17 December, Royal College of Surgeons.

Pesut, D. J. (1991) The art, science and techniques of reframing in mental health nursing. *Issues in Mental Health Nursing*, **12**, 9–18.

Rosen, S. (1991) *My Voice Will Go With You: The Teaching Tales of Milton H Erickson*. Norton, London.

Sharpley, C. F. (1986) Research findings on Neuro-Linguistic Programming: non-supportive data or an untestable theory? *Journal of Counselling Psychology*, **34**, 103–7.

Walker, L. (2004) *Changing with NLP: a Casebook of Neuro-linguistic Programming in Medical Practice*. Radcliffe Medical Press, Oxford.

Washington, S. (1978) *Mnemodynamic Therapy™*. Centre Training International School of Hypnotherapy and Psychotherapy: Course material circa 1998.

Zahourek, R. P. (2002) Utilizing Ericksonian hypnosis in psychiatric mental health nursing. *Perspectives in Psychiatric Care*, **38**(1), 15–22.

CHAPTER 14

Working with and supporting men with a learning disability who are gay, bisexual or attracted to the same sex

Neville Parkes and Nigel Hodges

This chapter is dedicated to the memory of Alf Facciponti (RNLD), whose life was tragically cut short and who, once met, was never forgotten.

Introduction

This chapter discusses practice issues that are specific to men with a learning disability who are sexually attracted to men or who identify as gay or bisexual. We stress that it is not our intention to minimise the issues for female service users who may express their sexuality in non-heterosexual ways, but this relates to our experience as male workers working almost exclusively with male service users in the arena of sexual issues and therefore reflects our expertise and clinical practice. The issues for women with a learning disability who are attracted to women are likely to have some commonality with their male counterparts, especially in such areas as homophobia, staff attitudes, responding to sexual situations, devising interventions and risk taking. However, the issue for women with learning disability who are attracted to women will *not be exactly* the same as the issues are for men. The reader needs to carefully reflect on the ideas and principles discussed in this chapter and how they might be adapted.

For services who support and care for people with a learning disability to be truly person-centred there is a self-evident need for a constructive response to service users who express or wish to express their sexuality, including sexual behaviours that are perceived as non-heterosexual. The issues outlined in this chapter will, to some, be seen as challenging, but to develop truly person-centred services for people with a learning disability may in some situations raise controversial issues.

Sexuality and sexual expression are a vital part of most people's sense of self-identity and esteem. It is imperative that learning disability services develop appropriate and in some cases courageous approaches to extend opportunities for sexual expression to service users. There is the conundrum of providing opportunities and facilitating sexual expression balanced with the duty of care to provide protection from ill treatment and abuse as well as keeping within the law. The authors of this chapter recognise the issues involved in such a conundrum. Simply because something may be difficult or controversial is not an excuse for ignoring it.

This chapter is intended to offer both a theoretical perspective and some practical responses to the issues raised when supporting men with a learning disability who may express or indicate their desire to express their sexuality in non-heterosexual ways. The ethos is not to give a prescriptive package to be replicated exactly, but to offer ideas and guidance that should be used by practitioners or support staff carefully in response to service users' needs.

This chapter contains a number of vignettes from our clinical experience to illustrate key theoretical points. To maintain anonymity specific details have been changed.

Sex and people with learning disabilities

People with a learning disability have historically frequently been subject to the curtailing of sexual opportunities and even the denial of their identity as a sexual being (McCarthy, 1999; Brown, 1994). Equally significant has been the concern of the dangers of uninhibited sexual expression by the learning disabled population (Marks, 1999; Brown, 1994). A comprehensive review and discussion on the historical responses to sexual expression by people with learning disabilities can be found in (McCarthy, 1999, Chapter 2). Anybody working with people with a learning disability in relation to sexual issues must be aware of the possible internalised negative attitudes the learning disabled individual may have about themselves sexually. Key people in an individual's life may also hold negative views (not always necessarily verbalised) in relation to learning disabled individuals expressing themselves sexually.

Mellan (2000, p. 13) discusses the responses to the sexuality of learning disabled men and comments that the negative perceptions that many hold can lead to either denial, minimisation or an overreaction to the sexual issues in focus.

In our experience of working with service users, reaction to same sex sexual relationships between men raises many differing reactions, but the level of concern expressed about such relationships is likely to be at a higher level than if the individual's relationship was perceived as heterosexual. It would be erroneous to caricature everyone working within support services for people with a learning disability as being hostile and negative towards this issue. Mellan (2000, p. 14) crystallises the situation in many services today:

Same sex relationships particularly between men can cause a number of anxieties often resulting in referring to specialist help services with a negative emphasis to contain, diminish or stop. A positive view of sexuality has not been on the political and social agenda in services working with people with learning disabilities.

Sexuality

It is not the function of this chapter to provide a lengthy discourse or theoretical treatise on the subject of sexuality. However, there are some key concepts that practitioners should consider when working with men who are attracted to men or who are gay or bisexual. Practitioners need to be wary of the indiscriminate use of terminology in this area of practice. Eliason (1996) highlights the indiscriminate use of terms such as 'sexual orientation', 'sexual preference' and 'sexual identity', although they do not actually mean the same thing.

The term 'sexuality' can be used either in a narrow sense to describe sexual identity and/or behaviour or in a broader more holistic sense (Adams, 2001). Kinsey *et al.* (1948) based on their research, described a continuum of sexual experiences from those he surveyed, ranging from exclusively heterosexual to exclusively homosexual. Figure 14.1 is an interpretation of Wilton's (2000) views on the need to differentiate between identity (how one may understand and view one's sexual self), behaviour (the sexual activities one does) and sexual attraction. It describes a level of congruence between attraction, identity and behaviour. Some individuals can have degrees of incongruence between their identity, attraction and behaviours. Examples could include 'gay' men who occasionally have sex with women or 'heterosexual' men who pick up men for sex (see Vignette 1).

Vignette I

Michael is a service user with a mild learning disability who makes numerous requests to his care workers to find him a girlfriend. At his day placement, he asks a male service user to partake in sexual acts with him.

Issues:

- Michael's behaviour indicates a need for caution in assumptions regarding his sexual identity
- Michael would benefit from exploring his sexual attractions and how this relates to his sexual behaviour
- Therapeutic work around making friendships and relationships would be of benefit to Michael

---

Homophobia

Richmond and McKenna (1998) described homophobia as 'aversion, anger, hatred, discomfort and fear that people have in dealing with homosexuals'. Many individuals who are lesbian, gay or bisexual are likely to encounter homophobia in their lives. Flowers and Buston (2001) state that the concept of heterosexism assumes that the heterosexuality of all is taken for granted. This is

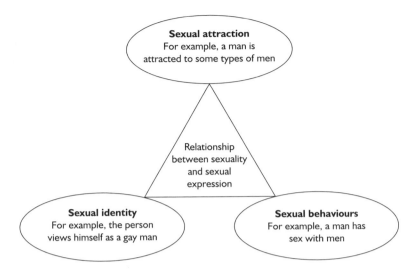

Figure 14.1 Sexual attraction, identity and behaviour.

exemplified by an example from our experience when a professional worker in learning disability services undertakes a series of sex education workshops with service users without covering any issues relating to same sex relationships. When questioned they said 'It's only a basic course'. (Does this imply that same sex relationships are too complex or may be seen to be more difficult to talk about or just less valid, or is the assumption that all the service users will be heterosexual?) This concurs with Wilton (2000) who suggests that heterosexism involves a process of demeaning any non-heterosexual sexual expression considering it to be less valued, abnormal or less moral.

Homophobia has been identified to be present within healthcare settings (Hayter, 1996; Morrissey, 1996; McColl, 1994). It is depressingly unsurprising that services for people with a learning disability are not immune to homophobia and heterosexism. Abbot and Howarth (2003) discuss homophobia in contemporary learning disability services, identifying negative attitudes by some carers and in some cases by the learning disabled individuals themselves. Davidson-Payne and Corbett (1995) report on the many complex issues associated with 'coming out' for learning-disabled gay men, including carers' negativity or lack of understanding and the lack of opportunity leading to isolation. Withers *et al.* (2001) and George (1988) highlight that men with learning disabilities who are attracted to men in many cases fear reprisals and punishment in response to their coming out. Hodges and Parkes (2005) outline a series of strategies that should be adopted by services that support people with a learning disability to tackle homophobia and heterosexism.

The attitudes and values of the supporter or worker and the working relationship with the service user

In services that aim to be person-centred it is imperative that the support workers in those services are able to examine their own values and beliefs. This is particularly important in the sometimes controversial area of sexuality, where personal values play a crucial role. The authors of this chapter advocate that the therapeutic relationship between the worker(s) and the man with a learning disability is crucial if an individual is to be effectively supported. The worker as a resource is seen as being pivotal to supporting people with a learning disability in sexual matters (Fanstone and Katrak, 2003, p. 15; McCarthy and Thompson, 1992, p. 14). The term 'therapeutic relationship' in this chapter is used to signify any *constructive* alliance that can exist between any worker and service user with a learning disability. Such relationships are not seen as the exclusive domain of workers who offer counselling or psychotherapy.

Stein (1985, p. 83), in discussing counsellors who work with gay men, recommends that therapists need to examine their own attitudes to homosexuality and specific sexual activities, their familiarity with 'gay' lifestyles (noting that this may not be always applicable to the needs of men with learning disability) and some knowledge of patterns and stages of gay men 'coming out'. Stein's recommendations are likely to be as valid for workers within learning disability services regardless of their professional role. Stein also highlights the need to consider the worker's view of masculinity. Parkes (2003) discusses masculinity within the domain of learning disability, in that a man having a learning disability contravenes many social normative values that subscribe to hegemonic masculinity.

Mohr (2002) highlights the need for counsellors to consider their own 'working models of heterosexuality' and the consequent impact upon how they will view homosexuality. This equally relates to workers in learning disability services. Four working models are outlined in Table 14.1.

Workers should use the four working models to examine their own viewpoints. If someone closely associates with the 'Democratic Working Model' or 'Compulsive Model' they may need to consider their responses to non-heterosexual lifestyles. The most helpful model to be closely associated with is the 'Integrated Model'. The ideas and concepts associated with this model provide a platform not to be dismissive of, deny, be hostile to or too over zealous in promotion of non-heterosexuality. The Integrated Model has a sense of balance and maturity, but is not without challenges. Working with a man with a learning disability who is attracted to men requires care staff and supporters to examine their attitudes towards disabled men and counter any ableist viewpoints that they may become aware of.

Mair and Izzard (2001) highlight the danger of the therapist or worker imposing what they see as a gay identity. Clark (1987, p. 34) highlights the issues raised by therapists who seek the client to become 'truly more gay' as limiting the uniqueness of the client and imposing a uniform identity. Similarly, Hari (2004) acerbically comments on the use of gay identities within the media as perpetuating 'camp-ness as being the dominant identity of gay expression and leaving some gay men confused and disenfranchised with how they are *supposed* to behave'.

Cambridge and Mellan (2000, p. 302) highlight the dangers for learning disabled individuals being supported by workers or services that are attempting to be liberal and accommodating of sexual diversity.

> It may prove tempting for some services to encourage men with a learning disability who have sex with men to adopt a gay identity as this initially appears a valid response. It is flawed as it disregards the impact on the man himself.

The working models should not be seen as being mutually exclusive or as fixed entities within individuals. Box 14.1 contains a list of reflective-type questions adapted from Mohr (2002) to enable one to consider how one views heterosexuality and homosexuality.

Table 14.1 Working models of heterosexuality (adapted from Mohr, 2002).

Working model	Brief description
Democratic model of heterosexuality	▪ All sexual orientation is essentially the same. Minimises differences between oppressed groups. ▪ May not fully appreciate the effect of homophobia. May see their own experience of heterosexuality as an adequate guide for working with lesbian, gay or bisexual clients; for example, Garnets *et al.* (1991) cite a therapist telling a lesbian couple to read a book about marriage. ▪ May minimise any oppression of the sexual expression of people with a learning disability.
Compulsive model of heterosexuality	▪ Assumes that heterosexual sex is the *only* morally or acceptable sexual orientation. Homosexuality or bisexuality threatens core values. ▪ May lead to problems in acknowledging and working with lesbian, gay or bisexual individuals with a learning disability.
Political model of heterosexuality	▪ Likely to view bisexual and gay individuals as being oppressed and requiring courageous survival skills to live in a homophobic society. ▪ May be zealous in their vigilance for homophobia. May have little patience with anyone who does not accept non-heterosexuality or with bisexual and gay individuals who struggle with internalised homophobia. May view bisexuality as the person 'denying true identity'. ▪ Essentially an 'all or nothing approach'. Can lead to regarding gay identity as being placed on a pedestal. May have little patience with individuals who are struggling with the 'coming out' process. ▪ Workers in learning disability services may find it frustrating to comply with multidisciplinary approaches that they may see as condoning homophobia.
Integrative model of heterosexuality	▪ Assumes that sexualities are participating within an oppressive system. Sexual orientation is seen as complex construct that can be categorised along a multi-dimensional continuum involving attraction, fantasy and other variables. ▪ Heterosexuality not seen as fundamentally different from other orientations, but acknowledges oppressive societal forces that impact upon gay and bisexual individuals. ▪ Probably the most helpful approach for workers in learning disability services.

Vignette 2

Robert is a service user with a moderate learning disability who referred to himself as 'gay' because he had sex with a number of men without a learning disability. During clinical work undertaken with him it transpired that Robert didn't like sex with his male partners. He only liked social activities, and it was highly likely that he had been exploited sexually and had thought that because he had sex with men this meant he was 'gay'. This vignette demonstrates that sexual behaviour and the service user's reported identity may be incongruent with his attraction. It also demonstrated the need to have therapeutic space for the service user to explore such issues in a truly person-centred approach.

Box 14.1 Reflective questions for exploration of heterosexual identity for workers in learning disability services (adapted from Mohr, 2002).

- Do my attraction, sexual fantasies and sexual behaviour mostly involve members of the opposite sex?
- Am I open to same sex attraction or fantasy?
- Have I ever been attracted to or fantasised about the same sex? So how do I explain this?
- What are my earliest memories of hearing others talk about sexual orientation?
- How did I learn about heterosexuality as a child or adolescent?
- How would you describe your working model of heterosexuality (refer to Table 14.1)?
- Do your attraction, fantasies or behaviour bring you into conflict with your working model?
- Does your work with people with a learning disability challenge how you view heterosexuality?

In a person-centred service there is a moral imperative that care staff and workers need to put aside personal values about sexuality and lifestyle that are in conflict with those of the service user. Staff members whose religious beliefs may be a significant factor should be treated with sensitivity and respect in accordance with employment law. However, they should not seek to influence a service user's valid choice of lifestyle.

A certain level of pragmatism and basic common sense needs to be applied by service managers. It is unacceptable for a member of care staff to espouse homophobic comments on religious grounds that are directed at a service user or worker. Equally, it is unlikely to be acceptable (or sensible) for services to insist that a staff member who objects on religious grounds should help a gay service user to, for example, purchase (legal) gay material.

Vignette 3(a)

Rob is a supporter who works with a man with a learning disability who is attracted to men. Rob is gay and open about his sexuality with his work colleagues. Rob discusses his work with his line manager and a multidisciplinary team at regular intervals (approximately fortnightly) and discusses the issues around disclosing his sexuality to this service user. It is agreed by the multidisciplinary team that it is likely to be helpful for Rob to take such action. Rob discloses that he is gay to the male service user, who finds this very helpful and feels less isolated.

Comment: Rob has acted professionally and thoughtfully, ensuring that his actions are in the best interests of the male service user.

Vignette 3(b)

Stephen is a care worker working with Uriah, a man with a learning disability who has stated he is attracted to men. Uriah asks Stephen where he can 'pick up men'. Stephen suggests a well know 'cottage' (public toilets where men meet for sex with men). Uriah later that day informs his key worker that 'Stephen has told him to go cottaging'. The key worker is very concerned and reports this immediately to his line manager: a lengthy investigation ensues.

Comment: Stephen is probably well motivated, but he has not worked in concert with the multidisciplinary team. He has not accounted for many significant issues, such as Uriah's personal safety or his knowledge of safer sex.

Workers who are gay or lesbian

A gay worker may offer positive therapeutic interactions in working with a learning disabled man who is attracted to the same sex. They may also be able to offer valuable insights into the service user's issues. This must not automatically be assumed. Cowie and Rivers (2000, p. 511) highlight the positive and negative issues about gay or lesbian therapists who offer personal insights within the therapeutic relationship. They may be positive, as they enable the client to feel a sense of identity with the issues that someone else has experienced. The negative consequences could be the blurring of the therapeutic relationship. Personal issues (for example issues of internalised homophobia, such as a worker seeking a cure for his gayness) could also cloud the focus of the work with the service user (Cowie and Rivers, 2000, p. 506).

Personal disclosures

Staff in learning disability services need to exercise caution before making personal disclosures about their lifestyle. This does not mean encouraging gay or bisexual staff to hide their identity (see Hodges and Parkes, 2005). They also need to be aware of what it is appropriate to disclose. If, for example, a service user asked a male worker 'Do you masturbate?', an appropriate response would be 'Most men do' rather than offering a personal account. Personal disclosures to service users may also be divulged to others. Where staff are comfortable with personal details about themselves being widely known they need to consider the impact on service users.

Undertaking supporting or working with male service users who are attracted to men

The following contains a list of guiding principles rather than exact and linear processes which would constitute a clearly defined package. The problem with a fixed approach is a lack of flexibility in tailoring it for individual service users' needs. The worker should be responsive to the service user and 'where he is at' at all times. This might mean returning to issues already raised or issues that the worker may have thought appropriate for the future. This is suitable for people with a learning disability, who may have difficulty in internalising abstract concepts and with memory, as well as with communication, or who may want to explore subjects when they want. In some cases there has to be a logical sequence; for example, to give sexual health information about safer sex the worker must ensure the service user understands the relevant terminology.

Below is what we refer to as the 'Adhesive Notes' approach. Figure 14.2 represents a series of adhesive notes, which serve as an *aide mémoire* to the worker to reflect upon their practice. This type of approach can be adapted to other types of work supporting people with a learning disability in relation to sexual issues. Each Adhesive Note is expanded in the following section.

Not all the 'Adhesive Notes' will be required for some situations all the time, and some will not be needed at all, depending on the role and function of the worker and the needs of the service user.

Is this within my caring or professional role?

The types of worker who are engaged in supporting or caring for people with a learning disability are very varied, ranging from peripatetic workers to direct care staff. In any sphere of work that one is engaged in it is a legitimate activity to ask whether this issue is relevant to the role. Figure 14.3 represents three levels of certainty, where staff, their manager or supervisor and the multidisciplinary team feel that it is within the worker's role (Level 1) or it is not within their role (Level 3). In Level 2 staff are unsure whether they have the appropriate skills and knowledge, feel unsure whether it is within their role or have personal reservations. They must seek clarification from their line manager, supervisor and the multidisciplinary team to resolve the issue.

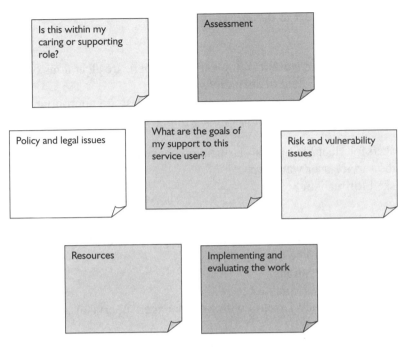

Figure 14.2 The 'Adhesive Notes' approach. Suggested processes to follow when working with gay/bisexual men with a learning disability that can be adapted for other types of sexual related service user issues.

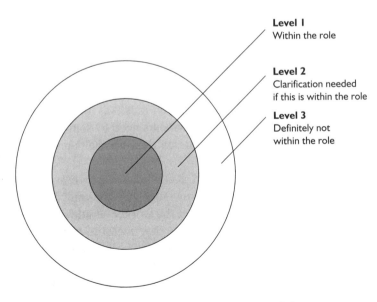

Figure 14.3 Is this within my role?

What are the goals of my support to this service user?

In any type of support and care work it is imperative that there are clear aims or goals of the work. This is particularly true in the field of sexuality work.

The following are key reflective questions that we suggest are appropriate when considering service user needs and defining the aim(s) of the work. This is not an exhaustive list.

- Is what is asked for clear? Is further clarification needed?
- What does the service user want/expect?
- Is what is asked for realistic?
- Is it legal?
- What are the implications for the services this person receives?
- Are there any risks to the service user/workers/service in what is proposed?
- How are any risks going to be managed?
- What are the policy implications?
- Are appropriate resources available?
- Is the work within my role? Discuss with line manager/supervisor and the multidisciplinary team.
- Do I have the knowledge, skills and competencies to undertake this work?
- What do I need to discuss this with multidisciplinary and multiagency colleagues?

Assessment

This section is biased towards workers whose role is to provide a therapeutic or educative relationship with the service user rather than being supportive.

Workers who have this role must recognise that it is important they are able to demonstrate a level of transparency to account for the actions and professional judgements they make. For example, nurses must adhere to the Nurses and Midwifery Code of Professional Conduct (Nursing and Midwifery Council, 2004). Varcarolis (2000, p. 4) identifies that the purpose of assessments is to identify and articulate specific client needs. Assessments need to demonstrate the process of how professional judgements have been made, which can then be evaluated and commented on and modified at a later stage.

Formalised inventories such as the Sexual Knowledge Interview Schedule (Forchuk and Martin, 1993) offer a structure to provide a knowledge baseline and later a tool to evaluate a service user's progress. However, it is stressed that the worker should consider the value of using any formalised inventory. Inventories measure what they measure and don't measure what they don't measure. The inventory may not fulfil the aim of the work required. The Sexual Knowledge Interview Schedule is not designed to assess an individual's level of internalised homophobia or an erectile dysfunction. Workers need to be cautious in using some inventories, in that they may, for example, be out of date legally, lack congruency with current attitudes or use language that is peculiar to its country of origin.

The following may impinge on the validity of the information gathered:

■ Service user embarrassment in discussing sexual matters.
■ Lack of understanding of the types of phrases or words in the inventory.
■ (Un)conscious prompting by the worker.
■ The understanding of the process by the service user; for example, they may be fearful of the consequences of divulging their knowledge/behaviour/attitudes or they may acquiesce.

The worker can use a range of resources to find out the service user's attitudes to sexual issues. The use of relevant material will provide a qualitative insight into the service user's views and behaviours. Using material from *Sex and the 3Rs* (McCarthy and Thompson, 1992) may result in responses ranging from 'he is dirty' (referring to, for example, a drawing illustrating masturbation) to a volunteering that he does this also, providing the worker with an insight into the terminology he uses.

Vignette 4 offers an example of an assessment process based on the Adhesive Notes type approach.

Resources

Resources need to be considered in terms of:

■ Staff to deliver the sessions
■ Timing of the session(s)
■ Venue(s) (see section below on implanting and evaluating the work)
■ Access to or purchasing educative packages
■ Time to prepare for the sessions
■ Clinical supervision (essential for this type of work)

There are a number of published sex education packages geared towards the needs of the learning disabled population. Each has its strengths and weaknesses. The worker needs to take time to become familiar with the package and ensure that the strengths and needs of the service user are kept in focus. In Table 14.2 we have given a brief résumé of the utility of some of the sex education resources designed for people with a learning disability that are available.

Implementing and evaluating the work

In developing any therapeutic or educative session the worker needs to regularly revisit the previous sections, in that they are able to define and modify the aims of the work and the assessment when new issues come to light.

Kiger (1995) highlights the fact that many healthcare professionals have health education within their role, but few know how to teach. It is important that workers consider the impact and the issues from the service users' perspective. The following is a list of key considerations.

Vignette 4

Kevin is man with a learning disability who was ' confused and distressed' about some aspects of his attraction to men. He was referred for some counselling type work. The following are some of the processes that were undertaken to assess his need. Note that the following was under-taken over several sessions after the therapeutic relationship was established with Kevin.

- Kevin's knowledge of sexual body parts (male and female) was assessed using *Sex and the 3Rs* to assess what words he used, any comments, positive or negative, he might attribute to sexual organs, and his attitudes towards sexual functioning, i.e. identifying any negative positive or inconsistent comments.
- Using discussion, and later the *Piece by Piece* video, his attitudes towards same sex sexual behaviours were explored.
- Internalised homophobia was assessed by discussion.
- Knowledge of sexual function of parts (erection, ejaculation)
- Check for any sexual dysfunction, e.g. erectile dysfunction, by non-threatening ques-tions in a later session about whether he can obtain and maintain an erection.
- Kevin's knowledge of social mores was assessed by asking a number of situation ques-tions, e.g. 'Where is OK to masturbate?'.
- Kevin's ability and opportunities to meet potential or actual sexual partners.
- Kevin's understanding of personal safety and vulnerability was assessed by scenario-type questions (based on some of his experiences).
- Knowledge of legal issues, age of consent, and sex in public was assessed similarly.
- Knowledge of safer sex/sexually transmitted infections was undertaken by asking a series of questions and use of a condom to ask him to explain what it was used for, where it was obtained etc.
- Knowledge of where to obtain suitable condoms via discussion.
- Knowledge of sexual techniques to make it pleasurable for his partner(s).
- Knowledge of homophobia – this was done by asking Kevin if he had anyone say any-thing to him which was possibly homophobic (using simpler phrases).
- Kevin's understanding of reproduction and contraception (may not be primary need for gay or bisexual men with a learning disability, but they have a right to know and may have occasional sex with female partners).
- Kevin's knowledge and attitudes toward unwanted and possible abusive behaviours toward himself were discussed (this was pertinent, as he had experienced experience of this type in the past).
- Knowledge and attitudes of Kevin's dealing with disappointments when faced with rejec-tion or ending of relationships.
- Kevin's level of support from social networks assessed by drawing a map of everyone in his social network.
- Independence and interdependence issues – this was assessed already via his commu-nity care assessment.
- Speech and language therapist reports utilised.

Table 14.2 A résumé of some sex education resources for people with a learning disability (not exhaustive).

Resource	Comments
Sex and the 3Rs (Pavilion)	Aimed at adults; could be used with adolescents. Contains line drawings and a guide. The worker needs to consider how to utilise this resource. Includes same sex relationships. Highly recommended.
Living Safer Sexual Lives (Pavilion)	Video and work pack using experiences of people with learning disabilities. Does not focus on sex education as such.
I Have the Right to Know (BILD)	Aimed at adolescents. May be difficult to use with adults.
Piece by Piece (West London Health Promotion Agency)	Demonstrates (using mannikin dolls) heterosexual and same-sex activity. Very clear and gives positive gay affirmation. Has a teaching package incorporated which has many strategies and ideas for sessions.
My Body and Sex Jason's Private World Kylie's Private World (Life Support Productions)	Three videos and booklets. Biased towards heterosexuality, but useful in parts for masturbation and same-sex relationships.
Health promotion leaflets	Language may be too complex and abstract for many learning disability service users, but could be adapted.
Developing own resources using clip art, drawings and similar	In some cases can be cheap and quick, and flexible to the service user's needs. The drawback is that it can be very time-consuming (searching clip art folders). The service user may not understate the graphics. Caution needed in using sexually explicit material, as it may contravene obscenity laws. May be problematic if searching the Internet for images (e.g. using the Google search engine) as it is highly likely to encounter pornography, which needs careful consideration before being using in a session, especially if there are alternatives available (e.g. in *Sex and the 3Rs*.
Learning Disabilities, Sex and the Law (FPA)	A useful guide to legal issues, although less in depth than its predecessor. Includes Sexual Offences Act 2003.

The service user's motivation and understanding of the work

■ *The service user's view* of the aim and content of the work needs to be explicitly agreed, probably at each session. Parkes (2003) discusses the importance of developing a contract within a therapeutic relationship.

- *Support and chaperoning.* This is recommended because of the subject matter. The service user may find the session difficult and may want a person to support them. There are benefits for the worker as this offers a level of protection for them from complaints. The chaperone/supporter needs to be the same person for each session, sensitive to the issues and able to work though their own issues after the session if they encounter anything they do not feel comfortable with. Clear guidelines for this role need to be agreed prior to the session; for example, agreeing that they will only interrupt the session in certain circumstances and about confidentiality issues. Having a supporter/chaperone in the session can make a qualitative difference to the type of work that is undertaken. This should be reviewed and the service user may state at some stage they may want a session on a 1:1 basis. Each issue should be judged on a case-by-case and probably a session-by-session basis.
- *The environment and timing.* Attempting to deliver a session in a cramped cold dark room just before lunch may be heroic, but is unlikely to achieve much. Ensure that the environment is private and comfortable, ensuring the service user's wishes are taken into account. Choose a time and a venue that will not detract from their concentration.
- *Interest and relevance to the aims of the work.* Tailor the sessions to the aims of the work. From anecdotal experience we are aware of situations where care staff have laudably attempted to offer sex education, but chose an inappropriate way to meet the service user needs: the service user exhibited inappropriate touching of others and the care staff responded by teaching him about fallopian tubes, uteruses and childbirth.
- *Evaluation of the work* in many cases is not simple. For example, if one was teaching a service user to make a sandwich or cross a road they could be observed doing the task, but if a service user needs to develop skills in putting a condom on it would be unethical to ask him to demonstrate this on his own penis, although a condom demonstrator could be used. The evaluation process must be transparent in demonstrating the way in which judgements are made about the progress that the service user has made in relation to the work undertaken.

Legal and policy issues

Workers supporting learning-disabled individuals need to ensure that any advice they offer a service user about the law is both accurate and understandable. This is complicated by additional legal constraints that affect learning-disabled individuals, principally designed to protect them from exploitation or abuse. This is particularly pertinent for more severely learning-disabled individuals and is linked to their capacity or lack of it to consent to specific acts or activities. Where there are concerns about an individual's ability to consent, the multidisciplinary team should initially explore the potential for capacity to be gained. A useful resource on legal issues is *Learning Disabilities, Sex and the Law* (Fanstone and Andrews, 2005).

It is important for services to have policies and good practice guidance in place in relation to sexuality issues. Without relevant policy and good practice guidance service users could be subject to idiosyncratic responses by staff (McConkey and Ryan, 2001) or their needs minimised or not addressed. However, there are clear issues in relation to the dissemination of such policies and staff adherence to them (Murray *et al.*, 1999). Service users also need to be clear about their rights and responsibilities and must be given accurate and understandable information (Frawley *et al.*, 2003). Equally, information given to staff needs to be understandable and not written in jargon. It needs to be clear that discrimination against individuals who are attracted to the same sex is unacceptable. The authors of this chapter have previously suggested that this is a key issue when working with individuals who have or are seeking same-sex relationships (Hodges and Parkes, 2005). Policy and good practice guidance need to be supported by staff training.

Risk and vulnerability issues

Studies into sexual abuse of people with a learning disability highlight the vulnerability of this group (for example Buchanan and Wilkins, 1991; Balogh *et al.*, 2001; Hard and Plumb, 1987). Services that support men who are attracted to men have a duty of care to ensure service users' safety within risk management strategies as agreed between the service user and the multidiscipli- nary team. Issues such as the service user's current sexual knowledge and capacity to consent need to be taken into account. The flip side of this situation is that services have a duty to ensure that individuals are enabled to develop friendships and relationships, including sexual ones (Depart- ment of Health, 2003). Figure 14.4 symbolises the duty of care that should be achieved in learning disability services in maintaining the rights to expression with the requirements of maintaining that the individual is not exploited sexually or otherwise.

Risk management is characterised by an analysis of the likelihood of an identified hazard occurring and the negative and positive consequences that can result from a particular activity (Titteron, 2005; Saunders, 1999). Fundamentally, risk management attempts to promote (or just recognise in some cases) positive consequences and to develop strategies to minimise the negative consequences associated with a particular action. Decisions made in risk taking should involve a multidisciplinary approach with the service user and/or their supporters.

Where possible, services should always attempt to work in partnership with informal carers, but keep the service user's issues paramount in the foci of decision making. The person-centred approach should be explicitly referred to in communication with the service user's informal carers. Services should be sensitive to the views of the service user's informal carers, but they should not

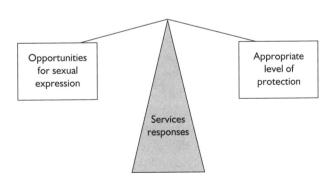

Figure 14.4 Balancing the individual's opportunities with the need for protection.

acquiesce to actions that may inhibit legitimate sexual expression; this should be incorporated into the risk management process.

Risk management should not be used to stop or limit opportunities for service users to legitimately express their sexuality. It should be utilised to develop approaches that facilitate service users to achieve their goals and may require skilful and possibly courageous approaches by services. In some cases the multidisciplinary team or relevant agencies may need to engage in a dialogue with their senior management.

When considering risk issues it is vital to consider the service user's perspective. Harding (1999, p. 36) asserts that for some, risk adds to the pleasure of the sexual encounter. Services need to be careful in the value judgements that they employ. Titteron (2005, p. 20) highlights that in health and social care services, aiming to completely remove risk from people's lives is unacceptable and is quite improbable.

Table 14.3 is a composite example of a risk management and risk-taking approach for a man with a learning disability (Andy) who accessed a gay venue. Note this is not a template, but one of range of ways in which issues such as this could be developed to help meet this and similar service users' needs.

Conclusions

Although this chapter has focused on men it is pertinent to comment that men and women with a learning disability who are attracted sexually to the same sex, irrespective of identity, potentially experience double discrimination. This is, in part, related to a historical legacy of prohibition or minimisation of their sexual lives. Lesbian, gay and bisexual people and people with a learning disability share some commonality of facing prejudice and hostile attitudes by members of society. It is likely that people with a learning disability who are attracted sexually to the same sex may have the double disadvantage of facing homophobia/heterosexism combined with the aforementioned negative attitudes towards people with a learning disability being sexual. However, both authors of this chapter are aware of many examples of 'success stories' where many people with a learning disability are leading successful and happy sexual lives. It is worth considering the progress made in more liberal attitudes towards people with a learning disability and their sexual needs in little over a generation. However, as Brown (1994) eloquently comments, progress made in other areas of the lives of people with a learning disability has exceeded the progress made in facilitating sexual expression for people with a learning disability. With this in mind it is imperative that progress is maintained.

The challenge for workers and services to be truly person-centred in their approaches to service users who are attracted to the same sex is to recognise the diversity of the service user's needs and circumstances. This means that workers and services have to take their lead from the individuals concerned and respect 'where they are at'. The worker needs to examine and be aware of, and in many cases set aside, his or her own values and beliefs. The worker also must not exercise undue influence over valid choices made by the service user and consider carefully what (if any) disclosures they make about their own lifestyle and their own choices.

Workers and services offering support to this group of service users (regardless of the care or support role they have) have to acknowledge the tensions between supporting legitimate sexual

Table 14.3 Risk management approaches to support a service user accessing a gay venue.

Andy wants to visit a gay venue.
Skilled worker undertakes an assessment What does Andy want and expect?
Does Andy have the capacity to make this decision? Multidisciplinary team decide that he has capacity to make this decision
A skilled worker assesses Andy's sexual knowledge and attraction
Risk assessment by multidisciplinary team identifies potential positive and negative consequences from undertaking the activity
Andy wants his parents to be informed Skilled worker discusses in depth with Andy Discussions then take place with his parents
Andy's parents do not agree with the proposed activity They do not wish to make a complaint or take any other action at this stage
Further risk management strategies are devised by the multidisciplinary team should Andy's parents: ■ Make a complaint ■ Attempt to withdraw him from his current care package ■ Attempt to exert undue pressure on Andy not to go to the gay venue Senior management of all involved organisations are updated
No volunteer can be found to support Andy Suitable member of staff identified who will support Andy
Andy visits the gay venue. He does not like it because it was too noisy. He feels very anxious Andy's wishes are respected
Andy and the multidisciplinary team evaluate the risk management strategies
No further visits are planned to that venue. Less noisy environments are sought

expression and managing the risks that may occur for the individual. Risk management can be used in a positive way to support service users to undertake particular activities. Utilising such strategies should have been agreed with the individual service user (unless there are overwhelming ethical reasons not to seek such an agreement), and the multidisciplinary team provides protection for the service user and staff in what remains a highly complex area of practice.

There is no single approach that workers can use with men who are attracted to men and women attracted to women that will fit every situation or individual circumstance. Indeed, to attempt to create such an approach ignores both the uniqueness of the individual service users and may fail to place them as the focus of the work. The 'Adhesive Notes' approach offers a worker a way to reflect and act on their role and is a flexible practical approach to consider their input or support, which can be adapted for the individual service user.

Whilst there is no one approach that can be adopted on every occasion, there are some areas of good practice that are common to most situations. It is important that workers utilise a multidisciplinary approach in complex situations, particularly where capacity to consent is involved. In managing difficult and/or potentially risky situations the agreement of the service user and the multidisciplinary team demonstrates good practice and should result in better quality decision-making. It also ensures that the service users' views are heard and acted on. Services also need to have policies and good practice guidance in place which are effectively disseminated to staff as well as ensuring that service users are aware of their rights and responsibilities.

We have attempted to offer in this chapter a starting point to assist those working with learning-disabled service users who are gay or bisexual, or who are attracted to the same sex. The utility of this chapter is to assist workers/supporters to consider how their work can support these individuals in facilitating ethical person-centred opportunities for this group of service users who have a right to such.

Finally, we accept that in some cases this will be a challenge, and we do not minimise the issues this raises, but if we are truly committed to ensuring that people with a learning disability receive person-centred support then the challenge will be well worth the effort, because sex can be exciting, pleasurable and wonderful.

Oppression can only survive through silence.
Carmen de Monteflores

References

Abbot, D. and Howarth, J. (2003) A secret love, a hidden life. *Learning Disability Practice*, **6**(1), 14–17.

Adams, J. (2004) *Explore, Dream, Discover: Working With Holistic Models of Sexual Health and Sexuality, Self Esteem and Mental Health*. Centre for HIV and Sexual Health, Sheffield.

Balogh, R., Bretherton, K., Whilby, S., Verney, T., Graham, S. and Richbold, P. (2001) Sexual abuse in children and adolescents with intellectual disability. *Journal of Intellectual Research*, **45**(3), 194–201.

Brown H. (1994) An ordinary sexual life. A review of the normalisation principle as it applies to the sexual options of people with a learning disability. *Disability and Society*, **9**(2), 123–44.

Buchanan, A. H. and Wilkins, R. (1991) Sexual abuse and the mentally handicapped: difficulties in establishing prevalence. *Psychiatric Bulletin*, **15**, 601–5.

Cambridge, P. and Mellan, B. (2000) Reconstructing the sexuality of men with learning disabilities: empirical evidence and theoretical interpretations of need. *Disability and Society*, **15**(2), 293–311.

Clark, D. (1987) *The New Loving Someone Gay*. Celestrial Arts, Berkeley, California.

Cowie, H. and Rivers, I. (2000) Going against the grain: supporting lesbian, gay and bisexual clients as they 'come out'. *British Journal of Guidance and Counselling*, **28**(4), 503–13.

Davidson-Paine, C. and Corbett, J. (1995) A double coming out; gay men with learning disabilities. *British Journal of Learning Disabilities*, **23**, 147–51.

Department of Health (2003) *Care homes for Adults 18–65 and Supplementary Standards for Care Homes Accommodating Young people aged 16-18 National Minimum Standards Car Home Regulations*, Department of Health, London

Eliason, M. J. (1996) Identity formation for lesbian, bisexual, and gay persons: beyond a 'minoritizing view'. *Journal of Homosexuality*, **30**(3), 31–58.

Fanstone, C. and Andrews, S. (2005) *Learning Disabilities, Sex and the Law. A Practical Guide*. FPA, London.

Fanstone, C. and Katrak, Z. (2003) *Sexuality and Learning Disability*. FPA, London.

Flowers, P. and Buston, K. (2001) 'I was terrified of being different': exploring gay men's accounts of growing-up in a heterosexist society. *Journal of Adolescence*, **24**, 51–65.

Forchuck, C. and Martin, M. (1993) *Sexual Knowledge Interview Schedule SKIS Instruction Booklet*. Hamilton Psychiatric Hospital, Hamilton, Ontario.

Frawley, P., Johnson, K., Hillier, L. and Harrison, L. (2003) *Living Sager Sexual Lives. A Training and Resource Pack for People with Learning Disabilities and Those Who Support Them*. Pavilion Publishing, Brighton.

Garnets, L., Hancock, K. A. and Cochran, D. C. (1991) Issues in psychotherapy with lesbians and gay men: a survey of psychologists. *American Psychologist*, **46**, 964–72. In: Mohr, J. J. (2002) Heterosexual identity and the heterosexual therapist: an identity perspective on sexual orientation dynamics in psychotherapy. *The Counselling Psychologist*, **30**(4), 532–66.

George, M. (1998) Private lives? *Community Care*, 4–10 June, pp. 30–1.

Hard, S. and Plum, W. (1987) Sexual abuse of persons with developmental disabilities. *Unpublished manuscript*.

Harding, J. (1998) *Sex Acts: Practices of Femininity and Masculinity*. Sage, London.

Hari, J. (2004) Why I hate *Queer Eye for the Straight Guy. The Independent*, 28 May.

Hayter, M. (1996) Is non judgmental care possible in the context of nurses attitudes to patients' sexuality? *Journal of Advanced Nursing*, **24**, 662–6.

Hodges, N. and Parkes, N. (2005) Tackling homophobia and heterosexism. *Learning Disability Practice*, **8**(3), 10–16.

Kiger, A. M. (1995) *Teaching for Health*. Churchill Livingstone, Edinburgh.

Kinsey, A., Pomeroy, W. and Martin, C. (1948) *Sexual Behaviour in the Human Male*. W. B. Saunders, Philadelphia.

Mair, D. and Izzard, S. (2001) Grasping the nettle: gay men's experiences in therapy *Psychodynamic Counselling*. **7**(4), 475–90.

Marks, D. (1999) Dimensions of oppression: theorising the embodied subject. *Disability and Society*, **14**(1), 611–26.

McCarthy, M. (1999) *The Sexual Lives of Women With Learning Disabilities*. Jessica Kingsley, London.

McCarthy, M. and Thompson, D. (1992) *Sex and the 3Rs. Rights, Responsibilities and Risks. A Sex Education Package for Working with People with Learning Difficulties*. Pavilion, Brighton.

McConkey, R. and Ryan, D. (2001), Experiences of staff in dealing with client sexuality in services for teenagers and adults with intellectual disability. *Journal of Intellectual Disability Research*, **45**(1), 83–7.

McColl, P. (1994) Homosexuality and mental health services. *British Medical Journal*, **308**, 550–1.

Mellan, B. (2001) Sex and men with learning disabilities. *Tizard Learning Disability Review*, **6**(1), 13–15.

Mohr, J. J. (2002) Heterosexual identity and the heterosexual therapist: an identity perspective on sexual orientation dynamics in psychotherapy. *The Counselling Psychologist*, **30**(4), 532–66.

Morrisey, M. (1996) Attitudes of practitioners to lesbian, gay and bisexual clients. *British Journal of Nursing*, **5**(16), 980–2.

Murray, J. L., Macdonald, A. R., Brown, G. and Levenson, V. (1999) Staff attitudes towards the sexuality of individuals with learning disabilities: a service related study of organisational policies. *British Journal of Learning Disabilities*, **27**, 141–5.

Nursing and Midwifery Council (2004) *The NMC Code of Professional Conduct: Standards for Conduct Performance and Ethics*. Nursing and Midwifery Council, London.

Parkes, N. (2003) Abuse and vulnerability. In: *Contemporary Learning Disability Practice* (eds. M. Jukes and M. Bollard). Quay Books, Salisbury.

Richmond, J. and McKenna, H. (1998) Homophobia: an evolutionary analysis of the concept as applied to nursing. *Journal of Advanced Nursing*, **28**(2), 362–9.

Saunders, M. (1999) *Managing Risk in Services for People with a Learning Disability*. APLD, Nottingham.

Stein, T. S. (1988) Theoretical considerations in psychotherapy with gay men and lesbians. *Journal of Homosexuality*, **15**(1), 75–95.

Titteron, M. (2005) *Risk and Risk Taking in Health and Social Welfare*. Jessica Kingsley, London.

Varcarolis, E. M. (2000) *Foundation of Psychiatric Mental Health Nursing: A Clinical Approach*. Churchill Livingstone, London.

Wilton, T. (2000) *Sexualities in Health and Social Care*. Open University Press, Buckingham.

Withers, P., Ensum, I., Howarth, D., Krall, P., Thomas, D., Weekes, D., Winter, C., Mulholland, A. Dindjer, T. and Hall, J. (2001) A psychoeducational group for men with intellectual disabilities who have sex with men. *Journal of Intellectual Disabilities*, **14**, 327–9.

CHAPTER 15

The person in a relationship: a systemic approach

Sandra Baum and Henrik Lynggaard

Vincent, a 20-year-old man with moderate learning disabilities, was recently prescribed medication by his general practitioner to reduce his anger outbursts. His family was told by the staff that unless Vincent's behaviour improved he could no longer attend the day centre. As the medication seemed to have relatively little effect, staff referred him to the local community team for 'anger management'. In their referral they stated that, 'Vincent needs to sort his anger out'.

The referral of Vincent is fairly typical of those received by many learning disabilities services. Historically, the professional response to this type of situation often consisted in conceptualising it from an intra-personal framework, in other words, situating the problem as an attribute of the individual (e.g. 'Vincent's anger'). Frequently, interventions included the prescription of medication, a behavioural modification programme, or a skills teaching course. In more recent times, a broader range of theoretical perspectives is influencing many professionals working in the learning disability field, and these approaches are starting to shape how we might try to work with – and alongside – people like Vincent and his network. In this chapter we will begin by describing the systemic approach, underline its usefulness in the context of working with people with learning disabilities, and then consider what it can offer to person-centred approaches.

What is systemic?

When we use the word *systemic* we refer to the fact that our living is always in relation to others. We may define or punctuate a human system in different ways. For example, we may focus on a couple, a family, a network of professionals, an individual and his or her significant relationships etc. It is precisely because of the broader scope of the term that systemic therapy is increasingly used in preference to family therapy, with which it shares a common history. Systemic and family therapy approaches seek to explore the network of significant relationships of which each individual is part. In doing so, they consider the beliefs that give meaning to people's actions and the communication patterns between people as they interact both with each other and with each others' ideas. Vincent, like all of us, exists in significant relationships. For example, when we met Vincent's family, we learned that he was the youngest of three children. His elder brother was married and lived away from home. His sister, Susan, had recently gone off to university in another city. He lived with his mother and father, who both worked long hours to give their family 'All that we didn't have'. Four months ago Vincent's maternal grandfather died suddenly of a heart attack. Vincent was very fond of his grandfather and they used to spend a lot of time with each other. Vincent had been told that his grandfather had gone to 'a better place' (an expression the family used for 'dying'), but he had not been given any further explanation for this sudden absence from his life.

We will return to Vincent a little later, but for now we want to emphasise that one of the key concepts of a systemic approach is that people are connected in relationships, and that they are affected by, and in turn affect, these relationships. So a systemic approach invites us to begin to explore how people such as Vincent are interconnected with others, in order that we 'work *with* him' and his system rather than 'work *on* him'.

The systemic approach developed out of dissatisfaction with the limitations inherent in psychological models where there was a predominant or exclusive focus on the individual, with little or no reference to the wider system of which he or she was part. There have been many developments within the systemic field and different traditions of systemic practice. It is outside the scope of this chapter to provide a comprehensive overview of the development of systemic approaches; however, Dallos and Draper (2000) provide a good introduction. In their overview of systemic family therapy, they emphasise that: 'One of the enduring contributions of systemic thinking has been to offer a view of problems... as fundamentally inter-personal' (p. 23). In systemic thinking, relationships are the prime focus, since all aspects of our social lives, such as our 'personality', are seen to be co-created through conversations and communication processes with other people (Hedges, 2005). As cultural and societal values are translated through the family, or an equivalent, throughout our most impressionable years, these relationships and the stories we have about them become very influential. Systemic therapists are interested in the influence of these relationships and the unique stories that people have. They note in particular that family transitions sometimes create challenges, which can (but need not) have long-term repercussions (Carter and McGoldrick, 1989; Hedges, 2005). Vincent, for example, had experienced a number of key transitions in his immediate family system. His sister had left to go to university and his grandfather had died.

In family and systemic approaches there is a long tradition of working in teams. Teamwork allows for the development of multiple perspectives and for more ideas to be generated that may be of help. Before meeting with the family who have been referred, the team come together to develop some initial hypotheses about the referral and the system's relationship to help (Reder and Fredman, 1996). Hypotheses serve to guide the therapist's discussion with the family. In terms of process, the therapist will then interview or talk with the family or people in the room, while the rest of the team (usually between one or three people) will be listening to the conversation. After a while the therapist will take a break and the team will offer their ideas and reflections while the family listens (this method is referred to as the 'reflecting team'). Families often comment that they like to hear the ideas of many people, as this offers more possibilities for change. (For more information on reflecting teams, see Andersen (1991, 1992)).

When hypothesising about a referral we often come up with a number of questions along the following lines:

- For whom is this a problem?
- What are the different systems that are involved in the problem?
- Which parts of these systems are asking us for help?
- What are they asking us for help with?

In our example, had our hypothesising led us to conclude that Vincent himself was asking for help with managing his anger, we would have arranged to meet with him to discuss whether we could help with this. Instead, our hypothesising clarified that we should be initially meeting with the staff at the day centre and the family who had referred Vincent to us.

When we met with members of the staff and Vincent's parents, the staff said that Vincent spent a large part of his day going from room to room as if looking for someone or something and pushing people who got in his way. Occasionally he was heard saying, 'Where's gramps?'. The staff team was unsure why Vincent's behaviour had changed and they were finding it increasingly difficult to manage him. Since the medication had been stopped because it was making him drowsy and disorientated, they had had to provide one-to-one supervision for him. Vincent's family were at first surprised to hear about his behaviour at the centre, as he rarely talked at home. They then told us that Vincent's grandfather died suddenly four months previously. They did not think that Vincent would understand about death because of his learning disabilities and therefore had talked about how his grandfather had 'gone to a better place in heaven'. When we asked how Vincent might have understood this, it occurred to the family that this could have been confusing, not least because they had also been using the phrase 'gone to a better university' as a way of explaining why his sister Susan had recently left home to transfer to a prestigious university some distance away. Over the next few meetings we worked with Vincent, his family and some of the staff from the day centre to find ways of talking together that were coherent with the family's belief system. This also helped Vincent to understand that his grandfather, unlike Susan, would not come back again. As more and more of Vincent's relationship with his grandfather was acknowledged in the conversations that we had together, new talk and stories were generated for describing different ways of leaving and coming back, and gradually Vincent's aggressive and bewildered behaviour diminished.

What did we do that was systemic?

As can be seen, we did not engage Vincent in anger management treatment in the manner that this is usually understood (for example, see Willner *et al.*, 2005). Instead, we thought that it would be most useful to meet in the first place with the staff team and Vincent's parents to think about their relationship with Vincent's behaviour. Were we to hold a more linear view of how problems evolve and exist, we might have chosen simply to meet with Vincent to address what was wrong with him and to treat this without recognising the significance of the relationships and contexts in which he exists. Our belief is that the client, and in this case the staff team and family, understand their own system and have a range of resources and skills that can be harnessed if we together create a system of problem-solvers. We think it is also useful to question our existing notions of expertise and redefine the concept in a different way which is more open to dialogue and the recognition of different perspectives. Therefore, rather than positioning ourselves in the traditional way as 'experts' (perhaps by doing observations, offering bereavement counselling, or providing training on anger management),[1] we prefer to create a forum in which we start to hear about the team and family's knowledge and experience in working with such issues. We assume that among the staff, the family and Vincent there are many possible constructive solutions to the problem. Moreover, we assume that the staff team, family and Vincent are already doing many things that are helping or preventing the problem from getting worse, although they may not yet have had the opportunity to 'story' their abilities (White and Epston, 1990). In common with many systemic practitioners we believe that as people begin to story their abilities they are more likely to *live* these and put them into action (Pearce and Pearce, 1998).

Why is a systemic approach useful in learning disabilities context?

The application of systemic ideas and principles in working with people with learning disabilities, their families and their service systems, particularly using the methods and techniques of family therapy, has grown in the UK since the beginning of the early 1990s. For example, Dixon and Matthews (1992), Vetere (1993), Goldberg *et al.* (1995), Fidell (1996, 2000), Salmon (1996), Baum *et al.* (2001), Lynggaard and Scior (2002), Fuchs *et al.* (2003) and Baum and Lynggaard (2006) have presented clinical reports and individual case examples involving adults with learning disabilities which suggest that systemic ways of working can be very helpful.

The wider context that surrounds this growth has been the change in the delivery of services in the 1980s and 1990s. With the closure of institutions, people with learning disabilities, their parents and carers having more choice and control over their lives, and the services and support they receive primarily through person centred approaches (*Valuing People*: Department of Health, 2001a). In community settings, the majority of people with learning disabilities live within complex networks consisting of family, carers and professionals on whom they may have a lifelong dependency. The way in which these networks interact with each other may affect how the person with learning disabilities presents for help to services, and will affect engagement, expectations and possible solutions to crises. As people with learning disabilities seldom initiate their own referrals, it is tempting to locate problems within them, ignoring the contributions of wider networks or systems. The application of the systemic approach can, in our opinion, help to provide a richer perspective. As we have already described, it seeks to understand concerns, problems or difficulties within the contexts in which they emerge and in the context of relationships. It offers a number of advantages over intra-personal frameworks by enabling conversations about the complexity of relationships and communications between different subsystems of which the person with learning disabilities is part. For example, Vincent's situation demonstrates that when receiving a referral it is good practice to consider who should be in conversations, with whom, and about what? Many people will undoubtedly be familiar with situations where it has been by virtue of inviting referrers and significant members in a network to be in conversation with each

---

[1]We do not want to imply that such approaches and methods could not also have had much to offer.

other that the 'problem' which was previously located in the person with learning disabilities gets reframed, relocated, dissolved or transformed. The systemic approach and its associated methods and techniques, therefore, can be used in shaping many aspects of work. For example, it can be used to inform conversations and interactions with individuals, with families, with staff teams and other networks. It can also be used in supervision and training. One of the key skills of the systemic practitioner is in asking questions that keep a relational focus, and that invite many voices to join in and be heard.

Person-centred approaches

In recent years person-centred approaches have become a guiding principle in national policies in the UK (Department of Health, 2001a), particularly in the form of person-centred planning (Department of Health, 2001b). This is defined as (Department of Health, 2001b, p. 12):

> a process for continual listening and learning, focussing on what is important to someone now and in the future, and acting upon this in alliance with their family and friends. This listening is used to understand a person's capacities and choices. Person Centred Planning (PCP) is the basis for problem solving and negotiation to mobilise the necessary resources to pursue a person's aspirations. Paralleling the developments in systemic work, person centred approaches have evolved in opposition to deficit models which are concerned with what is wrong with a person and how professionals can fix it. Instead, both approaches are interested in what the person's capacities, strengths and resources are and what supports they need to realise these.

The development of a person-centred plan begins by bringing together the person with learning disabilities and the people who are significant in his or her life to clarify what is most important to the person with learning disabilities from their perspective and how to accomplish their aspirations and wishes. Planning may be initiated by family or friends without any involvement from services. However, by and large, the people facilitating the plan tend to come from a range of service-providing organisations. The facilitators have a role to ensure that the process and the outcome reflect the person's wishes and goals. It is our impression that PCP has resulted in very significant and inspiring changes in people's lives, as has been documented in many publications (see the examples cited in Department of Health, 2001b). However, PCP can also be a complex process which places great demands on the skills of the facilitator (Kinsella, 2000). Some of these skills include taking the lead in sustained and careful listening to the person, in whatever ways the person communicates, in order to facilitate the plan. Other skills involve convening the significant people in a person's life, eliciting their views, and assisting them to consider different points of view. This may sometimes lead to situations where there are many and conflicting points of view about what the person with learning disabilities wants and needs. This can be further complicated if the person with learning disabilities has great difficulty in giving voice to their views or where these are strongly mediated by others. As O'Brien *et al.* (1997, p. 483) have commented, facilitation involves 'developing the courage to notice the potential in conflicting interests and to find ways to shift the circumstances that generate conflict to the person's advantage, no matter how slightly'. Kinsella (2000, p. 2) observes that 'Fundamentally, it requires sophisticated judgement, an ability to think quickly and think on one's feet, an ability to stay focused and recognise where focus should be and a propensity to not need to be in control'. In such situations, where there is conflicting interest or strongly voiced disagreements which potentially drown out the voice of the person with learning disabilities, we are not aware of any guidance to assist facilitators with these challenges. Perhaps systemic methods and techniques may have something to offer in terms of the facilitation and conduct of such meetings?

What might systemic approaches contribute to person-centred planning?

O'Brien *et al.* (1997, p. 483) asserted that 'PCP grew as a way to increase the power held by people with learning disabilities; this meant creatively stepping into conflicts among family members and with service practices and policies'. Systemic approaches have a number of methods and techniques for being in conversation with several people at the same time in order to discover ways of progressing together in conjoint action. Often people or families get into conflict when people hold a strong belief that their way of understanding a situation is the *only* way, or *the* truth, and that other views are inferior, bad or crazy. But how might one go about balancing the different voices in the system? Systemic practitioners attempt to gradually introduce the value of multiple perspectives, to move away from 'right/wrong' to 'more or less useful', from an 'either/or' to a 'both/and', from 'universal' to 'multiversal'. Situations where some people suffer emotional contradictions because of the strongly expressed dominant views of powerful others can be ameliorated over time by the questions that the practitioner ask from a position of genuine curiosity (Cecchin, 1987). For example, the practitioner may invite people to consider a situation from another person's point of view: 'Sue, from Vincent's point of view, how do you think that he understood your moving away from home?'. Another question addressed to Vincent's mother could be: 'What do you think that Vincent misses most about his relationship with his grandfather?'. Questions of this type seek to help people to step outside of their own particular view of a situation and to consider other's perspectives (this is referred to as 'circular questioning'; see Tomm (1988)). The intention of such techniques is gradually to loosen stuck systems. Variants of these questions can also be used to bring in the perspective of a person who is not currently present in the room, and as another way of introducing multiple perspectives. For example, we might ask both Susan and her parents: 'If Vincent's grandfather was here now, what advice would he have about what would help Vincent to understand what has happened?'.

Moving away from the specifics of Vincent's situation, facilitators may also consider a number of other questions that seek to unpack strongly held opinions and views of those in conflict with each other. These questions should be asked from a position of genuine curiosity and seek to help the network or system move forward in a way that does not alienate people. Examples include:

- What experiences in your life have informed this view/idea/belief?
- In what way have different contexts (i.e. gender, religion, culture, class, ethnicity, age, sexuality etc.) influenced this way of viewing things?

- Is there anyone else who you respect who would hold a different view?
- In what circumstances may a different view apply?
- What would need to be in place for you to have a different view?
- What would need to happen for you to be reassured?

Systemic practice not only involves asking questions of those we work with, but also involves asking questions about what informs and shapes our own ideas, beliefs and assumptions. This position of self-reflexivity is an inherent part of an ethical stance which enables us to minimise the likelihood of acting out of our own prejudices in a way that could be harmful or unhelpful to those with whom we work.

How do we include people with learning disabilities?

A systemic approach tries to include all of the voices of all the people involved, including the person with learning disabilities. It does this by trying to balance the particular voices by ensuring that everyone has an opportunity to have a say in sessions. The approach offers a particular way of asking questions that allows the person with learning disabilities to be involved in the conversation, but remains mindful of their particular system of significant relationships. In families where other people always talk *for* the person with learning disabilities, we do not try to 'rescue' the situation by over-inviting the person with learning disabilities to speak (and thereby disqualifying or silencing others). It is, in our experience, a question of gradually introducing different perspectives at a pace that remains comfortable to, and respectful of, the family. For example, Vincent's father said to us: 'It was not until I heard you asking for the third time: "I wonder what Vincent would say about that?", that I had even considered that he would have an opinion about things'.

Contributors to the book edited by Baum and Lynggaard (2006) have offered a range of ideas and practical suggestions for including and giving voice to people with learning disabilities. However, it is important to remember that people with learning disabilities have varied abilities and needs, and therefore we cannot be prescriptive about this guidance. We are only describing some suggestions in what follows.

One of the key responsibilities of the systemic therapist, as we have already said, is to create space for participation for the person with learning disabilities. It may require minimal adaptations of language and style to join in conversations with people affected by milder degrees of learning disabilities. However, the therapist may be severely challenged when communication in its broadest forms is limited or inconsistent, and when intent is ambiguous. In these circumstances, meanings may emerge only slowly and over time, and in a weaving backwards and forwards between the person and those who know them well. While such a view of meanings as socially constructed between individuals is coherent with some of the theories that inform systemic approaches, the therapist needs to be mindful of how differences in power can operate to fix or freeze meaning in ways that further disadvantage people. Participation and inclusion are enabled when the therapist and those who join him or her are able to remain curious and patient, are willing to struggle with uncertainty, and can voice the questions that ensure that people with more severe disabilities are 'heard'.

Involving people with severe and profound learning disabilities presents us with particular challenges. We have found the suggestions of Iveson (1990) useful in enabling us to do this. He suggests a way of inviting and imagining the voice of a person with no speaking voice and a very severe degree of disabilities by asking a series of questions that invite people to adopt, or to speak from, a different position. For example: 'If Saleha could speak, and if I were to ask her to choose someone to speak for her at this meeting, who do you think she would choose?' (Iveson, 1990, p. 82). The therapeutic intent in such an approach is to invite people to stand in and relate to a different position – a position that may otherwise become marginalised. Centring a position in this way may open up new understanding and opportunities for action.

Our language and sentences can often be complex and our pace too fast. Frequently checking the understanding of the person with learning disabilities therefore becomes important. There are several ways in which one can facilitate conversations and make things more concrete and accessible. These include: drawing a picture of all the important people in someone's life, or of all the things that are going well; showing or drawing the size of a worry/problem, which can often be easier to deal with in its externalised form; and writing down and taking notes of important events. Photographs of people and places can greatly enhance and facilitate conversations and understanding. Some people who may have difficulties in recalling or saying a person's name can join in conversations when photographs are available. Speech and language therapists can often be very helpful in suggesting how we build and maintain conversational bridges.

We are aware that we have only addressed some of the many ways that one may go about including and enhancing the voice of the person with learning disabilities. We are also mindful that person-centred planning has developed many creative ways for ensuring that the person's wishes and dreams are addressed and that their families and friends become supporters of this important task, for example though Planning Alternative Tomorrows with Hope (PATH), Essential Life Style Planning etc. (see Department of Health, 2001b). Some of these tools can in turn have much to offer to systemic practitioners who want to ensure that they include people with learning disabilities in ways that strive to be meaningful and accessible.

Conclusion

It seems to us that person-centred approaches and systemic approaches have much in common. They are all based on underlying principals that value inclusion, that are positive and hopeful, that seek to open up possibilities, and focus on people's strengths, resources and abilities. We have shown that systemic approaches are concerned with understanding people in relationships with others. It is our view that some of the techniques and methods developed from within systemic approaches could be useful in assisting in the facilitation of person-centred planning. It is our hope that other readers and practitioners will continue to explore the potential that these different practices have for mutually enriching each other.

References

Andersen, T. (1991) *The Reflecting Team: Dialogues and Dialogues about Dialogues*. Norton, New York.

Andersen, T. (1992) Reflections on reflecting with families. In: *Therapy as Social Construction* (eds. S. McNamee and K. Gergen), pp. 54–68. Sage, London.

Baum, S. and Lynggaard, H. (eds.) (2006) *Intellectual Disabilities: A Systemic Approach*. Karnac Books, London.

Baum, S., Chapman, K., Scior, K., Sheppard, N. and Walden, S. (2001) Themes emerging from systemic therapy involving adults with learning disabilities and their families. *Clinical Psychology*, **3**, 16–18.

Carter, B. and McGoldrick, M. (eds.) (1989) *The Changing Family Life-Cycle: A Framework for Family Therapy*, 2nd edn. Allyn and Bacon, Boston.

Cecchin, G. (1987) Hypothesizing, circularity and neutrality revisited: An invitation to curiosity. *Family Process*, **26**, 405–13.

Dallos, R. and Draper, R. (2000) *An Introduction to Family Therapy: Systemic Theory and Practice*. Open University Press, Buckingham.

Department of Health (2001a) *Valuing People: A New Strategy for Learning Disability for the 21st Century*. HMSO, London.

Department of Health (2001b) *Valuing People: Towards Person Centred Approaches*. HMSO, London.

Dixon, M. and Matthews, S. (1992) Learning difficulty in the family: making systemic approaches relevant. *Clinical Psychology Forum*, **39**, 17–21.

Fidell, B. (1996) Making family therapy user-friendly for learning disabled clients. *Context*, **26**, 11–13.

Fidell, B. (2000) Exploring the use of family therapy with adults with a learning disability. *Journal of Family Therapy*, **22**, 308–23.

Fuchs, K., Mattison, V. and Sugden, C. (2003) Reflections on engagement. *Context*, **65**, 21–2.

Goldberg, D., Magrill, L., Hale, J., Damaskindou, K., Paul, J. and Tham, S. (1995) Protection and loss: working with learning disabled adults and their families. *Journal of Family Therapy*, **17**, 263–80.

Hedges, F. (2005) *An Introduction to Systemic Therapy with Individuals. A Social Constructionist Approach*. Palgrave Macmillan, Basingstoke.

Iveson, C. (1990) *Whose Life? Community Care of Older People and their Families*. BT Press, London.

Kinsella, P. (2000) What are the barriers in relation to Person Centred Planning? *Paradigm*, November, pp. 1–12.

Lynggaard, H. and Scior, K. (2002) Narrative therapy and people with learning disabilities. *Clinical Psychology*, **17**, 33–6.

O'Brien, L., O'Brien, J. and Mount, B. (1997) Person-centred planning has arrived... or has it? *Mental Retardation*, 480–4.

Pearce, W. B. and Pearce, K. A. (1998) Transcendent story telling: abilities for systemic therapists and their clients. *Human Systems*, **9**, 167–84.

Reder, P. and Fredman, G. (1996) The relationship to help: Interacting beliefs about the treatment process. *Clinical Child Psychology and Psychiatry*, **1**(3), 457–67.

Salmon, A. (1996) Family therapy and learning difficulties: a case discussion. *Context*, **29**, 42–5.

Tomm, K. (1988) Interventive interviewing Part III: Intending to ask lineal, circular, strategic, or reflexive questions. *Family Process*, **27**, 1–15.

Vetere, A. (1993) Using family therapy in services for people with learning disabilities. In: *Using Family Therapy in the Nineties* (eds. J. Carpenter and A. Treacher), pp. 111–30. Blackwell, Oxford.

White, M. and Epston, D. (1990) *Narrative Means to Therapeutic Ends*. Norton, New York.

Willner, P., Brace, N. and Phillips, J. (2005) Assessment of anger coping skills in individuals with intellectual disabilities. *Journal of Intellectual Disability Research*, **49**(5): 329–39.

CHAPTER 16

Clinical supervision: the need for an integrative approach in supervising the experienced practitioner

Tony Viney

Introduction

This chapter seeks to examine the contemporary need for an integrative approach to clinical supervision in mental health and learning disability nursing. It will focus on supervision primarily as a 'space to think' (Mollon, 1997) and how the establishment of this collaborative forum can help in the process of appraising, articulating, and specifically, envisioning clinical difficulties. I will argue that the current clinical drive towards demonstrable efficacy, while in many cases much needed (Wessely, 2001), can lead clinicians to being 'outcome driven'. The pursuit of solutions can lead one to neglect or devalue the process of therapeutic exploration, which enhances articulation and understanding (Sturdee, 2001). I have referred to this process as envisioning, i.e. achieving a clearer and idiosyncratic clinical picture based on an empathic and contextual understanding. Ogden (1999) has termed a similar process 'reverie' and Winnicott (1974) has referred to it as 'play'. While there is much resistance to linking mental health work with the concept of play, with its associations of trivialising and infantilism, the author sees that the process is central to the identification of new or unique formulations more suited to contemporary clinical complexity. It is essential that the client be at the centre of the process, allowing them to be perceived as enmeshed within their context rather than as an endorsement of policy or ideology.

It is also the assumption of this chapter that the current field of psychological intervention is mired in a state of 'crisis' or rather a loss of confidence in its own effectiveness. This 'crisis' can be seen as the result of increasingly antagonistic environmental, ideological or policy-based responses to psychological interventions. This crisis has been referred to informally and variously as an 'inner city agenda' and the 'clinician's dilemma'.

This chapter will employ a narrative structure utilising anecdotal material, as I feel that this parallels the nature and structure of the supervisory experience. I will also draw on a range of diverse sources and suggestions taken from various psychological therapy models.

The problem: the clinician's dilemma

A colleague in a primary care mental health practice recently used the term 'inner city agenda' in referring to the high number of complex case referrals they were receiving. These referrals were distinguished by an increase in the cases reporting long-term abuse and neglect, clients with personality-related difficulties, inter- and intra-cultural dilemmas and an increased level of substance use and abuse. Linked with this is a perception often described as an ambivalence, suspicion and aggrieved entitlement from patients, relatives and politicians who appear to place unrealistic expectations on existing healthcare services. Recovery, also, is also reported to be impeded by a benefit system that is both antagonistic and disabling.

On a clinical level, presenting problems no longer neatly fit contemporary categories and as a consequence the traditional single school psychological interventions are seen to fall short when applied to situations outside private practice. Clinicians increasingly encounter clients with dual or multiple diagnoses where there are confluences of learning disability issues with either mental health problems or substance abuse.

Chris Williams (2001), in his justification for self-help strategies, referred to this situation as the 'clinician's dilemma', stating that clinicians are increasingly expected to work with more disturbed clients, in less time with fewer resources *and* provide proof of effectiveness.

In the field of psychological therapies there appears to be, if not the potential of détente among traditionally antagonistic single school therapies, at least a re-evaluation of the generalisation of original models. There are also greater confessions of interdisciplinary 'borrowing'.

Developments in cognitive behavioural therapies increasingly recognise the role of transference, counter-transference and resistance in the therapeutic relationship (Young *et al.*, 2003; Linehan, 1993; Leahy, 2001). Alford and Beck (1997) indicate a greater integrative role for cognitive therapy than solely with behaviourism. Linehan (1993) and Segal *et al.* (2002) have incorporated Buddhist meditation techniques into relapse prevention with depressed clients and borderline personality disorders. In psychodynamic therapy psychoanalysts like Patrick Casement (2002) call for the clinician to be guided more directly than by the emerging shape of the unconscious communication than by theory, echoing Sandler (1993) in suggesting that not everything is projective identification or that clinical perceptions can be too readily shaped by a too zealous application of theory to the client. Maroda (1991) calls for a greater degree of mutuality and reality within the therapeutic relationship, particularly in the exploration of counter-transference issues. McLeod (1997) proposes the use of narrative approaches to counteract the:

> ... recent vogue for manualized training, in which therapists learn to practice in conformity to a set of guidelines defining and specifying a particular model of therapy.

Client-centred therapists Prouty *et al.* (2002) suggest that the universality of the core conditions be reconsidered, with greater emphasis being placed on the primary importance of psychological engagement, particularly in relation to working with more disturbed cases.

While each suggested innovation provokes counter-argument, Leahy makes an interestingly pragmatic and yet contentious statement:

I have found the emphasis on theoretical purity to be more common amongst novices and among people who do not see many patients in clinical practice. Many experienced clinicians regardless of their orientation are willing to borrow or steal from any modality simply to be more effective as a clinician

The effect

What is the impact of this dilemma on the clinician? Faced with this situation, clinicians can feel that they are in 'frontier territory' at the limits of their knowledge and skill, relying more on their wits and armed only with a will to get to their next holiday. A clinician I once worked with, who had many years of clinical experience, was engaged in a process of transition from psychological therapist to Community Psychiatric Nurse (CPN). In our informal discussions the clinician talked about how he was doing a lot of anxiety management. 'Are there a lot of patients with anxiety problems?' I asked, not recognising the ironic tone. 'It's not for the patients, but for me!', the clinician replied.

While clinical supervision is seen as providing an important containing function for the clinician (Casement, 1985; Bramley, 1996) most literature appears to be directed at the new and developing therapist or clinician. However, little of it directly refers to the experienced clinician. Seligman (1975) perceives that when caught in such irreconcilable circumstances the tendency is to try either emotionally or physically to distance themselves from intense and unrelenting stress. However, if such relief is not available the only option is a sense of resignation and despair. The current exodus of experienced staff from the clinical sphere via early retirement, long-term sickness, high staff turnover, and moves into management or education all seem to support an increase in the fact that this conflict is not being resolved. The tendency of seeing the responsibility for this situation as solely situated within the ability of individual practitioners can result only in high levels of burnout (Edelwich and Brodsky, 1980). Experienced clinicians, rather than feeling confident, competent and integrated into their role, may often feel disillusioned, cynical and marginalised. In this sense the supervisor has what can only be termed as a pastoral role in listening and understanding experiences which have led to their current situation. While in many cases their predicament may have no immediate resolution, the result of a successful supervisory alliance can be a more personalised clinical re-engagement and the regeneration of curiosity with their own professional process.

Clinical supervision

Clinical supervision is perceived as an essential and necessary aspect of case work. However, attempts to define what it is can be both misleading and confused. The adoption of clinical supervision into mental health and learning disability nursing has been received with a mixture of welcome and suspicion. The term 'clinical supervision' is itself inaccurate and ambivalent in describing what it constitutes, suggesting either management surveillance or extrasensory perception. A blanket definition of supervision still proves elusive. Wright (1989) described it as:

... the meeting of two or more people who have a declared interest in examining a piece of work. The work is presented and they together will think about what has happened and why, what was said and how it was handled and could have been handled better or differently and if so how?

While this definition focuses on the dialogic value of reflection in action (Schön, 1983) it is purely descriptive. Another more inclusive definition states that it is:

A term to describe a formal process of professional support and learning which enables individual practitioners to develop knowledge and competence, assume responsibility for their own work practice and should encourage self assessment, analytical and reflective skills. (Vision of the Future, 1993)

This definition, while stressing the professional educative and developmental role does little to explain the nature of support or it's containing function. Faugier and Butterworth's (1994) less precise, but nonetheless valuable, reference to supervision as 'Pit-head time' is important in its implication of support as an essential function. The term refers to the union struggle for miners to be able to wash the grime of work off in works time rather than in their own time. This implies that management has a duty of care in addressing the wear and tear of the environment of its employees.

Within the literature this supportive or containing function of supervision appears to be addressed essentially as a non-specific factor or by-product of the supervisory encounter, yet I would argue that it is a core factor which enables the supervisory relationship to move from tokenism or ritual to an engaged and valued dialogue (Cottrell, 2002). Proctor (2000) suggests this move as being from self-focused to case-focused. The author's own experience of this shift was connected with the experience of using audiotapes in CBT supervision. Prior to submitting the tape for scrutiny, the author was highly anxious due to his own perceived limitations and vulnerability in exposing his clinical work to a supervisor. Anticipating a punitive response led to a defensive presentation. When a rebuttal did not occur, but instead a genuine, supportive response and recognition of the difficulty of the case, the author was led to both trust and value the supervisor's comments. This in turn led to a less defensive stance by the author in using audiotapes in sessions and also a genuine curiosity in the author's self-evaluation of his practice.

Psychoanalysts have long held the belief that supervision is more than education and less than therapy, and Sterba (1934) referred to the need to establish 'islands of contemplation'. Supervision, paradoxically, is both a process of re-engagement and disengagement where the clinician is able to reflect, more cognitively than emotionally, on clinical events, but where re-engagement can also engender a greater understanding and more effective responses.

Integrative supervision

Integrative models of psychological therapy are familiar, such as Egan (1998) and Cognitive Analytical Therapy (Ryle, 1990), and essentially seek to impose a logical, sequential and objectifying

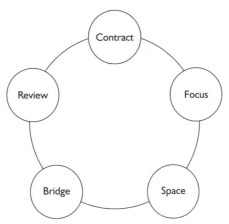

Figure 16.1 The cyclical model (Wosket and Page, 2001).

structure on the subjective, amorphous and often contradictory experience of psychological inter-vention. While many supervisors may utilise an integrative or eclectic approach on an informal level there appear to be few models of Integrative Supervision. Wosket and Page's Cyclical Model (2001) seeks to address clinical supervision as a 'discrete' phenomenon with its own theory rather than as an subsidiary of a single-school model of therapy. It takes a 'common factor' approach to supervision in which the similarities within many reported supervision experiences have been identified. They describe a five-stage cycle which they term as:

Contract, Focus, Space, Bridge and Review (Figure 16.1)

Each stage is subdivided into five further factors. The contracting stage refers to the need to estab-lish ground rules, boundaries, issues of accountability, mutual expectations and the establishment of the working relationship. The focus stage entails the establishment of an appropriate working format, such as identification of issues, objectives, methods of presentation, overt approaches and priorities. The space stage refers to the explorative tasks of the supervisory relationship such as collaboration, investigation, challenge, containment and affirmation. The bridge stage refers to the re-connective link between the supervisory work and its application to practice. This consists of consolidation of insights, information giving, goal setting, action planning and the client's perspective.

The review stage enables the supervisee and supervisor to evaluate the effectiveness of the supervisory alliance.

I find this model highly pragmatic and increasingly valuable as an organising structure, but feel that far more exploration of the space and bridge stages are needed. If the model is inter-preted too narrowly there is a danger of compartmentalising or undermining the reflective nature of supervision. While agreeing with their claim that it is essential to counter act 'bumbling intro-spection and wild eclecticism', I would like to explore this more fully in relation to the clinician's dilemma with particular reference to the experienced clinician.

As a supervisor of predominantly experienced clinicians I have seen two main themes emerge within recent years: firstly, issues around role transition, and secondly, a perceived mismatch between their current level of skill and expectations and limitations of their treatment remit.

In the first instance, supervisees have actively sought independent supervision when either appointed to a new role or are involved in a significant change to an existing role, such as the move from clinician to manager, secondary to primary care, health centre to community, or CPN to clinical nurse specialist. An important aspect of the initial phase is to identify and establish what could be termed as the supervisory 'task'. This is essentially a long-term goal of supervision. This has a baseline function in establishing where the supervisee feels they are currently in relation to their perceived goal of where they would like to be. In this sense the role relates to what Morton-Cooper and Palmer (1993) refer to as Contract Mentoring, which they see as:

> A collaborative relationship of personal equality involving the development of new skills and the shouldering of new responsibilities.

Secondly, new initiatives which place clinicians in a time-limited therapy setting or in a purely screening capacity can prompt feelings of being deskilled, isolated and overwhelmed. Early sessions involve practitioners engaging in a process of identifying skill and knowledge deficits. There are often requests for information about training courses and new therapies. On a more personal note, clinicians may discuss doubts or negatively evaluate their often considerable skill and experience. This negative evaluation has been referred to by Peggy Macintosh (1989) as feelings of fraudulence, where therapists may feel:

> illegitimate in doing something, or appearing as something; one feels apologetic, undeserving anxious, tenuous, out-of-place, misread, phony, uncomfortable, incompetent, dishonest and guilty

Teaching colleagues have often stated that, at times, the perception of them being experts sits uncomfortably with them as that they often feel only one chapter ahead of the student. When DeAngelis (1987) carried out a study amongst 62 doctoral level therapists as to whether they had ever felt like 'impostors' in their role, they reported that 79% of their sample stated 'occasionally', while the remainder reported 'frequently'. Macintosh proposes that while these feelings may seem somewhat alarming and demoralising to both the supervisee and managers, that they are to be trusted and pursued. She suggests:

> The trick is to trust the very feelings of discomfort that are giving us the most trouble, and try to follow them where they may lead.

Nyatanga (1990) refers to a similar process occurring among post-registration student nurses in higher education. They describe an experience they term as Regressive Progression:

> Having previously gained mastery, control, confidence and perhaps having acted as a role model to others, some students in this research found themselves having to go back to the drawing board. But they were actually restarting at a higher level or deeper level

Both of the above references suggest that this is a personal process of self-directed learning and reflection, part of the steep learning curve involved with any major change. However, this is also much of the containing function of clinical supervision for the experienced practitioner. This process of change and re-visioning calls for specific skills on the behalf of the supervisor. Supervisors in these situations need to have what the poet John Keats (Gittings, 1995) referred to as a negative capability, where, in this case, the supervisor:

> Is capable of being in uncertainties, mysteries, doubts without any irritable reaching after fact or reason

In this sense it calls for a view of supervision as far more of a collaborative dialogue rather than as a didactic passing on of information. Anderson and Swim (1995) talk about supervision as occurring within a mutual learning context, where both supervisor and supervisee can learn from each other's experience actively working towards clarity and meaning. In this sense clarity is something of a shared gleaning, as there may not be a well-defined answer or procedure.

In this sense supervision can be an exciting, creative and challenging forum. Supervisors within the creative therapies and *Gestalt* therapies have suggested that supervision should be more active and utilise more non-verbal and less chair-bound approaches. In particular Ireland and Weissman (1999) suggest using drawing and diagrams as an effective method of aiding therapeutic clarity. Hoffman (1990) in her use of narrative and metaphor put out a challenge to create new metaphors and stories about family therapy. I would suggest the same could apply to clinical supervision.

Conclusion

While much has been written about the models, content and stages of integrative approaches in therapy, little has been written about the role and function of clinical supervision within the experience of integrative practice. Local accounts suggest that the internalisation of integrative practice involves both an interpersonal and intra-psychic process, which is at times difficult and emotionally painful. Some clinicians have referred to it being like having to learn a new language only to find very few other people can understand it.

Tom Main (1990) talked about learning as an emotional process:

> New knowledge, concepts, facts and skills can also give pain, for they sometimes demand the abandoning or modification of old beliefs and practices that have been long cherished as familiar possessions; and now the enforced loss of favourite ideas and techniques can give rise to the protest, rage and despair of mourning processes and to sad or resentful, nostalgic wishes for the good old days and the good old ideas

Guttmann *et al.* (2005), while recognising this process of disillusion, also recognise that it can also be a process that can lead either to a more realistic assessment of situations or to a new configuration. Either way clinical supervision has a very important role in the containment and engagement of experienced clinicians in contemporary practice.

References

Alford B. A. and Beck, A. T. (1997) *The Integrative Power of Cognitive Therapy*. Guilford Press, New York.

Anderson, H. and Swim, S. (1995) Supervision as a collaborative conversation: connecting the voices of supervisor and supervisee. *Journal of Systemic Therapies*, **14**(2), 1–13.

Bramley, W. (1996) *The Supervisory Couple in Broad Spectrum Psychotherapy*. Free Association Books.

Casement, P. (2002) *Learning from our Mistakes: Beyond Dogma in Psychoanalysis and Psychotherapy*. Brunner-Routledge, London.

Casement, P. (1985) *On Learning from the Patient*. Routledge, London.

Cottrell, S. (2002) Suspicion, resistance, tokenism and mutiny: problematic dynamics relevant to the implementations of clinical supervision in nursing. *Journal of Psychiatric and Mental Health Nursing*, **9**, 667–71.

DeAngelis, T. (1987) Therapists who feel as if they are not therapists: the impostor syndrome. *APA Monitor*, 14–15.

Department of Health (1993) *A Vision for the Future*. NHS Management Executive, London.

Edelwich, J. and Brodsky, A. (1980) *Burnout: Stages of Disillusionment in the Helping Professions*. Human Sciences Press, New York.

Egan, G. (1998) *The Skilled Helper: A Problem Management Approach to Helping*, 6th edn. Brooks Cole, New York.

Faugier, J. and Butterworth, T. (1994) *Clinical Supervision: A Position Paper*. Manchester University.

Gittings, R. (ed.) (1995) *Letters of John Keats*. Oxford University Press, Oxford.

Guttmann, D., Van der Rest, F., Tennier-David, J., Verrier, C. and Millat, J. (2005) *Disillusionment: Dialogue of Lacks*. Karnac Books, London.

Hoffman, L. (1990) Constructing realities: an art of lenses. *Family Process*, **29**(1), 1–12.

Ireland, M. and Weissmann, M. (1999) Visions of transference and counter-transference: the use of drawings in the clinical supervision of psychoanalytic practitioners. *American Journal of Art Therapy*, **37**, 74–83.

Leahy, R. L. (2001) *Overcoming Resistance in Cognitive Therapy*. Guilford Press, New York.

Linehan, M. M. (1993) *Cognitve-Behavioural Treatment of Borderline Personality Disorder*. Guilford Press, New York.

Macintosh, P. (1989) Feeling like a fraud: Part two, Stone Center. *Work in Progress*, **37**.

McLeod, J. (1997) *Narrative and Psychotherapy*. Sage, London.

Main, T. (1990) Knowledge, learning and freedom from thought. *Psychoanalytic Psychotherapy*, **15**, 59–77.

Maroda, K. (1991) *The Power of Counter-transference: Innovations in Analytical Technique*. Wiley, New York.

Mollon, P. (1997) Supervision as a place for thinking. In: *Supervision of Psychotherapy and Counselling: Making a Place to Think* (ed. G. Shipton). Open University Press, Milton Keynes.

Morton-Cooper, A. and Palmer, A. (1993) *Mentoring and Preceptorship: A Guide to Support Roles in Clinical Practice.* Blackwell, Oxford.

Nyatanga, L. (1990) The ET penumbra. *Senior Nurse*, **10**(7), 12–14.

Prouty, G., Van Werde, D. and Pörtner M (2002) *Pre-Therapy: Reaching Contact-impaired Clients.* PCCS Books, Ross-on-Wye.

Ogden, T. (1999) *Reverie and Interpretation.* Karnac, London.

Proctor, B. (2000) *Group Supervision: A Guide to Creative Practice.* Sage, London.

Ryle, A. (1990) *Cognitive–Analytic Therapy: Active Participation in Change.* Wiley, New York.

Schön, D. A. (1983) *The Reflective Practitioner: How Professionals Think in Action.* Temple Smith, London.

Sandler, J. (1993) On communication from the analyst to the patient: not everything is projective identification. *International Journal of Psychoanalysis*, **74**, 1097–107.

Segal, Z. V., Williams, J. M. G. and Teasdale, J. D. (2002) *Mindfulness-Based Cognitive Therapy for Depression: A New Approach to Preventing Relapse.* Guilford Press, New York.

Seligman, M. E. P. (1975) *Helplessness: on Depression, Development, and Death.* Freeman, New York.

Sterba, R. (1934) The fate of the ego in analytical therapy. *International Journal of Psychoanalysis*, **15**, 117–26.

Sturdee, P. (2001) Evidence, influence and evaluation. In: *Evidence in the Psychological Therapies: A Critical Guide for Practitioners* (eds. C. Mace, S. Moorey and B. Roberts). Brunner-Routledge, London.

Wessely, S. (2001) Randomised controlled trials: the gold standard? In: *Evidence in the Psychological Therapies: A Critical Guide for Practitioners* (eds. C. Mace, S. Moorey and B. Roberts). Brunner-Routledge, London.

Williams, C. (2002) Unpublished conference paper. *Innovative Techniques and Applications in CBT*, University of Manchester.

Winnicott, D. W. (1974) *Playing and Reality.* Pelican, Harmondsworth.

Wosket, V. and Page, S. (2001) *Supervising the Counsellor: A Cyclical Model.* Routledge, London.

Wright, H. (1989) *Groupwork: Perspectives and Practice.* Scutari Press, London.

Young, J. E., Klosko, J. S. and Weishaar, M. E. (2003) *Schema Therapy? A Practitioner's Handbook.* Guilford Press, New York.

Index